BREAKFAST

WITH

SHARKS

BREAKFAST
WITH
SHARKS

A SCREENWRITER'S GUIDE
TO GETTING THE MEETING, NAILING THE PITCH,
SIGNING THE DEAL, AND NAVIGATING
THE MURKY WATERS OF HOLLYWOOD

MICHAEL LENT

FOREWORD BY MICHAEL MEDAVOY

THREE RIVERS PRESS
NEW YORK

Published by Three Rivers Press, New York, New York.
Member of the Crown Publishing Group, a division of Random House, Inc.
www.crownpublishing.com

THREE RIVERS PRESS and the Tugboat design are registered trademarks of Random House, Inc.

Printed in the United States of America

Design by Meryl Sussman Levavi/Digitext

Library of Congress Cataloging-in-Publication Data
Lent, Michael, 1963–
    Breakfast with sharks : a screenwriter's guide to getting the meeting, nailing the pitch, signing the deal, and navigating the murky waters of Hollywood / Michael Lent.— 1st ed.
    1. Motion picture authorship—Vocational guidance. I. Title.
PN1996.L427 2004
791.43'7'02373—dc22

                                                                    2003025953

ISBN 0–609–81043–X

10 9 8 7 6 5 4 3 2 1

First Edition

To my wife, Sonia.

You are the be-all, end-all,

love of my life and living proof that

beside every good man is a great woman.

And to our beautiful new son

Willem Spencer

Contents

PART TWO

THE SCRIPT-TO-SCREEN PROCESS

CHAPTER 4

SECTION 207: A GLIMPSE INTO HOLLYWOOD SCREENWRITING

CHAPTER 5

SECTION 215: SPECS AND ASSIGNMENTS

CHAPTER 6

SECITON 243: PITCHES

CHAPTER 21
SECTION 530: ALTERNATIVE EMPLOYMENT—
THE JOB-JOB   214

PART SIX
EXTRA CREDIT

CHAPTER 22
SECTION 605: Q&A   227

CHAPTER 23
SECTION 612: RESOURCE LIST   245

Acknowledgments

Carrie Thornton, my editor.
I am truly fortunate to work with an excellent editor like Carrie. Thank you and the terrific Three Rivers Press team for all your hard work on behalf of this book.

Erik Bauer, my long-suffering editor at *Creative Screenwriting* magazine.
In addition to being the most even-keeled publisher I have ever met, you are a good friend.

Daniel Greenberg, my agent.
Thank you for making this project happen.

Mary Lent and Walt Heinbach, my grandparents.
Both had an extraordinary work ethic and truly believed in the power of knowledge.

Inez Bauer, my copy editor at *Creative Screenwriting* magazine. Thank you for your help proofing and correcting this manuscript.

Masako Oshiro Beckwith, my mother-in-law.
You have taught me the true meaning of perseverance and determination against all odds.
Domo arigato.

Janet and Joseph Hirschoff.
Thank you for being the sister and brother who encouraged me day in and day out.

Paul Lazarus III.
Thank you for sharing your experiences, which inspired me.

Norma Brokaw
Thank you for your words of encouragement when I needed them most

Playwright David Rambo
Theodore Heyck, Esq.
Dr. Valarie Clemente-Crain
Lee Hamilton Knight
Dr. Nitin Patel
Thank you for your friendship, wisdom, and encouragement throughout my journey in Hollywood.

FOREWORD

Navigating the depths of the Hollywood shoal is as difficult as venturing into a Minoan cave without a ball of string, especially if you weren't born into a place of wealth or position. My own start in this industry was in some way the norm. I started at the bottom, like most people who gain entry into the business of moviemaking by delivering mail or as readers at a studio. However, to succeed here, you will need—among other things—help and guidance. *Breakfast with Sharks* will provide that help and guidance, but nothing beats jumping in headfirst and starting your career yourself.

This business, more than any other industry, is constantly changing; tastes change and people in power change positions frequently. Many who come to Hollywood and make a go of it are driven out by the undertow and the vicissitudes of time. The sine qua non is the passion for their craft, lots of patience, and the ability to stay at the table long enough to get people to notice you. You have to know that a career in Hollywood is a marathon and not the hundred-yard dash.

Millions of people are trying to open doors in the movie business, but only a few will make a living at it. Luck and, most of all, talent are the most important ingredients. Experience comes after that. The thing to remember most is to find a friendly ally quickly. Also, think about what is important to you. In my opinion this isn't money. That will come if you love what you do. You have to keep your priorities in order. In my view, family and a few friends come first. These values and what you do for others will determine your character and will put you in good stead. Be honest, first to yourself, then to others. If you take the easy way in, you will suffer the easy way out.

That said, read *Breakfast with Sharks*, learn, and then go ahead with it and enjoy the journey.

—Mike Medavoy, Chairman of Phoenix Pictures

INTRODUCTION

Hollywood is one place in the world where you can die of encouragement.

—DOROTHY PARKER

Graduate film school was the best two and a half years of my life. The next three years that followed were definitely not. Since way back, I had focused on this singleminded dream of writing movies for a living. All was going according to my master plan until just after my relocation to Hollywood in the autumn of 1993. Upon arrival, I hit the ground running with three completed specs and three student films made for under $1,000 each. Luckier and maybe more persistent than most, I quickly landed my first production company writing assignment, along with a high-profile agent at one of the Big Five literary agencies (those being CAA, ICM, WMA, UTA, and Endeavor) in Los Angeles. A studio executive at Disney was also championing my spec script. Life was sweet. Indeed, my Barcalounger was oiled and ready for a victory lap down Sunset Boulevard. But wait . . . within my first forty-five days, the assignment project was dead, the executive was fired, and my agent let me go with a blunt 7:30 a.m. phone call saying, "I shopped your spec, but couldn't find a buyer. I read your new spec. It's okay, but frankly I was unimpressed. You had one friend in this town [the aforementioned exec] and now you don't. I don't think there's any more I can do for you." My first thoughts were *Who conducts business at that ungodly hour?* and *Now what the hell do I do?* While the questions came quickly, the answers took years. In the difficult days and weeks that followed, it would hit me like a brick hurled from hell that although I had watched both *Eraserhead* and *The Seventh Seal* frame by frame seventeen times, and understood as much about binary character theory and restorative three-act structure as anyone else, I was still desperately unprepared for this brave new world of trial and many, many errors. Unfortunately, writing a script, or making a short film, or taking a dozen film theory courses in no way prepares you for what Hollywood is really like.

Aside from my fellow film-school plebes who were scrambling and being cut from the sled dog races just like me, my now ex-agent was right, I was out here alone in the harsh wilderness of botox injections and *Chuckie VII.* I soon discovered that broken deals and fickle fortune were part of the initiation process for a place where ex-lawyers sort mail at talent agencies while hoping soon to land as agent trainees. In the ensuing months I realized that my formative academic background meant very little in Tinseltown. I was qualified for a place at the starting gate, but not guaranteed a career. The day you finish law school and pass the bar exam, someone will hire you to practice law, but that is not the case with film school. In fact, I had little practical experience or even a reference point to cope with the business and day-to-day aspects of life here. Meanwhile, a tsunami of student loan debt—$60,000 to be exact—threatened to wash away my flimsy thatched hut of patience and self-confidence.

I remember once talking to an aspiring director who had been out here for three years. She said, "I'm struggling so much here I can't bring myself to tell people I have a master's." After listening to her plight, I promised myself that no matter what, I wasn't going to be back on the bus, another casualty on Hollywood's Walk of Shame. What actions I took next would determine whether or not I was to have a career in film. So I scoured the bookstores for material pertaining to my situation. I was a writer who could write but who didn't have a clue how to navigate the hierarchy of Hollywood—on the bookshelves I found little that pertained to my situation. Unfortunately, to this day, few sources exist for those looking to go beyond how to shoot a movie, how to write a script, how to find an agent. Actually learning how to be a full-time screenwriter, how to make the leap from competence in the art to the business side of the craft, would have to come the hard-knocks way. There was no guidebook to be found. That process for me took more than four years with cumulative writer earnings of $6,500. By then, all but a few from my graduate and undergraduate film-school classes were long gone, back on that bus.

Each year, upwards of 20,000 films are independently shot and 50,000 screenplays are written on spec by in-the-trenches screenwriters, usually in the wee hours after the tykes are put to bed, or at dawn before classes, or following a ten-hour work shift. And every year, tens of thousands of intrepid souls with so much to offer the world descend upon Hollywood. These hopeful, huddled masses yearn for fame, fortune, artistic expression, and a respectable table at L.A. hot spots. Most of these arrows shot at the sun will hit dirt. The independent films they made that never found distributors to show them will find a place in the family video archive, and the script will serve nicely as a drink coaster. And the dreamers seeking to nibble their chunk of the $6-billion-a-year entertainment industry cheese will instead go hungry and leave town just in time to make room for the next wave of eager beavers. Ninety-nine out of a hundred would-be Spielbergs, Goldmans, Ovitzes, and Bruckheimers fall short of their aspirations, in part because the stakes are so very high and the knowledge that comes from mistakes, failures, and lost opportunities quickly takes its toll on the psyche and on the wallet.

Because film is the most dominant art form in contemporary culture, and the need for information, for "a way in," is so great, more than 2,500 film schools and professional programs with more than 30,000 students currently exist, according to the American Film Institute (AFI). While film school is invaluable for teaching theory and history, most of what is taught is by definition academic. Film is a young art form, and the film industry is constantly in flux. So a cottage industry of seminar-meisters and their books have leaped into the breach, charging as much as $500 a day for promises of secret handshakes granting passage onto the inside track to Hollywood. Many pay it because actual Hollywood experience is relatively hard to come by.

Every minute of every day, people arrive in Hollywood and want to know where to live, how to get a job, how to get a life and a foothold in the business. There are definitely ways into the Hollywood system. For six of the last ten years that I have been a working Hollywood screenwriter, I have provided such information teaching at Santa Barbara City College and for UCLA, as well as sharing personal experience in my "Belly of the Beast" column in *Creative Screenwriting* magazine, as well as through two other industry publications, *Screenstyle* and *Tournages.* During that time I have optioned, sold, or have received studio assignments on ten projects, as well as co-producing the feature film *Hard Scrambled.* I have pitched on dozens of scripts, perhaps even a hundred or more. I've also been a judge in four writing competitions. If any of the above terminology is baffling to you, don't worry, it will all make perfect sense by the time we're through.

With *Breakfast With Sharks,* I set out to write a book that would be loosely organized like academic courses, but would provide a real-world education and an intimate glimpse into the movie industry. It would be filled with "take this and use it right now" information, as well as innovative tactics for the business side of Hollywood. Readers will learn such information as

- how to pitch a project to a producer over the phone within thirty seconds
- how to shop a script without an agent
- how to cut through agent-and-producer-speak
- how to turn a spec into an assignment
- how to structure your deal
- where can you meet other creative people to build your community and enhance your chances of success

In addition to prescriptive advice, I also explain the subtext of many of the situations you will encounter in the industry. In other words, you'll learn how to "read" a room and recognize certain situations even before you encounter them. I have attempted to deconstruct many of the various business and creative processes you will face as a Hollywood writer, then put it all together for a broader perspective.

This book is about making things happen for yourself in Hollywood, and taking charge of your career. It's for anyone hoping to get a toe over the trapdoor of show business or looking to move to the next level of their profession. Within these pages, I have worked to provide real-world experience in an easy-to-read, practical, concise guide for navigating the highways and byways of the film industry. For the cost of this book, less than twenty dollars, far below the cost of a film school education or a $500 seminar, you will gain real-world understanding of the business side of Hollywood. Further, you will learn the guerrilla tactics that are sometimes required to make dreams of a career in show business come true. In other words, this is a real-world education for writers and anyone else who has ever contemplated a career in Hollywood. Because so many parts of the movie industry are difficult, whenever possible I'll try to add a spoonful of sugar to help the medicine go down.

I believe persistence always pays off—both on the business side and in perfecting your craft. Only the exact time line is indeterminate. This book is about learning from such experiences as you build first a nest and then a career in Hollywood as a writer. Through strategic planning, perseverence, and taking responsibility for your own career, you can have the kind of career you want. We writers are a unique breed. But always remember that no matter how big the desk is, most likely, the person sitting behind it once tried his or her hand at writing, too. In fact, many who have tried quickly realized that the endeavor was much harder than it looked and wisely began to pursue a career in Hollywood on the other side. By organizing your career into a structure in which you can create, you maximize your odds of succeeding.

Okay. Ready? Good. Let's get started.

PART ONE

Basics—
Your Decision to Go Pro

SECTION 101:

INTRODUCTION TO TINSELTOWN

- Overview of Hollywood
- What Does Hollywood Want?
- "What Just Happened?"
- Effort, Access, Timing
- Passion vs. Pa$$ion

EXTRA CREDIT READING:

What Makes Sammy Run by Budd Schulberg

Adventures in the Screen Trade by William Goldman

The Writer's Journey by Chris Vogler

OVERVIEW OF HOLLYWOOD

There's an old joke about the studio exec who has read a script and someone asks what he thought of it, and he says, "I don't know. I haven't talked to anyone yet." The jest works on two levels: Hollywood is a startlingly tiny community, and in L.A. everyone plays the "six degrees of separation" game to figure out how you already know each other, as in "You just sold Matt at Sony? Ohmigod, I pitched him on *Ninja Clown Posse* six months ago. We gotta have lunch." As for the second part of the joke, ideas may be king in Hollywood, but this place is not about reinventing the wheel. "Uniquely familiar," a phrase coined by veteran producer Joel Silver (*The Matrix, Lethal Weapon*), is the stock and trade of Hollywood. In other words, you should think outside the box, but don't try to bring your own box to L.A., because over the past hundred years or so, Hollywood has developed a way to do business and make movies that it is quite comfortable with, thank you very much. The system works in an imperfect way, but it does work. So there's little use in trying to force the town to do things *your* way. The logic behind the Hollywood development process for a motion picture goes something like this: no matter where you are making movies in the world, if you are producing a product for a mass audience, the various funnels through which your story (the entertainment you are creating) must pass will narrow in order to appeal to the most people waiting on the other side. Typically, mass audiences reduce characters to white hat/good guy and black hat/bad guy. Consequently they like the familiarity and comfort of a twice-told tale. As we shall see, the trick for the successful Hollywood writer is to create a script that is intensely personal, yet still manages to resonate with a mass audience by virtue of its universal themes. A quick scan of the American Film Institute's list of "America's 100 Greatest Movies" shows a number of masterpieces that have accomplished this difficult feat. These are films like *Casablanca, The Graduate, On the Waterfront, Schindler's List, All About Eve, Raging Bull, Midnight Cowboy, Rebel Without a Cause, Rocky, Platoon, Easy Rider, The Apartment, Goodfellas,* and *Pulp Fiction.*

While most of us are uncomfortable judging, say, Japanese calligraphy or a Wagnerian opera based on our limited exposure to those art forms, we are all experts on Hollywood simply by virtue of having seen hundreds or thousands of movies in our lifetimes. Few moviegoers have qualms comparing and contrasting *The English Patient* with, say, *Scary Movie.* But from inside Hollywood, what you see is an imperfect system that contains vast armies of smart, usually young people in their twenties and thirties, working tremendously hard to make mainly mediocre movies. Why? Because moviemaking looks deceptively easy, but is, in fact, very, very hard. It's a highly collaborative endeavor with dozens and often hundreds of people involved. Perfecting your craft to work in tandem with other craftsmen can and does take many years. That's why even great fiction writers like F. Scott Fitzgerald and Dorothy Parker were never better than mediocre screenwriters.

WHAT DOES HOLLYWOOD WANT?

I think film schools serve as a good training ground, but there isn't really a replacement for doing it.

—BRIAN GLAZER, PRODUCER,
IMAGINE ENTERTAINMENT

This book isn't about teaching you how to write. There are lots of other sources to help you with that part of the process. I will state, however, that the fastest, most time-honored way to learn structure and form is to take a favorite movie and, as you view it, type it out into a script. But if you're reading this book, I assume you have already achieved the laudable goal of completing a screenplay. Congratulations on having written a movie on paper! Now you're ready to ask the next logical question: "What do I do with this thing that I've written?" How will you realize your dreams of making a living as a writer in Hollywood with a chance to see your work on movie screens all over the world? That's what this book is about.

One of the first realizations that arrivals to the movie capital of Planet Earth make is that despite having the world's biggest stage, Hollywood is an amazingly insular place. Catch-22s abound, such as that "no one important will read your work unless you have an agent, and you can't get an agent to read your work unless you are referred to them by somebody important who has already read your work." So, as soon as you get here, intent on befriending anyone with access who will read your script, you discover that everybody seems to be a producer or working on a hot project. You feel as if you're chasing your tail as you deal with some of these people, because, although they promise the moon, from them you see very little in terms of money or the all-important access to the real players of the town. It's so hard to find out who is really who. Believe me, you will get frustrated as you try to cut through the miasma—"What's up with this !%*$ town? What is really going on?"

I know exactly how you feel because I've been there, and I want to tell you right now that if you learn from your hard-knocks experiences and persevere, these early days in Hollywood will become war stories that you can share and laugh about later. As mentioned in the introduction, during my first ten years in the film business, I have co-produced one movie, sold outright one screenplay, taken on four production company and studio assignments, and optioned or "rented" my work to producers five times. What follows is my very first war story.

"What Just Happened?"

I arrived in September and, several weeks later, landed my first pitch meeting at a production company based at Warner Brothers. The company had made two successful films in the past two years, one of which is still considered a minor classic. Initially I had used my film school alumni contacts and then the big-budget script I had just completed as a sample to get a meeting with the senior vice-president of the company. The VP told me right away that although they really liked ("loved!" is the way the exec put it) the script I'd written, the project was well out of their budget range. However, they had German funding for a science-fiction project in the $2.5–$3-million range for which they believed I might be perfect. So I was asked to come back in a week with three ideas based on the one-sentence "concept" for a story they had given me. To be honest, I have forgotten what the concept was, but I think it involved a single location in a futuristic, postapocalyptic society—people hiding in a warehouse with a killer android/alien/mutant on the loose. Something like that. Later I was to learn that a week is actually quite a lot of time by Hollywood standards, but back then it seemed incredibly cruel and short. Working frantically for five days and nights straight, I turned in my best three stories on time, then went home to bed and waited. And waited. One week and then two excruciating weeks of silence followed. And then, finally, the call came. It was early November. I suppressed tears of joy as the VP told me over lunch that they wanted to go forward with one of my story ideas. In fact, the contracts would be submitted to the production company's business affairs department that very day; and I should anticipate a "deal by Christmas" that would pay me a total of $30,000 up front, in addition to an opportunity to earn a production bonus if my script was made into a movie. The VP smiled and said he intended to fast-track this project. We would get started as soon as the contracts were signed, most likely right after the New Year.

"Nope. It will never happen," said the jaded veteran director who lived in my building. I had already lined up a young, aggressive entertainment lawyer to handle things from my side, and all was right with the world. A few days later my fiancée and I were on our way out to celebrate our good fortune when I ran into this director in the parking garage. "I know the chief accountant for the company. They're dead broke over there." "That isn't what I've been told," I said haughtily, while wondering to myself what this guy's problem was. "We're fine, so you're fine," was the gist of the phone conversation I had with the VP the next morning. I hung up feeling silly, but in the back of my mind I wondered if I had detected just a whiff of *something* in the executive's power pep talk. Sure enough, the VP began to avoid calls from the lawyer and me in the ensuing weeks, before phoning me one morning in early December to say that no projects were going forward at this time. In fact, he was leaving the company, but he hoped we could find something to work on together where he was going. That was it.

Postscript: My deal never got off the tarmac, and the production company closed shop soon after, but the exec and I did indeed find another project to work on. Through this I learned the valuable lesson of never celebrating before the check clears, as well as to be a little more low-key (and a little less public) about any "success" I might have. I used to run into that director long after moving out of the building. "Hey, Mr. Deal by Christmas!" he would shout at me from across a crowded restaurant, guffawing and mock-toasting me with his water glass. (Avoiding his level of cynicism was another important lesson.) Later I discovered that the scenario of a production company promising more than it can deliver is well known to nearly all veteran screenwriters. But such a situation is hard to imagine until you've gone through it.

Effort, Access, Timing

The old saw that you must "know somebody" in Hollywood to succeed isn't completely untrue. Having a famous relative does help, at least initially. Sooner or later you'll be judged on your own merits. "Talent always wins out" my old film professor used to say. Success in Hollywood can be boiled down to a trilogy of components: Effort, Access, and Timing.

Effort is the diligence you exercise by writing *every day,* as well as by pursuing all the various career opportunities that may come your way.

Access comes from continually educating yourself about the process, then finding the right decision-makers who may be interested in your writing, and immersing yourself in their world.

Timing is about having the talent and skills to seize opportunities when they are presented. If you can combine timing with effort and access, you and your work can be in the right place in the right time.

Here's a story of how I used and then failed to use these components. In my first year as a Hollywood writer, I worked long into the night to finish a new script (my second "Mr. Professional" project). This script incorporated everything I was learning about the craft, post–film school. That diligence paid off when I attended an industry screening of a new movie, and met an ambitious young assistant to a well-known director whose work I had long admired and felt very passionately about. That introduction or "access" led to drinks with the assistant whereby I pitched my new project. Not only did he like the pitch, but he agreed to read the script and liked that, too. Another hurdle was overcome a couple weeks later when the assistant called breathlessly one Friday morning to say, "I just pitched your project to my boss, and he's interested. Get me a two- or three-page synopsis tomorrow so we can make his weekend reading." Talk about great *timing!* But I had never done a truly professional synopsis of a script, and I didn't have one ready with this particular project. So I struggled mightily over the next seventy-two hours to boil my movie first down to twelve, then six pages.

Early Monday morning I faxed a four-and-a-half page synopsis—two pages too long and two and a half days too late, as it turned out. When I called the assistant, he simply said, "Michael, you're not ready for this," and hung up. He was slow to return my subsequent calls, and then stopped all together. Clearly my efforts, while noble, were undercut by my inexperience. Thus I had failed to fully take advantage of an opportunity when it was presented. Of course, it's quite possible that the director would have passed on the script based on my synopsis, but at least I would have been one more step further in the process. In the end, I at least took comfort in the fact that responsibility for this failure clearly rested on my own shoulders. That meant it was a lesson to heed and something that I could address. I spent the next two weeks writing formal synopses for all my preexisting work.

Make no mistake—it takes a certain kind of person to follow his or her dreams here in sunny California. Aside from cloudless skies and chronically pleasant weather—the thrill of pumping gas into your Ford Festiva while standing within ring-toss distance of Al Pacino, who does not drive a Festiva—Hollywood is a very tough place to make an easy living. The cost of living rivals New York and San Francisco. Many people have more than one job. Meanwhile, the craft of filmmaking is difficult to perfect—the results can be very unforgiving. And if the craft is unforgiving, the industry is even more brutal.

My First Hollywood Lessons

1. Attend screenings and premieres where I might meet industry contacts.
2. Know the market and make sure I'm offering a suitable project to my potential buyer.
3. Follow instructions and recognize the importance of making my deadlines.
4. Recognize my mistakes and take the time to correct them.

PASSION VS. PA$$ION

Some writing that we writers do for the market may be less than satisfying creatively. However, no writer should feel compromised artistically just because he or she must pay bills or dues. Conversely, some writers can develop pa$$ion for a paycheck by writing exclusively what they think studios want to buy at the expense of fully realizing their craft with themes that resonate or ambitious characters that are fully fleshed out. While Hollywood screenwriting can be very lucrative financially, solely running to the whistle of money will guarantee neither career longevity nor satisfaction. That's where passion comes in. Passion (not pa$$ion) is still caring about the end result even after you've completed draft after draft of a project. Passion means that you're willing to "go back in" one more time to get it right. When financial concerns dictate what most studios and movie producers are willing to make, the most direct impact is on the filmmaker. First, we creatives delight in spinning words into images. Telling visual stories is our particular passion. And passion is what agents, producers, and executives alike seek out. It is a powerful ally in choosing the kind of projects you want to do and the kind of career you want to have. Passion is the manna of inspiration from heaven—a currency passed from writer to producer to executive, then director and actor, down the line from key grip and best boy to editor, on to the promotions department and, ultimately, to the viewing audience. And therein lies the rub.

Above all else, Hollywood is a business. Writers should always be aware of what's going on in the market. Hollywood likes to couch the uncertainty that a new movie represents in as much financial security as possible. Go to any development meeting and you will quickly discover that producers and decision-makers crave track records and paradigms. They tend to go with established story elements from established writers. What this means for you, the writer trying to break in, is that it's going to require a special effort on your part for any studio to be comfortable in taking a chance on you, the unknown quantity. But it can be done. Check out AFI's list of "100

Greatest American Films" in Chapter 24, and you'll notice a predominant trait that I mentioned before: uniquely personal stories that resonate with universal themes with which many audiences can identify. Take, for example, *Casablanca,* written by Julius and Philip Epstein and Howard Koch. Here the personal sacrifice and moral dilemma of Humphrey Bogart's cynical expatriate, Rick Blaine, is played out against a backdrop of idealism and patriotism. The result is a powerful perspective on war, as well as the best closing scene ever written.

So what does Hollywood want? Writers who can tap into their own life experience or perspective to create stories for a wide audience. Scripters who can accomplish that will quickly find a place here. Meanwhile, omitting such voice from one's writing in a pursuit of pa$$ion may or may not result in short-term financial gain, but is guaranteed to produce long-term cynicism about the industry because following this path means you lose your grip on your beloved craft. That's a perspective that no writer attempting to realize his or her dream of making movies can afford.

-2-

I'm sure it's better than it sounds.

—A "FRIENDLY" PRODUCER, AFTER HEARING MY VERY FIRST PITCH

Don't believe the hype. You don't have to make a tremendous impact in your first year as a writer. Matt Damon and Ben Affleck's *Good Will Hunting* was five years in the making. Tom Schulman's *Dead Poets Society* was ten. Billy Bob Thornton spent nineteen years in the wilderness to get to *Sling Blade*. Notice a pattern? The Greeks *wish* they had a mythology as elaborate as our star-studded, gold-paved Hollywood myths of instant success. There is the fantasy of Hollywood and the reality of Hollywood. In other words, don't mistake Hollywood sizzle for steak. The reality of Hollywood requires patience and hard work. Lots of your favorite films were more than a decade in the making. On the real road to fame and riches, there are many, many potholes, and much rejection in them there Hollywood Hills, so much so, that I decided to include the section at the front of my book, just so you'll think about this reality as you read the rest of the tips I share. Literally hundreds of people will say no, in the form of nondecisions and passes, for every one that says yes on your project. But even one "yes" can make for a successful career. Often luck happens when preparation meets opportunity.

ADVICE ON REJECTION FROM A SEASONED, AWARD-WINNING WRITER

Some of the best advice I received came early in my career from Emmy Award–winning writer Cynthia Cidre (*Mambo Kings*) who has more spent more than twenty years in the business. She recommended the following Hollywood timetable: "Five years for overnight success and ten years to have a career." That's because even after that initial affirmation of all your hard work, dedication, and talent, rejection will still remain a big part of the business. So, for any sort of longevity, you must glean what you can from the naysayers, and discard their rebukes. Admittedly, when Cynthia Cidre imparted her hard-earned wisdom to me, I remember thinking, "Five years? Yeah, right! Maybe for other people, but I've got an advanced degree and Master Plan." But when, four years, nine months, and two days later, my first studio assignment came through following a string of small production company options and writing gigs, I heaved a huge sigh of relief and told myself I was right on track. A career in Hollywood is less a sprint than a marathon with intermittent bursts thrown in. That's why the kamikaze approach—"I'll blow into town for seven months while scoring up some meetings and big-money deals!"—is shortsighted. Writers should think about the big picture of what they want to accomplish, and then brace for the long haul. In practical terms you should definitely accept a midnight shift editing someone else's opus—or the thousand-dollar option on your masterpiece—just to keep yourself working and in the game. So here are three things to take into account when planning out your career strategy:

1. True-career building usually has a long, slow, logical progression that is more cyclical than linear.
2. Many ups and downs can occur during the three to four years that the average movie requires to go from script to screen.
3. Don't be in a hurry. Perfect your craft.

> *The business side never gets better. Only your craft improves.*
> —Ed Solomon, Writer, *Men In Black*

HOW TO HANDLE REJECTION

Rejection is a big part of the Hollywood landscape, but you can learn to deal with it. In fact, the sooner you do, the better off you'll be. It's a fact that upon achieving a certain proficiency with your work, you have zero control over the biblical pestilence of things that may go wrong—a three-picture deal hangs up in Legal Affairs, meanwhile the production company loses its development funding and your two-year deal is dead—or maybe a $46-million studio deal that would pay you $600,000 against $750,000 (the price paid for the project up front; "Against" refers to total additional monies paid if the screenplay is made into a movie) comes apart over $2 million for cable rights. Both war stories happened to me—and to just about anybody else you talk to here. The industry is a behemoth whose actions may feel crushing but are rarely personal. So when bad things happen, take a time-out. Get away from the situation as fast as you can. Yes, you have a lot riding on the result, but the sooner you gain perspective, the sooner you'll be able to correct a problem or come back with a new action plan. Sounds easier said than done, doesn't it? What follows is a quick story showing how I put the above into practice.

I once gave a new screenplay to a top producer with whom I had already worked. The producer called three weeks later, saying she would like to meet on the project. We did, and I walked away thinking we had a deal in the works. When none materialized, my agent couldn't illuminate the situation beyond saying that "they [the producer and her company] are slammed over there. They'll probably revisit the project in the spring." A call to the producer was returned by her assistant, who verified what I'd been told. Of course, my first reaction was to seethe. This seemed to me like months and months of work and careful strategy apparently down the drain for seemingly unfathomable reasons out of my control. Instead of continuing to stew, I called an independent film producer friend who happened to live near Santa Monica. The script was much too big for his budget, but I respected his opinion. We met for lunch, watching Rollerbladers on the boardwalk and taking in the midday sun and surf. At the end of the afternoon, I gave my friend the script to read. Five days later I was already feeling like myself again, busy with pitching on another project, when my friend e-mailed his thoughts. According to this producer, the script was a winner, but the setup was overly complicated and the first act too slow to develop. Most likely, the A-list producer who was known for getting projects made quickly had had reservations about taking time to correct the problems. While I might have felt "betrayed" by the A-list producer's apparent flip-flop and lack of commitment, instead I was euphoric at reading my friend's e-mail, since these were both issues I could easily correct. My time had not been wasted, and the project still had a bright future. Responsibility for my career was squarely back on my shoulders.

To repeat: Bad news in the form of a passed (rejected) script or dropped deal is inevitable. Again, it's nothing personal and it happens to EVERYONE. But you can always go walk your dog or hike into the canyons or drive out to Santa Monica to clear your head, then get back to the business of building your career.

> ## Five Keys to Dealing with Day-to-Day Frustrations
>
>
> 1. Be patient. Rome wasn't built in a day, and neither are most careers.
> 2. Give the process its due. Be willing to write and rewrite.
> 3. Choose only projects that challenge you—stories with themes that you are passionate about.
> 4. Passion is infectious. Learn to harness and communicate your excitement to others.
> 5. Try to glean information from every criticism you receive. Your focus should be on your work and ways to improve it. Avoid getting embroiled in personality conflicts.

Remember that even professional writers who spend six months completing a screenplay may give in to frustration when they receive critiques from the studio. These same writers may become unwilling to spend another month or two on the project. If a contract or accolades aren't immediately forthcoming, sometimes it's easier to abandon the project and start fresh on the next sure-fire million-dollar idea. Entitlement is a killer in our business. Getting a little success and thinking you're granted a secret handshake for life is dangerous. That's a problem I have perceived as a young writer regarding *some* older writers who seem to be hermetically sealed in their own sense of entitlement. Usually this "old attitude" is not related to their writing ability, but is a business conceit whereby these writers feel that they are owed a living by the industry. For example, the very first writing group I audited upon arrival to Los Angeles felt like the cast of *Twelve Angry Men*. Project discussion deteriorated into teeth-gnashing at "the system" even before I had time to put on my "Hello! My Name is Michael" name tag. I never went back. Of course, what these writers wanted was to recapture that moment long ago when it all seemed *so easy,* and what they were really railing against was a system where writers now have to prove themselves over and over again. A successful veteran writer once told me that writers especially tend to devolve into whiners over time. He blamed this on "the process." He was referring to that conga line of execs and above-the-line people who can wipe out six months of a writer's work in a single afternoon of notes, without giving the writer a chance to plead his case. I used to run into a writer/director who wrote series television in the early eighties but has worked sporadically since. Every time I saw him he repeated the same mantra: "Lemme tell you something, those executives (or producers, directors, agents, lawyers, valets, stevedores) are idiots. Don't let them screw you, because they will. Believe me, I know!" One day I was surprised when he suddenly asked me to read one of his new scripts. I was only slightly curious, but felt obligated to give it the ol' colleague try. A few days later I came back humbly with detailed comments that I felt would elevate the material beyond its current state, which was that of a good concept mired in a fog-bog of hastily executed clichés. After we talked it over, the writer admitted as much, but then said, "You gave me some great ideas, but that sounds like a lot of work. I just want to sell this thing and let somebody else figure it out. I think I'm gonna go with what I've got." All I could say was "Good luck." I realized then that the old timer's frustration with the industry was based on the fact that the industry doesn't award sloppy and lazy writers. Here I must tell you that no matter what level you reach as a writer in Hollywood, producers will almost always pressure you to bleed the edges—i.e., do free changes (if not free drafts). The request for revision is another kind of rejection, one that may still lead to ultimate rejection. You just have to be willing to view revision as further attention you can pay to your craft.

REVISING YOUR WORK IN THE FACE OF REJECTION

There are some frustrations that can be easily avoided. Never, never, never send an agent or a would-be producer a script that is hot off the presses (the only exceptions being unavoidable situations like assignments and revisions to shooting scripts under tight deadlines), because such a project is not ready for the market yet. The scriptwriting process means that a writer is trying to juggle a couple of dozen subtle and not-so-subtle story elements, and a few obvious problems may slip through the cracks. So a time buffer is needed. Remember, most agents are inundated with flawed material—they get their best possible rush from receiving a script that they can sell TODAY. Consequently, agents tire very easily from too much development and need for revision. In other words, they quickly lose enthusiasm for the specific project and for you as a client. Writers who continue to send out green scripts do so at the peril of their careers. As will be discussed in more depth later in this book, Hollywood literary agents are, first and foremost, *deal brokers*. That is their primary training. Despite what some agents may claim, few are motivated by hunkering down in the trenches, participating in hand-to-hand combat with a writer on an unsold spec. With all of the above in mind, I devised a system of Five Trusted Readers who understand the pitfalls of reading first drafts. This system provides me with a first line of response and rejection, but also clear instruction on how and why I need to revise my first drafts. It is a very valuable tool.

Five Trusted Readers

I use a system of Five Trusted Readers to check out my work and give feedback BEFORE I send my projects on to producers, or even to my agent. These readers are peers, former instructors, or industry people I have befriended who are willing to read my new project and whose opinions I value and trust. I made five the number because it's a tie-breaking odd number (if two like a story element and two don't, I always have a tie-breaker). Also, I found that three were too few opinions while seven meant I was waiting longer for more people to read my work. The makeup of the group shifts depending on circumstances and the type of project. For example, I won't give a science-fiction script to someone who has no interest in science fiction. So I look for a replacement reader.

No matter what deadlines I'm under, I always show my work to my readers first. Then it's rewrite, revise, rewrite. Remember Cynthia Cidre's little gem of a movie *Mambo Kings*? Thirty-two drafts of the script were required to get to the screen. Meanwhile, veteran playwright and screenwriter Craig Lucas wrote 26 drafts of *The Secret Lives of Dentists* before it reached the screens.

Writing is hard, and rewriting is inevitable. Not every moment of the creative process can be a Mardi Gras parade. As writer and psychotherapist Dennis Palumbo points out in his excellent book, *Writing from the Inside Out,* fear and doubt, procrastination, loneliness, and even creative blocks are all a normal part of the creative process. We fear failure and rejection, but these feelings are actually part of the process. Even the most established writers and directors experience profound doubt on a regular basis. That's because such a sense of discordance and isolation, and fear that "time is out of joint," is our very motivation to create. As Palumbo points out, without such feelings we would have story structure but no unique story. Those things that we often perceive to be inadequacies or defects are actually the building blocks of our creative process. If you don't put something of yourself in the frame or on the page, what's the point?

The Challenge to Write About One's Experiences

My first teaching job was a screenwriting course in a prison. In the class was a folksy older inmate whom I liked to think of as "Oregon Woods." He had lived in various communes in the desert and the Pacific Northwest during the 1970s, and wrote fluffy stories about teenage parties and "love-ins." One day he came to see me in my office and I said casually, "You lived in such an incredible time, but write such nonsense—what's up with that?" Oregon Woods shifted in his chair and there was a long silence before he told me that one morning more than two decades ago, he had dropped acid and decided to go for a drive at dawn along the California coast. Until a cop pulled him over, Oregon Woods knew nothing of the jogger he had struck and killed five miles back.

Oregon Woods's life spiraled down from there. He was haunted by a horrific event of which he had no memory. The room with just the two of us in it became very still. I quickly realized that this man's depth of despair and grief was beyond my experience or skills as an instructor. I said the only thing I could: "Can you write about it?" He paused, then replied, "I don't think I can . . . I guess I'm not cut out to be a writer." I said, "It's your call." Oregon Woods showed up a few more times, but didn't say much, then one day stopped coming to class. I never saw him again.

-3-

In this chapter we analyze factors that will help determine whether you are prepared to come to Los Angeles, as well as the feasibility of living and working outside of Hollywood. Recently a fellow screenwriter, a good friend I've known since film school, packed it in and jetted town. Hopefully, this writer will try again soon. The old saw that people in Hollywood succeed not on ability but by persistence remains true. No one ever really fails here, they simply quit. That my friend is talented, disciplined, and driven, but somehow has yet to catch on here, speaks volumes about how difficult it is to carve your personal Mount Rushmore into these Hollywood Hills. Film is the most dominant art form in contemporary culture, and, as a sought-after vocation, has considerably more sparkle than, say, iron smelting. Such allure makes ours one of the most difficult industries to break into, and great personal ability and pricey film school training may not always be enough to ensure that one will make it. Indeed, the odds against thriving here, or even surviving, can be daunting. Every day, however, many beat the odds and make it. The very same week my colleague made the decision to move on, another friend, a director, who deferred his migration to L.A. for several years and tried to work from the Right Coast, finally arrived in town. His first words to me were, "Man, I'm just thrilled to be here. Now I can commit one hundred percent to the dream."

WHAT ARE YOUR CRITERIA FOR COMING TO L.A.?

Hollywood is the land of laptops, cell phones, designer water, and decaf caramel mocha latte. It's the best town on the planet in which to create and express yourself—when things are clicking. You can peer at mountainscapes (white-capped in winter, smog-capped in summer) as you write in the early morning, then catch a dynamite story meeting at the studio with an exec who is as excited about your project as you are. Afterwards, you may be invited to attend a private screening of a new movie directed by a friend, followed by a drive out to Santa Monica to watch the pounding—if sometimes dingy brown—surf beneath a glowing California sunset. That can be a typical day. But it takes time to get to that point.

So, should you say good-bye to your cat and U-Haul just your Craftmatic bed and toaster oven to be here? Your decision to move to L.A. boils down to this:

- Anything that creates forward momentum is a plus, and moving to L.A. is real forward momentum. Anything that creates inertia or self-doubt is to be avoided.
- If your prime motivations for writing are "money!" and "everybody else in the solar system seems to be doing it," don't come.
- Don't come if comparing your feet to Arnold Schwarzenegger's size-elevens in front of Mann's Chinese Theater is the first thing you intend to do upon arrival.

Instead, ask yourself these three simple questions:

1. Is there an original and unique voice in my writing or in my films?
2. How will I find time to make money and write when I get to Hollywood?
3. What are my immediate goals? What are my long-term goals?

HOW DO YOU KNOW WHEN YOU ARE READY TO MOVE TO L.A.?

The simplest quantifying answer is that because living, working, and writing in Hollywood presents many unique challenges—cost of living in particular—you should complete at least two *solid* short films or sample screenplays before making the move. These are works whose merits have been recognized by any of the more than a dozen major film festivals and competitions around the United States. Beyond having these complete, polished works, each writer's creative process and time line is unique. Because there are several important pros and cons to living in Tinseltown, you will need to establish your own criteria for determining whether the time is right for your relocation to Los Angeles, based on the factors I present in this chapter.

THE PROS AND CONS OF LIVING IN L.A.

Filmmaking is a relationship business because it involves the extremely intense collaboration of hundreds of people for weeks, months, and even years at a time. Frequently, producers and directors use military jargon like "going to war on a project." It can get that tight. You're all putting in interminable hours and pulling for the same thing. By day three, that A-list actress you thought was so aloof is asking how your dog is feeling. That's why the notion of "build it and they will come" doesn't work here. A writer should be in the trenches, too, ready to be his own best advocate for his work.

Producers, directors, and writers have to get out and push their work by constantly generating new leads, working the trades and the pitch fests, and researching buyers in the trades and around town. A writer/director I know who recently completed a $650,000 independent film has been working every film festival from Cannes to Lake Arrowhead, attempting to set up theatrical distribution theater by theater, country by country. For this kind of face-to-face connection, being in town is a decided advantage. You never know when an exec may call impromptu to say, "If you're not busy today, let's hang out and kick this thing around." Or, at the gas station, you may run into the star who would be *perfect* for your project. It happens. For example, actor Jim Gandolfini was my wife Sonia's former client. That connection eventually resulted in a meeting and interest in one of my projects. A "creative" on the move takes a lot of meetings and knows all of the projects in development—especially those that pertain to their genre. That's pretty tough to do on a regular basis when you're in Piscataway, New Jersey.

It's hard to believe that a hundred years ago Hollywood was little more than a sleepy enclave in the desert, specializing in silent films called "short reels." The movie industry, still in its infancy, had chosen a Southern California location both for its abundance of good weather and natural sunlight and to avoid the cost of electricity. Thus, Ithaca, New York's loss (it was the first home of the film industry) was California's gain.

The idea of conducting business over a meal is a holdover from those simpler times. Remember that Hollywood is a place where success can be proportionate to the number of times you eat breakfast, "do" lunch, dinner, or drinks, and have other, more formal meetings in a single day. If you're physically here, there's much greater opportunity to meet the people with whom you're eventually going to be working. "When are you going to write me that part?" is a running joke I have with a TV actor whom I run into around town seemingly every month. One benefit of film school is that you'll probably come out here and travel in a pack with a class of fellow plebes. That means that as soon as one person in your posse hears about an opportunity, you'll learn about it, too. For example, a director who gets a shot at a new show will solicit the writers he or she knows for scripts. That sort of thing happens all the time, and is the means by which many of us writers commonly obtain work.

There are disadvantages to living in L.A. as well. Rent a house with a yard in New Hampshire for $350 a month, write full-time and have a part-time job to cover the essentials—*or* get a modest two-bedroom apartment in the San Fernando Valley for $1,600 a month and work two jobs and write on weekends and in the hours between midnight and 3:00 a.m. Rejection of your work can be expensive at these prices. My life during my first three years in Hollywood, as I hunted for crappy $1,500 options, was augmented by teaching college courses in a prison, working as a weekend manager of a real estate office, and sometimes filling in as a paralegal for a city attorney who handled a few private cases on the side. So you have to hustle to live here. However, having a day job that you enjoy and that consistently pays the bills, yet provides an opportunity to write on the side and let the process move forward, is a solid buffer against becoming a broke, angry writer who is no fun at parties. Striking such a balance isn't easy. One key is discipline—establishing a time to write every day and then sticking to it. Having a writing group where you are expected to submit pages for the group read each month is one way to ensure you stay on track.

Another strategy is to figure out exactly how much money you need to live, then find the base level employment that meets that criteria. For example, what's the point of being a corporate executive earning $125,000 a year if you're miserable because you can't find free time to write? Perhaps you'd be happier running the night shift of a copy shop where no one cares if you write while the print jobs are processing or business is slow. And if the copy shop is in Southern California, chances are your co-workers will also be "creatives," and many of the jobs you process will be projects coming from production companies. A writer/director/producer I know learned a lot about the kinds of scripts that made it into production by scanning such projects as they came through the copy shop he managed.

Temping is another good alternative, especially here in Los Angeles, since some agencies specialize in placing you at studios and production companies. It's a good way to get a worm's-eye view of the moviemaking system in action. The jobs can last as little as a day or can stretch out to months, and are great opportunities for networking. Often, good temps are offered permanent positions since most producers and execs like to hire from the inside. A friend of mine who temped at Disney ended up as a writer twelve months later just by being in the right place at the right time. Such an occurrence is unusual, but it *can* happen.

Hollywood Temp Agencies

Ad Personnel, Beverly Hills
310-284-3939
(Advertising agencies)

Apple One, Glendale
818-247-2991
(Disney, NBC, Warner Bros)

Friedman Agency, West Hollywood
310-550-1002
(Various)

The Right Connections
310-657-3700
(Disney)

Star Personnel, Beverly Hills
310-278-8630
(Paramount Studios and Talent Agencies)

Ultimate Staffing, Century City
310-201-0062
(Fox)

Venturi Staffing (formerly Thomas Staffing) Los Angeles (Mid-Wilshire)
323-931-9400
(Paramount Studios and E! Entertainment)

Websites for Film, TV, Writing, and Job-Jobs
www.mediabistro.com (writing jobs)
www.sunoasis.com (writing jobs)
www.writerswrite.com/cgi-bin/listjobs.pl (writing jobs)
www.journalismjobs.com
www.Film.com (nationwide crew placement)
Castandcrew.com (payroll and talent services)
Crewcalldirectory.com (nationwide crew placement)
Filmstaff.com (nationwide crew placement)
Mandy.com (film and TV job postings)
www.showbizjobs.com
www.entertainmentcareers.net
www.showbizdata.com
www.craigslist.org
www.awn.com (animation jobs)
www.cooljobs.com
www.flipdog.com
www.hotjobs.com
www.monster.com
www.techies.com (computer jobs)
Planet Shark.com
EmployNow.com

Temporary Housing and Sublets
LosAngelescraigslist.org

Working for free, or interning, is another tried-and-true way to build the necessary credits to land an industry job. Cull through the *Hollywood Creative Directory,* which is the leading source for contacting nearly 10,000 producers and studio and network executives representing over 1,750 production companies, studios and networks. The *HCD* includes addresses, phone and fax numbers, staff and titles, credits and studio deals. You should find a spot within days. The downside, of course, is that you will be working without pay or benefits, so you'll need savings or a part-time job. One friend who is now a Hollywood producer got her first break by interning three days a week for a well-known actress. She was offered her first assistant position within six months. Note that some writer/producers have interns, but the practice is less common than with full production companies or at the studio.

THE THOMAS GUIDE

Los Angeles County comprises some 312 cities and communities. Unless you are coming from New York or London or another great international city, the vastness of Greater Los Angeles can be overwhelming. In fact, according to the *Newcomer's Handbook for Los Angeles,* discussed later in this section, this city is large enough to fit St. Louis, Milwaukee, Cleveland, Minneapolis, San Francisco, Boston, Pittsburgh, and Manhattan all within the city borders. Studios and production companies are spread out across Los Angeles from Santa Monica to Beverly Hills, from Hollywood to Santa Clarita. It can take over an hour and a half to drive from one place to another over freeways, mountain roads, and surface streets. Not knowing where something is, or how long it takes to get there, is not a viable excuse for missing a meeting or being late. So the first book you buy upon arrival should be a *Thomas Guide,* a map book that's more than one inch thick, is updated annually, and is indispensable for getting around Southern California. Based on personal experience, I highly recommend that you study this good book a bit before the time comes when you actually need it. During my first visit to Los Angeles,

I purchased a *Thomas Guide* the night before my very first two meetings in Hollywood. These meetings just happened to be with executives with studios at the opposite ends of the city. Sweating and swearing through rush-hour traffic on L.A.'s notorious freeways, I somehow managed to crash-land my rental car at Disney Studios in Burbank on time. It was certainly no way to take my very first industry meeting. Afterwards I opted to return to my hotel in Hollywood, drop off the car, and call a cab to take me to Sony in Culver City. I was on time there, too, but the ride cost nearly fifty dollars, which was my meal budget for the entire week.

WHERE TO LIVE

L.A. is composed of many city-states, each with its own character, its own pluses and minuses. Your objective should be to find a place that's in line with your habits and interests. For example, one friend is willing to pay a little more in order to be minutes away from the museums along the Museum Mile district of Wilshire Boulevard. It's probably not a good idea to sublet a place just above Sunset Strip if you're not into the club scene. Despite the panoramic views, such a place will have you locked in your living space by 10:00 p.m. each night as you avoid the crowds and grit your teeth at the ceaseless honking and squealing of cars. One rule of thumb is that rent is cheaper the deeper into San Fernando Valley you go, mainly because of the sometimes searing desert heat in summer, where temperatures can reach as high as 112 in places like Santa Clarita. If the prospect of watching children turn sand into glass on the sidewalk right outside your apartment alarms you, then moving too far inland probably isn't an option at any price. Of course, it's only uncomfortably hot for about three or four months of the year. Conversely, the cost of living rises the closer you get to the Pacific Ocean, which remains temperate and cloaked in a morning sea mist even during the hottest months. Here, it's not uncommon for people to pay $600 to $2,000 a month or even more to live in apartments as small as 200 square feet.

To figure out what area will work best work for you, I highly recommend the *Newcomer's Handbook for Los Angeles* by Joan Wai and Stacey Ravel Abarbanel. The authors have profiled most neighborhoods within Los Angeles County. Most of the resources you will need are covered, including utilities, local banks, cable, mail, publications, public transportation options, child care, and public school districts. The book also covers recreational activities, museums, public parks, shopping districts, and annual events throughout the city.

What Should You Have Before Arriving in Hollywood?

1. The security deposit on an apartment, as well as enough money to tide you over for eight weeks (figure on a total of $2,500) while you look for work to pay the bills and until you receive your first check.
2. An idea and strategy for obtaining a full-time or part-time job that will still allow you to pursue your writing career.
3. Two polished screenplays and/or two short films that have been transferred to video or DVD.
4. A productive writing regiment.
5. A reliable automobile.

WHAT IS A WRITER'S "VOICE," AND HOW DO YOU MAKE YOURS STAND OUT IN HOLLYWOOD?

As I've said, it's not enough just to show up in L.A. with a burning desire to be a writer. You will need something that sets you apart from the competition. In Hollywood, the corollary to success having many fathers, and failure being an orphan, is that the career ladder to success has many, many rungs, all of which are slathered with Krazy Glue. So it's important to have the following four virtues in your arsenal: *voice* in your work; *patience* for a process that may take several years; the desire to build your support *community;* and the *commitment* to make sure you work every day.

First, let's put things into perspective by doing a bit of math. In a given year, 50,000 screenplays will be registered with the Writers Guild of America (WGA). Of that number, about 5,000, or 10 percent, will earn money through optioning (a studio, production company, and or producer pays someone for the exclusive rights to a literary property for a set amount of time. At the end of that time period, the material can, in most cases, be optioned again, but if not, the rights revert back the original owner, i.e., the writer). That's means 45,000, or 90 pecent of the 50,000 scripts will never earn a dime. However, of the 5,000 screenplays that are purchased or optioned, only 200, or 4 percent, of the money-earners will be made into movies. So the odds of a script being bought are ten to one, and the odds of a script being turned into a movie are 250 to one. Pretty sobering, huh? Of course, you'll cut those odds down considerably just by applying what you learn from reading this book. But you're still going to need a script that cooks with heat, that gets people's attention. I have been paid for more than half of the projects I've written. I'm proud of that fact, even though the monetary compensation has sometimes been limited to as little as five hundred dollars. My "secret" is not competing with the other 45,000 writers. Okay, so how does one do that? VOICE.

Around once every two weeks, a reader of my magazine column queries me about relocating. I wouldn't recommend packing the Yugo until you at least have the seeds of what will become your most important commodity and currency, your *voice*—that wonderfully magical, ethereal word the industry uses in sometimes hushed, reverential tones, as in, "This writer has a fresh voice." The term connotes everything from a writer's uniquely personal style or perspective to a grasp of specific themes or an ability to work with subject matter that is commercially viable.

In practical terms, a voice means having something to say, whether about teen angst, the detachment we all feel in the midst of the "communications era," etc. It is a point of view, a style, and an intimacy or urgency flowing through your work. Veteran screenwriter Jon Cohen (*Minority Report, Riptide*) explains his voice this way: "My one rule is write big. No matter what they tell you, if your sentences are rich and compelling, then you're telling the story that way as well. Somehow be spare and get to the good parts fast, the standard rule, but when you're doing the good parts fast, remember fast does not mean skeletal and lean. Let them smell the copper in the blood and the slippery lick of the tongue."

Every time one of those enthusiastic "New Guns Taking Hollywood by Storm" articles appears in a magazine or a newspaper, 10,000 people across the planet drop what they're doing and move here. What will they say with their words and images when they get their opportunity? What part of the human condition means something to them? *What is their voice?* Too often writers leave that part of the equation blank. People get here, quickly lose their way, and start writing and rewriting the same two or three scripts over and over in an attempt to work an angle for a perceived opportunity. Often you'll hear writers say the most improbable things, like "I'm reworking my slasher script into a romantic comedy period piece because that's what's hot." Such an attitude can become a one-way ticket to the land of cynicism, which can poison a writer's creative process. And if you do have a distinct voice, it can be hard at times to get that voice heard.

Hollywood seeks out fresh voices via film school programs and best-and-brightest competitions like the Sundance Institute and the Nicholl Fellowship. As will be discussed in more depth in Chapter 20, doing well in the competitions is a good way to clear the first hurdle to getting your work read and noticed by professionals, that is, getting your "voice" heard. Another opportunity can be had at industry-sponsored pitch fests, where writers pay for the privilege of pitching their projects, for periods as short as 120 seconds, to low- to mid-level executives and producers. Such pitch fests are advertised on sites throughout the Web. Simply search for the keywords "screenwriter pitch fest." Unfortunately, these grope encounters between scribes and gatekeepers can be pricey, ranging from about twenty-five dollars into the hundreds. Be aware that competition is fierce and there is no "top secret," foolproof way to get noticed. As I will repeat throughout this book, the best way to get noticed is to write a polished, bulletproof script. Sounds easy, right? Unfortunately, ninety percent of the scripts submitted to Hollywood do not meet this criterion. A nifty concept poorly executed won't be enough to set up your career.

Don't, however, try to develop your voice once you get to town. Because many of us here came from someplace else, we quickly discover that we are far from our sources of life experience and creative inspiration. Although a writer will learn a tremendous amount about the craft of moviemaking just by being here, you have to have a strong foundation of writing experience and voice *before* you arrive. One of the hardest parts about being an "artist" in Tinseltown is the white noise of the industry, by which I mean that everyone you meet here seems to be working on developing movie projects and writing screenplays. Everyone. That's an odd feeling for writers who are used to being a rare, rogue breed in their hometowns. The buzz of the entertainment industry is ever-constant here. For example, a couple of years ago, a studio exec insisted on holding a story meeting with me at a trendy coffeehouse on Sunset. Initially the place was so loud that I couldn't hear myself think. Within minutes, however, clusters of people at every table around us had abruptly stopped talking, hanging on every word as I pitched revisions to my climactic third act. The exec loved the attention, but for me it was freaky, and I struggled to stay focused.

Learning Patience Once You Get to L.A.

You also have to be emotionally set for Hollywood. Rejection and still more rejection is an integral part of the business, as we'll discuss further in later chapters. The average period needed to go from script to screen for a single project is about three to four years, so there's an enormous time investment required by all involved to make a movie. It takes time to prepare a script that is ready to be checked out by an agent and then ready to be read by a producer or director. Many writers who come here seem unwilling to make such a time commitment, and attempt to leapfrog steps in the process to get a deal, usually with disastrous results. Once a *green draft* (a raw and unpolished, usually first draft of a screenplay) has been circulated to and passed on by potential buyers, that script is effectively dead. All your work is wasted. So, along with your financial cushion and your keen voice, you have to bring the virtue of patience to Hollywood. If you don't have it, don't make the effort of moving.

A Question to Ask Yourself

Do you want to pursue a full-time job with a career and have less time to write, or take a day job at Kinko's that affords more time to write, but is markedly tougher on the ego? The answer is that you should do what makes you happiest. Hiding from creditors and bill collectors is a certain path to personal misery and a short career. As a case in point, I know a producer who didn't date or socialize for ten months because his projects weren't going well. When I told him that I thought that was a pretty crappy way to live, he shrugged and said, "First of all, I'm broke. Second, I can't deal with all the questions. I mean these are the same people I'm trying to sell to. So it's easier to just stay home." About twelve months later he was out of the business.

BUILDING YOUR SUPPORT COMMUNITY

While attending grad school in Miami, well outside of Los Angeles, I used to meet with three other writers on a weekly basis to share work. Friday was set aside for screening and discussing new movies, often with a member of the faculty. I look back at that period very fondly. In some ways my community there was stronger and more focused than anything I've found here.

People outside of L.A. can join a film or screenwriting group in their area. And they can attend seminars and other events hosted by the Directors Guild of America (DGA), the American Film Institute (AFI), and the Writers Guild of America (WGA), where they will have contact with agents, producers, and other established professionals in their chosen field. Actually, it would be more helpful for you to volunteer to work at these seminars rather than simply attending them, because you'll get more one-on-one contact with the people you're trying to meet, and you'll make more of an impression on them. For example, several years ago, I was interning at the Key West Film & Literature Symposium in Florida when the program director assigned me to escort a distinguished screen-writer, novelist, and playwright who would be speaking on panels throughout the day. The writer was William Goldman, legendary author of *Butch Cassidy and the Sundance Kid,* and many others. The time spent with him changed my life. Because cinema involves so many people, it's crucial to know others at your career level and above for emotional support and guidance. The Internet has made it easier than ever to build your community. Look up writers' group chat rooms and discussion boards like the DoneDeal message board at http://pub130.ezboard.com/bdonedeal.

Bottom line: Working outside of Hollywood may add to your frustration and sense of isolation, but it can lessen your cynicism about a place where the day-to-day ebb and flow takes its toll. How-ever, people outside of Southern California must be proactive about building their film community. Community is an indespensible virtue if you want to make it as a screenwriter.

The Most Important Virtue: Commitment

As stated above, upon arrival here, you will most likely have to lead a dual life with a part-time job. Yet the simple but undeniable truth is that you must make time to partake in your craft *every day,* even if only for fifteen minutes. Shooting a film or writing a script requires muscles that quickly atrophy with disuse. We creative types are innately curious beings—we seek out and attempt to unlock the mys-teries of existence. The danger is that we can easily become side-tracked with other interests. Many fledgling directors and writers come up with the seeds of brilliance, then put them aside, assuming those seeds will still be there when they return to start anew. Usually they're gone. Instead, think of your craft like Sharon Stone in *The Muse.* She's maddeningly precocious and flighty and requires constant nurturing, but the rewards are great, and you can't make it without her. In the end, it costs nothing to hit the pad and start writing.

Ten Tips for Keeping Your Commitment to Write Every Day

1. A well-kept secret among pros is that they "get it all down ASAP." In other words, these writers write as quickly as possible to get everything down on the page in order to complete the script. When blocked, I have occasionally resorted to using a stopwatch to sprint-write my way through a tough section of pages.

2. Rewriting is when the real writing begins. That's why it's so crucial to get the first draft down on the page quickly. Relieve yourself of the pressure to hit the ball out of the park on the first draft.

3. Obey your biorhythms. If you're a morning person, schedule time to write then. Write at the same time every day.

4. Don't mix activities. When you take time to write, do that exclusively. For example, if you have scheduled your writing from 7:00 to 11:00 a.m., don't also answer phone calls or surf the Net during that period.

5. Don't allow yourself to be distracted while you work. If your living space isn't conducive to writing, go somewhere else, such as a library or coffeehouse.

6. Reach out to your local or online writing community. It's easier to stay on pace when you're discussing your work with colleagues. Sometimes it's helpful to think of yourselves as heirs apparent to the Algonquin Round Table or the American expatriates of 1920s Paris.

7. Keep a tracking board. Use a dry marker to color-code script submissions, charting their progress in the marketplace—including follow-up dates, etc. Likewise, keep a work journal that charts how many pages you have completed in a given day, as well as schedule projections, story issues to resolve, and marketing contact leads.

8. See as many movies and read as many produced scripts as you can. Learn what elements cause a film to succeed or fail. Early on in my writing career, I attended bad movies on purpose to see where they went off course and how I might have fixed them.

9. Develop pre-writing rituals. Take a brisk walk, answer e-mail for thirty minutes, sharpen pencils, or prepare coffee or tea before starting to work.

10. This is your dream. Keep in mind that you are making this commitment for yourself. Nurture your dream with patience and dedication to your craft.

FINAL NOTE

We of this industry are risk-takers by nature. Many who heed the cry of "location, location, location!" and leave their comfortable setups back home quickly realize they can't write or direct as effectively here. Many writers have a more comfortable setup for writing back home, and the white noise and pressure of suddenly being in a town where *everyone* seems to be a producer, writer, or director can sometimes throw them. Others stay put, but feel disconnected from the pursuit and target of their dreams. The key to a successful choice is deciding whether you'll benefit more from an autonomous existence or from seeing the hooks, wires, and mirrors of Hollywood up close and personal.

The Script-to-Screen Process

PART TWO

-4-

Those who dream by day are cognizant of many things which escape those who dream only by night.

—EDGAR ALLAN POE

A SNAPSHOT OF THE ACQUISITION PROCESS

For your project to find a home at the studio, it must navigate the following minefield:

A script is submitted by an agent to the production company or studio for consideration by the *story editor,* who manages a stable of script readers who will then evaluate or *cover* the project. If the project garners good coverage, a young executive may choose to read it. This executive is either a creative executive or a director of development (the titles are virtually synonymous). The clout of these CEs and DDs is mainly by recommendation of a project to their boss, usually a VP. Note that a great amount of material is going through smaller and smaller funnels.

The next step up is the VP of development. These execs bring in material, networking with agents, and lead projects through the development maze. Above the VP is the president of production, who is empowered to greenlight projects for acquisition. Every script arriving at a production company must fight its way up to every level until there is a critical mass of executives backing it. Once the president of production comes on board, then the project is optioned or purchased, or it is brought to the studio for the same purpose.

Meetings with the writer of the project begin after contracts have been drawn up. Note that guild writers are guaranteed at least one rewrite draft. The writer is brought in to meet with the development executives on the project (usually one VP and one C.E.), where the notes that the C.E. wrote are presented; either verbally, or actually on paper. A lot of prodcos use story notes internally, preferring to dispense their thoughts to the writer verbally in discussion form. Now, the writer goes off to knock out the rewrite. The meeting-rewrite process continues as many times as the contract requires, until the studio either decides that the script is ready to go into pre-production, or a new writer is hired.

WHY EVERYONE WRITES AND YOU SHOULD, TOO

In Hollywood there are many, many golden doors leading to career opportunities, but all of those portals seem to be surrounded by razor wire. Aside from self-generated projects in the form of independently financed, low-budget movies, which we will discuss in depth later, specs are the keys to the Hollywood realm and the lifeblood of the industry. They are the best way to control your destiny. Producers need intellectual properties to develop into films, and the vast majority come in the form of spec scripts. That's why everybody writes. Producers, directors, actors, studio executives, and, yes, even writers. And what they write are specs, which we discuss in depth later in this section.

WHAT YOU SHOULD BE WRITING

The best answer to this is a mix of everything: specs, assignments, and "passion projects." For example, for several years now I have been conducting research for a spec about baseball leagues in the Japanese-American internment camps of World War II. Writers who work exclusively on assignments work with ideas and story lines generated by someone else. Such filtering limits the potential for artistic and personal expression. While such projects can be lucrative, the downside is that your writing will become extremely formulaic and derivative. When that happens, the industry will brand you a *hack*, the pejorative term for a writing gun-for-hire who delivers strictly formulaic work. Eventually, such writers are shut out of the best projects in Hollywood. It is presumed that with specs you are writing whatever you want to write, while assignments entail writing what someone else tells you to write.

There is also a distinction between specs with a decidedly market-oriented slant, which can showcase your talent and help you find a place in the industry during the early stages of establishing your career, and the more personal writing you may opt for later on. Many established writers who shift over to doing predominantly assignment writing (which can be extremely lucrative) once their careers are on track soon feel that something's missing artistically. And so these writers may pass on assignments in favor of working on passion project specs. For example, Ed Solomon, who is primarily known for writing *Men In Black*, wrote and directed *Levity*, based on his experiences mentoring prison inmates.

"What are you working on?" is a perfectly good conversational segue in a variety of social circles, that will generally solicit information about someone's passion project. If what everyone "really wants to do is direct," one may decide that the shortest means to that end is to write specs. That's because Hollywood will break many "rules" in order to obtain a hot script. A legendary tale is the story of an unknown Sylvester Stallone holding out for the lead role in *Rocky*, which he wrote. Similarly, Chaz Palminteri refused to sell his screenplay for *A Bronx Tale* unless he was given one of the leading roles.

Writing to Direct

If you write two hit movies, you can demand to direct the next script you write. At other times, if you sense that a company wants your project (a preemptive offer in advance of the script going out into the market is one such clue), you can insist on directing the project yourself. Nine times out of ten, the purchaser will opt to pay you more money *not* to direct.

Except for a few executives who are career studio people and are not on their way to becoming producers, everyone else in Hollywood is essentially an independent contractor. As an independent contractor, you work for yourself, and your time is literally your own. Unfortunately, the downside is that there isn't much security in Hollywood, but writing is the one way of creating something of potentially great worth out of nothing. That's because writing a spec is the single endeavor in Hollywood that makes you self-sufficient. Think about it: actors cannot act without a script, nor can directors direct. The screenplay is the basis for all other work in the industry. If your goal is to be able to create and make a living wherever and whenever you want, then this is the occupation for you.

WHERE DO PROJECTS COME FROM?

Studios receive potential movie projects from producers and would-be producers that they put into development, the process of "going from the page to the screen." Only one in twelve projects will ever get made into movies. Projects come from two sources: *specs*, which are original source materials written specifically for the screen (*Lethal Weapon* and *The Sixth Sense* were both spec scripts shopped in the market for producers and studios); and *adaptations*, or translations of finished written work into film. Adaptations mainly come from the following sources:

- Books: literary works with a strong narrative line that can be translated into a visual medium. Both *Lord of the Rings* and the Harry Potter series came from books.
- Plays designed for the theater and converted to the big screen. Think of Mel Gibson's *Hamlet*, which might have been called *Dis Dane!* if the project had been produced by Jerry Bruckheimer.
- Comic books. Two of the following three projects originated from comic books. Can you guess which one didn't? *Men In Black*, *X-Men*, and *Sophie's Choice*.
- Journalism: newspapers or magazines. *The Rookie* first appeared as a newspaper story.

Of course, such speculation involves inherently long odds. As stated earlier, something like 50,000 scripts are registered with the Writers Guild of America (WGA) each year; however, you can bet that about 90 percent of those scripts will be poorly written retreads of successful movies that came out the year before. So you can rise immediately to the top 10 percent of all screenwriters simply by avoiding that trap. Remember that the top 5 percent of scripts registered with the WGA in a given year are the only ones that will receive monetary compensation, and you can enhance your odds 100 percent by just using the standard Hollywood three-act storytelling of setup, complication, and resolution to express what is otherwise your own story and unique perspective. Of course, both new and more experienced writers sometimes chafe at the limitations of such a rigid structure. As Ken Dancyger and Jeffrey Rush point out in their excellent book *Alternative Scriptwriting: Successfully Breaking the Rules*, there are philosophical limitations to the three-act or "restorative" three-act structure. With this storyline, your main character or protagonist must recognize and address a personal flaw or Achilles' heel that impedes greatness and threatens to destroy him or her. For example, actors like Tom Cruise have created a cottage industry of stories about young men who must overcome the ghosts of their father in films like *A Few Good Men, Top Gun,* and *Rain Man.* Resolution of this internal struggle ("I deserve my own destiny!") leads to a triumphant conquest of an external goal (saving the world, winning the game, vanquishing evil, having a loving relationship with others, etc.). Much like the Book of Job, the protagonist's world is first destroyed and then "restored" to a higher level than when the story began. If you detect a bit of the "pull yourself up by your bootstraps" puritan work ethic and self-determinism that is the bedrock philosophy of our culture, you're right. And such a paradigm may not jell well with a story about, say, Eastern culture, where events and circumstances are perceived to be well beyond the control of an individual. American movies as disparate as *Memento* and *She's Gotta Have It* have eschewed three-act structure. All I can say is that if you decide upon another structure for your story, check out *Alternative Scriptwriting* and make sure you nail your story cold.

Low-Budget Filmmaking As Another Way In

The low-budget, straight-to-video world is a good way to start working as a writer in Hollywood. Budgets generally range from $350,000 to $3 million, often arrived at by selling in advance the foreign distribution rights, literally based on who the actor is on the video cover. Certain B- and C-list, mainly action-oriented actors command a certain price in the foreign market place. Most of this kind of work is non–Writers Guild union, so a writer can anticipate compensation in the $20,000–40,000 range—far below WGA minimum standards. That sounds like a lot of money for a story about a vampire rock band, but your agent will take 10 percent and the tax man's take is about 32 percent, leaving you with as little as $11,600 to live on. If, however, you can write fast and deliver a script in about three weeks, the endeavor can be quite lucrative.

The following are some criteria for low-budget filmmaking:

- Limited locations save money and help with short shooting schedules that last only a couple of weeks versus the ten weeks or longer of a typical mainstream Hollywood production. A big-budget production team will consider shooting two pages of script in a single day to be a very good day. A low-budget crew must find a way to shoot as many as ten pages in the same amount of time.
- Limited use of computer-generated special effects (CGI), because they are very expensive. Instead, low-budget filmmakers like gunplay and car chases, because they are guaranteed adrenaline-inducing but cheap thrills.
- Horror, martial arts, and action are the predominant genres of low-budget films, so avoid submitting a romantic comedy as a writing sample unless the script happens to be *Bride of Chuckie.*
- Many LB projects are conceived with money in hand first (mainstream studio projects start with a piece of material and *then* financing). For example, a Hong Kong company partners with an American company to make a karate vampire movie for a budget of $1.5 million. Rather than attempting to read hundreds of spec scripts, the American producers may listen to a week or two's worth of pitches before hiring a writer. That writer should be prepared to write very fast. Five to ten pages a day is a typical pace for a production schedule that may only be six weeks away.

An element to consider here is the fact that many unsavory characters swim in the low-budget waters. Checks bounce or sometimes fail to arrive in this bottom-feeder's netherworld of the industry, so a writer must go in with eyes wide open and research the company's reputation in town and over the Internet. For example, the MO of one producer I've come across is to start production on three movies simultaneously, all the while well aware that he has financing in place for one. Crews are already hard at work when the checks stop coming or start bouncing, and so are forced to make the painful decision whether or not to work for free in hopes of compensation from the finished product. When enough ill will and creditors have built up, the producer simply disbands the company and, with his limited-liability protection, starts up a new one. People are always desperate to break in to the business, so very soon the producer is fully staffed for a new set of projects. Everyone in the industry knows about this character, but people who fail to ask around will pay the price.

On the other hand, low-budget Hollywood films can be a great training ground. I can honestly say I have tried to elevate every one of my "gene-spliced lizard people addicted to ozone" assignments above the ordinary fare. It's important not to be condescending about taking on one of these projects. Remember that the humble, low-budget *Piranha* (the 1978 version) was directed by Joe Dante from a script by John Sayles. One key to landing these assignments is never to project an attitude that says, "I consider myself way too good for this kind of work." One time I received a message from a talented colleague who stated that he was going through some rough times professionally, and was now "willing to take a cabana boy assignment" if I knew of one. In response, I offered to do what I could, but knew that the writer's poor attitude would never see him past the initial meeting with a low-budget producer.

THE PITFALLS OF TRYING TO WRITE FOR THE MARKET

Screenwriters are nothing if not resilient risk-takers, so if you say that it only requires one script to knock down the walls of Jericho, you're right. However, writing specs designed specifically to chase the capricious market is a mistake. One studio reader tells me that ninety percent of the hundreds of scripts he covers each year fall into this category. So the question remains, "How does one particular script, your script, rise above others and be the one?" Director

Sidney Lumet answers with a series of *what* questions in his excellent book, *Making Movies*: "What is this movie about? . . . What is it about emotionally? What is the theme, the spine, the arc? . . . What does the movie mean to me?" In other words, "Is there a voice?" The unsolicited spec is your best opportunity to put something of yourself on the page.

The best solution to the "specs taste great"/"assignments are filling" debate is to pitch on projects that interest you (your agent should have boards on every project in development in Hollywood, and will pursue projects closest to your aesthetic). With a little luck, assignments can tide you over financially, even as you continue to write your own stories. These specs should be less encumbered by market considerations. To that end, my own personal goal is to write market-driven material for six months of the year, and for the other six months to write or produce independent films that have Hollywood-level craftsmanship.

WHO OWNS WHAT YOU WRITE?

The answer is, "You do . . . until the moment you sell it." Of all artistic pursuits, only the screenwriter loses intellectual proprietorship of his finished work. Someone else literally owns the scenes, and the very words we write, and can mold them in any way they see fit. Imagine if Kenny G bought the rights to Beethoven's Fifth and proceeded to rewrite the symphony until the point where he could claim creative authorship, or if a Louvre curator used Crayolas to increase The Mona Lisa's bustline, then renamed her *Moaning Leeza* to boost ticket sales. Many producers and execs are motivated to help the writer realize his vision. But this is not always the case. Take, for example, a co-opting process in which J. F. Lawton's poignant and bittersweet screenplay about decaying urban life and a Cinderella fantasy gone wrong was transformed into Disney's hooker-with-a-heart-of-marzipan-feel-good-flick-for-the-whole-family-megahit *Pretty Woman*. Although the commercial viability of Lawton's original concept is debatable, the point is that the transformation from pure art to pure market occurred despite Lawton's very public protestations. Along with the collaborative nature of film, such loss of ownership comes thanks to Hollywood's Golden Era of the Studio System, which made writers into apprentices and contract craftsmen. I have experienced this situation firsthand after rejecting a producer's request for a free rewrite of a pivotal scene in my optioned script (I had already given several freebies—"taking one for the team," as the producer called it). Following my refusal, this producer simply removed the entire scene (leaving a gaping hole at the end of the first act), then submitted the work around town. The result confused readers, and the producer was eventually forced to return to the previous draft. The only way to protect yourself from such an experience is to know as much as possible about the company with which you will be doing business. What is their track record of produced projects (check out credits on the Internet Movie Database (imdb.com), or ask around. What kind of projects do they have in development? Check the Done Deal message board at http://pub130.ezboard.com/bdonedeal for writers who have worked with these producers. Unfortunately, once you're under contract, there's little you can do to protect the integrity of your work aside from ensuring that you have a buy-back clause in your sale contract if the producer fails to put the project into production by a specified time period, usually a few years. Then, as the buy-back opportunity draws near, you can shop the project as you envision it to other producers who may be willing to pick up the soon-to-be-previous producer's development costs on the script. *Beverly Hills Ninja* was one film that went through this process. Of course, rights will automatically revert back to you if the project has been optioned or "rented."

-5-

Writing is easy. All you do is stare at a blank sheet of paper until drops of blood form on your forehead.

—GENE FOWLER

What Is a Spec?

Spec screenplays are original source material written by a writer not under contract who "speculates" that he or she will create a market for a particular project by writing it. Specs are scripts for movies that no one has paid you to write, but that you believe might entice someone to purchase the finished project. Remember that voice in *Field of Dreams*? "If you build it, they will come." A writer working on a spec relies on that same concept, except that at this exact second, about 50,000 other people besides you and Kevin Costner are hearing that voice. And they all believe that a spec is a lottery ticket to fame, wealth, and excitement. At this writing, the top fee that has been paid for a spec is $4 million for *Panic Room*. Despite what you hear about scripts being churned out over a long weekend or bus ride from Newark to Trenton, good specs take time to create. Unfortunately, time is the one luxury none of us has, especially in Hollywood, where time is measured at twenty-four frames per second.

Of course, you may spend months on a script for which there will be no buyer is a risk, hence *speculation*. That's because some ideas are deemed to be commercially unviable enterprises for a mass audience. For example, the courtship of James and Dolley Madison has very limited appeal, but even without such marketability, a spec is the best means to show what you can do. A screenplay polished to perfection is the way to gain access to key decision-makers who are constantly seeking that one wild-card plot or character element that the studio can use to freshen up an otherwise formulaic project. For example, *Die Hard* had a blue-collar cop with a penchant for Will Rogers and family values battling suave and ruthless German thieves. Without such unique elements, *Die Hard* would be no different from dozens of other heist movies. If you can consistently deliver such elements, that will be your calling card.

SPECS VS. ASSIGNMENTS

Beginning writers are encouraged to "write what you know or what you're passionate about," but the logic doesn't seem to jibe with a Hollywood determined to churn out high-concept fare. Often the realities of the marketplace do not correlate with such passion, and the writer's voice may be lost during a struggle between the commercial and the personal. Indeed, the script-to-film developmental process is such a rollercoaster ride that sometimes we forget why we even became writers.

You may have spent two years perfecting your spec script before it ever saw the market. If you intend to get assignments, however, you have to be willing to work fast. Usually drafts of assignments are turned in within a time frame of ten to sixteen weeks. For example, my very first studio writing assignment was for Miramax Studios, a place that is notorious for hands-on development, or for extremely intrusive micromanagement, depending on your perspective. Assignments occur when a studio or production company owns a project or has an idea for a movie, but needs a screenwriter to develop it into a screenplay. Potential writers are selected via writing samples and past credits. These hopeful scribes are paraded through like a conga line of harem girls—each must "pitch" or tell to a producer or studio executive various possible story lines that might be suitable for the existing project or concept the producing entity would like to bring to the screen. These pitches can last from as little as a minute and a half to forty-five minutes, which can feel like an endurance test. In my own case, after driving hard to get the gig over a two-month period—sometimes pitching a new take on the project as often as three times in a week—I was then asked by the head of production to turn in Act One (the first thirty pages) in two weeks.

Where Do Assignments Come From?

Relatively few spec scripts sell in a given year, so most working writers make money by doing assignments from concepts that are not their own. The ideas for these assignments usually come from three sources: material previously acquired that is still in development; ideas generated by executives and producers themselves; adaptations of novels, magazine and newspaper articles, or plays.

For the working professional screenwriter, an argument can be made that competence and craft are more important than a singular point of view. In this case there is a clear distinction between specs and assignments. Often the demands of the assignment dictate the form and style. Assignment writers go about their business with expert, craftsmanlike efficiency. The average filmgoer would be hard pressed to correlate *The Joy Luck Club* with *Rain Man* or *My Best Friend's Wedding*, but they are the work of a single writer, Ron Bass. Undeniably, the very best screenwriters have elements of voice by virtue of their ability to assimilate many environments and points of view, and to encompass disparate genres and subject matter. The best writers understand the demands of studio writing: the numerous story meetings and eyes over the shoulder; rewriting fellow scribes while acquiescing to directors and star talent. Often these writers are brought in to a project in the last stages of preproduction to script-doctor an element or two into the work of another writer. At this phase, millions of dollars, as well as careers, are at stake, so the pressure is enormous. The payoff for such a skill is indeed lucrative, but this kind of writer is anonymous outside of a sliver of the industry.

Nailing down what's missing in someone's project is called *cracking the story*. Writers who land assignments regularly must be able to quickly mix and match story elements, often while the producer is sitting before them. Note that some professional writers prefer assignments because the groundwork for shaping the story and characters has already been done. All that's required are a few elements that are the particular writer's specialty. For example, perhaps a script that is otherwise tight lacks quips or one-liners. At other times a writer who specializes in giving stories emotional resonance may be called in to "punch up" a story, as in a science-fiction script, that is gadget-laden and complex.

Working writers also take assignments because they're guaranteed a paycheck and aren't subjected to the ever-changing whims of the marketplace. Such screenwriters aren't as emotionally invested in the project's outcome, either. The downside is the difficulty of making a story "your own," particularly when much of the work has already been done by someone else, and many people will be telling you what to write next. Such projects can have a nine-to-five workaday feel that may chafe those who chose writing as an escape from such a world. Further, much assignment work is market-driven, as in "Disney owns the rights to this franchise and wants to make a sequel," or "We have money and a space in our schedule for a teen slasher project." Again, such projects may be less than satisfying creatively. And while spec markets have a sky's-the-limit California Gold Rush feel, fees for assignments are more rigidly defined by a studio or producer's budget and are usually far less lucrative. While a complete unknown can pen a script that could potentially sell for a million dollars, a working writer may be limited to the amount of his or her last assignment plus 15 percent (basically a raise for landing a second project). An agent may refer to this amount as his client's "price." So a writer paid $100,000 on an assignment can ask for $115,000 on the next. Of course, the studio may have allocated only $70,000 for a rewrite, and you will have a tough decision to make. If it gets out that you worked for a much lower quote, then studios will try to get you for that lower amount. Your agent will be challenged to come up with a reason why you accepted the lower amount, as in "He wrote that for half his price because Tri-Star is giving him first crack at their *Wendy Witch* project." But, usually, executives will save time and trouble by only bringing in writers of a certain level and price range, and you will soon be familiar with all the other writers on your level. Thus, it's doubtful that you'll run into legendary writer William Goldman (*Butch Cassidy and the Sundance Kid*) in the reception area also waiting to pitch on *Evil Sock Puppets II*. Personally, I once found myself going head-to-head with the same writer on three projects in two years. I landed the first, he the second, and neither of us got the third.

Deadlines can be generated by circumstances beyond the script when working on assignment. The studio may have a bankable star (a recognizable actor like Brad Pitt, whose participation in the project guarantees a certain level of publicity, audience anticipation, and budgetary commitment by the studio) or director under contract who is only available during a certain window of time. For example, say Denzel Washington is only available for three weeks in November before moving on to another movie for which he is under contract. Or the studio may have a space in its release schedule, say May, so it needs to fill that spot with a film shot in September. Given the constraints of time and energy to make such a deadline, it is no wonder that movies are such a pragmatic art.

The writer's Pyrrhic victory from surviving such pressure is finally realizing the dream of seeing his or her work on the big screen. I should tell you that at that exact second of the above studio assignment, I had no more than the three-page outline and only a whiff of a clue where to go from there. The prospect of two weeks to turn in thirty to forty pages of story that would be scrutinized by executives on both coasts had me apoplectic. You see, the story I'd sold the studio had been reworked and revised at least a dozen times in the space of a month. In other words, I had nothing more than a rough concept that my REM-addled mind had burned rubber on at 5:30 a.m. the very morning I pitched it as the latest installment of "Michael Lent hangs on desperately to land this assignment." But many of us ultimately thrive on and do our best work under such pressure. If that isn't the case for you, then that is another reason to keep writing specs.

How to Turn Specs into Assignments

Excellent specs that tell a story well or have a strong voice, but are hampered by a perceived limited appeal to a mass audience, are considered to be "writing samples." Such work can still get you work on more-mainstream Hollywood projects. It's an exec's job to be acquainted with writers doing interesting work. Often a development person will bring you in seemingly to tell you how much they loved your script, but then lament the impossible realities of actually getting such a project made. Actually, the exec is trying to ascertain whether you have or are open to more-commercial fare. This is how spec writing often turns into assignment writing.

To turn specs into assignments, your goal is to be prepared with the following:

1. A list of all your existing projects, each of which can be described in a sentence or two.

2. A list of projects on the executive's development slate (see Chapter 9 for how to obtain this).
3. A list of completed films produced by the production company, so that you have sense of budget and content considerations. Obviously, you don't want to discuss your groundbreaking nineteenth-century Hopi Indian project with a company that makes teen comedies.

Streamlining the presentation of your work is crucial, but be prepared to open closed doors and provide details if called upon to do so. There's really no faking preparation.

I once submitted to Miramax Films a character-driven screenplay that had recently fallen out of option with the previous production company. My manager stated up front that we would not accept an option on the project. In other words, all outright purchase of the script or nothing. Within two weeks, the script went all the way to the top, came back down, and we got nothing. End of story? No. The script was liked by several execs, and my manager had the foresight to request a meeting to discuss the project, even if the result was a pass. Since passes are typical for scripts that do not already have the elements of known director, producer, or star attached, the reasons for rejection often have no bearing on the talent of the writer or merit of the project. Thus it's in your best interest to get over the initial disappointment and awkwardness (remember that the exec championing your project has lost some face), and begin building the long-term relationship as quickly as possible.

So, this kind of meeting at the studio begins with a discussion of the merits of the passed-on spec and some circumspect analysis of the nature of the pass. Next comes the other project at hand. The exec's main objective here is to determine whether this particular writer understands the mythology and lexicon that distinguishes the project as marketable. Once it's established that you "get it," further information about the project is dispensed. Your objective should be to adapt to a new story line as quickly as possible each time a concern or agenda is raised by the executive. And the best way to "adapt" is to stay loose and calm, not sweat small details of the story, and not be "married" or beholden to any one specific element, like how a main character should be defined. Strive for fluidity. Note that adapting is not the same as being a rubber-stamp yes-man. No studio exec worth his Platinum AmEx expense account wants his thoughts parroted back verbatim. A writer quickly learns that the court-stenographer method of developing material often leads to disaster. Instead, immediately embellish anything that seems to excite the exec. Take the good ideas and make them great.

The process of acquiring a coveted assignment can be tough. However, despite enormous difficulties, here is a seven-point strategy to turn your specs into assignments:

1. Understand that a spec that garners some interest but no sale *is* a powerful entrée.
2. If a producer contacts you about a writing sample, request a meeting to discuss this project and others—even if you live outside L.A. and must pay your own way.
3. Meet-and-greets are the lubricant of the industry. Execs must maintain relationships with material sources (writers) at all times, even though they may only have the capacity to hire a tiny handful of the many people they meet.
4. Arrive at your meeting with a couple of other film ideas to pitch.
5. During the meeting, find out specifically what the exec liked about your script. Later, casually ask what else the exec is excited about working on these days.
6. All production people enjoy discussing their slate. Following that discussion, segue back to the particular strengths of your own spec. If the exec mentioned that your dialogue was memorable, now is the time to say, "I'm sure you'll put me on the short list if you need a dialogue pass on [X] project." It may seem like some kind of Jedi mind trick, but long after the exec has forgotten the specific script you were brought in on (and they will), you will be remembered as that "dialogue guru," "action scene specialist," etc. I have even heard of producers saying to their staff after such a meeting, "That writer is really great. What do we have around here?" In that situa-

tion, the company had passed on the writer's spec but was looking to bring in a beginning scribe for a $10,000 or $20,000 assignment on owned material, just to build the relationship.

7. If you don't have representation, ask if the exec likes any of the agents with whom he or she is dealing. This is a bone many execs will gladly throw.

WHAT KINDS OF ASSIGNMENTS SHOULD YOU TAKE?

The Secret About Assignments

Many writers only tolerate spec writing as an escalator to what they assume will be the more secure and financially lucrative world of assignment writing for production companies and the studio. Often that's not the case. Not long ago, a friend who had sold a high-profile spec was being inundated with assignment offers. All of the potential projects seemed well below his talent. "But the money is right there!" he pleaded. When we hooked up again a few months later, I asked which project he had chosen. "None," he said. "I chased a couple and went to a bunch of meetings. I'm back working on my new spec." We shared a lament about the dirty secret of assignments: They often require lots of free work and can take months and months to lock down. The reason is that a producer may know that a project has problems, but has no clear idea of how to fix them. So writers are brought in by the dozens for their "take," or potential story suggestions, on a new version of the story. This can be a difficult and protracted process for the writer, since some producers have little more in the way of discernment than "I know the right one when I hear it." And when a producer does shout "Eureka!" he or she still has to convince the studio that this is the right take. That's no easy task, either. Abandoning your own writing of spec scripts in favor of assignments can negatively impact your career.

"*Our project is* Seven *meets* American Pie *with a* Terms of Endearment *twist. We already have the script, it just needs a polish. Interested?*"

Here I assume that money is either not an issue, or is the only issue for you. Maybe you've just sold your first spec. Maybe you're coming off an assignment and need a new project. Maybe you've been approached by a would-be producer in a writer chat room. Or maybe you're mainlining classic Syd Field three-act structure, while dreaming about any one of these scenarios. When you are working on an existing project that has a profile bigger than a dung beetle mound, inevitably you will be offered such commerce-driven assignments as the above at the production company or studio level, or at least asked to pitch them. Should you take the above-offered *Seven Terms of Pi*? Or should you pass on the e-z $$$ and finish that new spec? It depends. Can you do both? Some writers don't work that way. More than any other factor, your decision should be based on your nature and work habits. Of course, the amount of money involved is a big determinant, but so is the amount of time required.

Recently I was offered a "polish assignment," or what is often referred to as script doctoring. The project was a novel-turned-script that was billed as a cross between *The Fugitive, James Bond* (pick any one), and *Eraser*. I took the existing script home after meeting with the producer. Actually, I didn't even make it out of the parking lot. Right from page one, in my estimation, it was clear that the project was definitely not a polish (a final tweak of the dialogue and story elements that will make a screenplay ready for production). Besides a bland protagonist, there were abundant structural problems to go along with the threadbare, hackneyed story line. While a tongue-in-cheek tone would at least have made things more festive, instead, formulaic action scenes dragged on like the Siege of Leningrad. Conflict was manufactured in Spam-like blocks, and dialogue flowed like a groin pull. The compensation offered was mid- to high five figures ($50,000–$99,000), which is not bad— especially for what was billed as a four-to-six-week polish. It was nice money at this stage of my career.

I passed for two reasons. First, there was little chance the producers and I would ever be on the same page, especially since we already didn't agree on the project's condition, and the source novelist who did the initial script drafts was also on board as an executive producer. Second, I wasn't willing to take four to six months out of my life, the amount of time I figured it would require to make the project somewhat viable. Admittedly, the initial elation that came from having the guts to turn down a purported sure thing was soon replaced by my fear of the unknown. What if I was wrong and the script was better than I thought? What if I woke up tomorrow with a "U" sutured into the side of my head like that astronaut in *Planet of the Apes,* and no one ever hired me again? Why didn't I just clean up one or two elements and leave the rest be? Is it ethical to do derm-abrasion when a quadruple bypass is required? There were many questions. Luckily, life goes on. A week later I felt fine about my choice, and started work on a new spec I was very excited about. A few days after that, a production company optioned another of my scripts. So all was well in the end.

Many writers will be quick to note that anytime you're being paid to flex your pen is a happy occurrence. They're right. However, the flip side to that argument is that a writer's career is finite. We all come with invisible bar-code expiration dates on the backs of our heads. Most of us don't spend our nights dreaming of a chance to write *Count Chocula: The Movie.* (Note to self: concept could be a gold mine. Must flesh out.) So finding the balance between commerce, craft, and artistic expression is crucial. There are chutes and ladders whether you choose to chase work or create on your own. Few writers would like to be mired in straight-to-video Purgatorio forever, no matter how financially lucrative it might be. Meanwhile, too many writers choose to hide behind craft and leave their voice off the page, while allowing their careers to oscillate between fear and complacence. A crucial question to ask yourself is: Could any excrement-hurling gibbon at the zoo complete this assignment? If your specific expertise isn't required, and it's not do or die in your wallet, move on. Don't forget that the alluring power of spec writing is the blank page. That applies whether or not you've sold your previous projects.

THE WEEKEND READ

Friday through Sunday is the time that executives use to catch up on incoming scripts, aka "the weekend read." The exec's objective is to take a look at the week's best half-dozen or so scripts in preparation for discussion during the creative team's Monday-morning meeting. As a writer, if you're turning in an assignment, your goal is to make the weekend read. Otherwise, a script turned in Monday morning will most likely sit on an exec's desk until the following weekend, unless it is a high priority for the studio. If the production company or studio has development teams in Los Angeles and New York or Canada, as is the case with Miramax, the pressure to catch the weekend read increases exponentially because you also have to make the overnight pouch to other teams outside of L.A. In that case the deadline is pushed up to Thursday morning.

Writers are constantly rushing to make these deadlines because, if you don't, you find yourself in a situation where a cranky exec has to read your project midweek, in addition to his or her normal load of twelve- and fourteen-hour days involving other projects on the slate, which all require budgets, screenings, casting, shmoozing, etc. Worse, if your project has a lower priority than everything else on the slate, you will miss the window and will be pushed to the following weekend read. That means you will race to make a deadline, miss it, and then wait. Such a situation translates into your being on hold for a week, with that horrible feeling that you will have to make up the time later, in a frenetic flurry of writing during "Crunch Time," which is the period when time is short because the script is needed for production.

POST-WEEKEND-READ NOTES

The Most Common Notes from Execs and Producers After the Weekend Read

1. Protag (protagonist) feels opaque. Make him more compelling and less reactive. (Many writers create heroes who have either too much backstory or too little. A good protag operates in the moment with an eye for the future.)
2. Ratchet up the stakes. (If a single family is in peril, the producer will want the jeopardy to be more amplified and universal.)
3. Second act feels flat and confusing. (The middle part of a script is the toughest part to write because it entails character development and playing out subplots. Many second acts tend to meander and sag until jolted into action by the fast and furious finish of Act Three.)
4. Beats are off. Compress story. (Most first drafts are flabby because you're still trying to find your way in each scene.)

Most writers will try to anticipate the sorts of notes they will receive from execs after the weekend read in order to avoid the worst aspects of Crunch Time. Notes can be extremely annoying. They are an inevitable part of turning your spec into an assignment.

Notice that you can cede most Common Notes to the execs because they're usually the first things you'd change if you just had a few days of quality sleep. Often, even before the notes come back, you're off and running again. Difficult as this process can be, don't look for outside help to bail you out. Buckle down.

Although particularly odious to a writer's creative process, it's not unusual for a scriptor to be pressured into submitting work in sections. However, once you've proven yourself, you won't get micromanaged quite as often. But in the meantime, don't look for your agent or manager for help. As will be discussed in greater depth in Chapter 13, the main job of your representation is to keep things moving smoothly between you and the gatekeepers. Always remember that even though they represent you, the client, they still have to maintain their relationship with the studio, no matter what happens.

Such gray areas of conflict of interest are part of the entertainment business. Agents really represent the industry, and their attentions are heavily stacked in the industry's favor, so they'll patiently listen to your rants and offer to put in a call to the film executive, which will go something like this:

> AGENT
>
> How was Fiji?
>
> EXEC
>
> Bunjee surfing. You gotta try it, bro'.
>
> AGENT
>
> Indeed. So Michael loves you guys. He's really eager, really loves the challenges on this project.
>
> EXEC
>
> Cool. I'd love to get those pages with a little more lead time. New York wants to see everything, and David wants a January start.
>
> AGENT
>
> I'll tell him. How about drinks Thursday?
>
> EXEC
>
> Sounds good. I'll have Jim [assistant] set it up.

Because this is a "people business" where the same names disappear and pop up elsewhere over and over, Hollywood people are notoriously nonconfrontational. Notice that in the above conversation the agent has fished around via subtext to find out whether there might be some wiggle room with the deadlines. In response, the exec has basically said that he has people looking over his shoulder, and he's expected to deliver a go-picture by January. So, if anything, the writer can be expected to rachet it up a notch or two. Note that such time pressures are common.

FINAL THOUGHTS

There's an old story about a guy who sees a snail on his doorstep. He picks up the snail, flings it across the lawn, and four years later there's a knock at the door. The guy opens it and finds the very same snail, who says, "So, what was *that* all about?" Steven Spielberg once said that all films begin with the word. However, life in Hollywood for the writers of the word is a lot like that snail. Endless rounds of pitches and meetings, often punctuated by seemingly random comments from a gatekeeper such as, "You should rethink the protagonist's arc, and the whole second act needs work, but I can't figure out exactly where." Back to the drawing board we writers go, to do our part in this highly collaborative process. Because writing is so very time-consuming, when a writer finally comes back with a revised spec, say, twelve weeks later, the whole landscape may have changed. Landmasses have shifted, mountains have risen up where once were valleys, producers and executives have moved on, and someone else's project is now being hyped. Your battle-hardened shell of resilience, determination, and attention to craft is the one thing that trumps hype.

Remember this: Being on the losing side of a close call to sell your spec can be frustrating. However, if you only obsess bitterly about how initial interest in your screenplay did not turn into a firm sale, none of the above will be yours to reap. Millions of dollars and sometimes careers are riding on a single project, so extend yourself and get back in the game. The logic may seem obvious, but you'd be surprised how many writers do not take the next step.

-6-

If you would not be forgotten as soon as you are gone, either write things worth reading or do things worth writing.

—BENJAMIN "INVENTOR ON SPEC" FRANKLIN

WHAT IS A PITCH?

September is the time of year when we writers scrape off the barnacles and slime of past frustrations and disappointments to grease up like channel swimmers for the upcoming high spec season, which is traditionally from September through early December and from the end of January through the end of May. That means trips to the studios and production companies in the form of sub-missions, queries, and pitches. Pitches are meetings where writers are asked to see production or studio execs on their stories, their talent, and themselves. What follows are some battle-tested and timely tips for navigating those shark-infested waters.

Breathless, my arms waving like sheared-off propellers, I was once right in the middle of revealing my *incredible* Act One complication when the senior studio exec picked up his phone. "Is he summoning the late Irving Thalberg to get in here at once?" I wondered. "Maybe they're checking to see how much money they have in the Big Giant Vault which we screenwriters all know is kept expressly for such emergency bidding situations." No, the exec instructed his assistant to set up a lunch reservation at a trendy Chinese restaurant. He then proceeded to dial around the studio lot to see if other execs wanted to join him. "Sorry," he said, winking at me. "These guys have the most amazing shrimp, and they're always jammed." Several minutes later the exec turned back to me and said, "Go on. Where were we?" Why do they do it? Because they can. It's a development exec or producer's job to hear *incredible* stories in the form of pitches, *all day long*. While there's not much excusable about the above incident, such behavior is part of doing business in Hollywood. Give somebody that much power, and that's what can happen.

THE MEET-AND-GREET

If a studio likes a writing sample and wants to meet the writer behind it, this is commonly referred to as a "meet-and-greet." The purpose of such a gathering is not only for the exec to find out if you have other interesting ideas to pitch, but also to determine "what you're about"—meaning whether you are normal and sane, or if you froth at the mouth and mutter darkly to yourself. Oddly enough, while execs enjoy movies about lunatics, they don't want to have meetings with them—unless, of course, the lunatic is star talent, which then requires dinner and drinks. Your hope for this kind of meeting is that the executive will pigeonhole you as a writer with a penchant for story elements—for example, vivid scenarios or strong characters. Come prepared to discuss or "pitch" your other work, even if it's little more than a rough outline. Your objective here is to showcase the range of your work, as well as to push the executive to deepen the relationship, whether by interest in something else of yours, or via an in-house project already owned by the production company, and which may be in need of a rewrite.

THE ACCORDION PITCH

The first thing you'll notice as you're ushered into the producer or executive's office is that there's a big desk with an expensive designer chair where the occupant is already seated and is usually busy on his or her telephone headset. Once, I was brought in just as the exec was finishing a call with actor Mike Myers on speakerphone. If this is a small company, there will be a pair of leather chairs across from the desk. One will be for you, the other will be available for the producer's assistant who will take notes, if necessary. Often, these spaces are designed to project the trappings of power with original artwork, awards and posters from successful movies produced by the company on the wall. If you feel vaguely uncomfortable upon entering the room, that's the point. You're entering "territory" that's been strongly staked out by someone else, much like a big cat entering the lion tamer's circle at the circus. Stifle the fight-or-flight urge to take the chair nearest the door. Instead, if you're right handed, take the chair to the right which will be more in line with your natural body movement and flow of energy.

However, if your meeting takes place at a large production company or studio, the layout of the room will be different. The exec on the phone will nod and make a gesture toward the separate conversation area consisting of a comfy couch and two adjacent overstuffed chairs. (One company where I pitched had a Moroccan theme and we all sat cross-legged on giant pillows.) TIP: Don't sit on the couch if you can help it. It's sure to be low to the ground and too soft to maintain your posture. Remember that since this is your meeting about your projects, you're expected to be the most energetic and enthusiastic person in the room. That's going to be tough to do if your spine is compressed like a Slinky six inches off the floor. Actually, the stiffer the chair, the better you'll do at maintaining good eye contact while keeping your energy level up. Here, any jitteriness you feel will be mistaken for *excitement!*, while the same motions on the comfy couch will look like flailing or leather asphyxia.

After a bit of small talk, your meet-and-greet will segue into a discussion of your work. The producer might say something like, "So, what are you working on now?" or "What have you brought me today?" Congratulations, you are about to pitch. You should respond with "Wait until you *see* what I have." Here's where your planning and preparation is most crucial. Take a deep breath, compose yourself before you begin. Maybe create a mental image of lifting a lid leading to the Ark of the Covenant.

Myself, and many working writers deliver their stories via a series of steps that can be expanded or compressed to fit the situation. These steps are referred to as an *accordion pitch*. The key is to start small with memorable, take-away phrases that remain long after you've left the room, expanding to more details that will flesh out and add distinction to your memorable first impression.

The Accordion Pitch

1. Start with the one-sentence "high concept." (Make sure that major beats of the story can be summed up in three minutes.)
2. Expand out to a three-minute fire drill, with main beats delivered in a staccato fashion, like Walter Cronkite narrating the taking of Omaha Beach. If the executive shows interest and asks questions ("Tell me more about the protag. What's his backstory [prior history]?"), begin introducing major characterization elements. Keep answers brief and to the point.
3. Prepare your fire drill to be further unfurled from six- up to twenty-minute expanded pitches—be ready for whatever the situation dictates. If the executive continues to show enthusiasm, tell him or her

some of the subplots of the story. Deliver these story lines in a "confidential aside" fashion. A complete telling of the story, including subplots and characterization, selected minor beats, personal inspirations for writing the story, and any particularly relevant themes, should take no more than twenty minutes. If the exec's body language seems to indicate waning interest, wrap up the particular topic immediately and move on to the next major story beat.

4. Shift into your six-minute pitch, which should include more character details and subplots. Your strategy should be to give the executive a fairly complete idea of the story, but leave him wanting more, leave him wanting to read the script or invest in its development. Hunker down for the full twenty-minutes telling, and include character backstories.

5. Should you be faced with interruptions or a glazed-over, walleyed expression coming from across the desk, time to wrap up and contract the accordion.

To streamline the work to its most essential components is critical, but be prepared to open closed doors and provide details if called upon to do so. There's really no faking preparation.

How Not to Take a Beating at the Meeting

In the Trenches : How to Relax During a Pitch

Either I give a great pitch or a lousy pitch, depending on the initial "temperature" or reception I receive from the room. One trick I have for loosening up is by telling a very brief story about something else before going into my pitch. For example, minutes before a meeting before a senior studio exec and her cadre of development people, I was stuck in traffic behind a famous director who was driving a very expensive Italian sports car but was clearly not a good driver, as his slamming into and over a median strip curb seemed to indicate. The story got a big laugh that melted any anxiety I was feeling about my material.

Relax. Simply put, the best advice I can give you is to relax. Here's a huge secret: most producers and execs know, even before we enter the room, that most of us are borderline incompetent regarding the business aspects of filmmaking. For months and months, we labor over every stage direction and snatch of dialogue ("Is it 'Huh' or 'Hmm'? Let me stay up all night analyzing it."), then struggle to remember our protagonist's name when we're in the conference room. Conversely, execs, by virtue of having done these meetings thousands of times, exude cool confidence or detached boredom, as they feel the situation dictates. In other words, they're playing three-tier chess and we're still on Chutes and Ladders.

I know an A-list writer who goes in to pitches with his twenty pages of single-spaced treatment. As soon as the meeting starts, this writer proceeds to read the treatment, never looking up from the pages, which are kung-fu-gripped so hard that the paper is permanently crimped with sweat stains. Producers and execs put up with this jittery-guy-on-the-edge persona because they know that this writer can deliver the goods. While most of the rest of us are given trapdoors instead of such latitude, I think it helps to be aware that those apparently sentient beings across the desk are prepared for the worst when we sit down.

What Kind of Writers Do Executives Like to Deal With?

- Open-minded to story suggestions.
- Optimistic and upbeat. Passionate about their craft. The kind of person an exec can imagine working with on a regular basis for the next six months. Secret: execs like to "discover" writers, so being fresh in your perspective about the business of writing will distinguish you as the kind of writer who deserves "discovering."
- Willing to go the extra mile to make a project work.
- Limited ego.
- Never hides from deadlines.

Here's a trick to make pitches and story meetings go more smoothly: Imagine that your script is printed on hundred-dollar bills. In other words, you'll feel a lot less stress and pressure if you can convince yourself that no matter what happens, you don't need this fantastic gig or their sweet money. Remember the Buddhist maxim that action is clouded by desire. True self-confidence (as opposed to the easier-to-summon but more transparent bravado) strikes a chord with industry types and makes them wonder what you might be lining up should they pass. Right. I know, "Good luck with *that*," but remember, you're not *asking* for something, you're *offering* something. Be a true professional and do everything in your power to make sure you have the goods to back up your self-confidence, but then detach your emotions from the proceedings. Lack of confidence comes from feeling that you or your project is somehow unworthy. Instead, prepare as best you can, and if they don't want what you're offering, it's their loss, not yours. Reward yourself by generating new leads as soon as you can—even if that means plundering their Rolodexes while they're ordering the afore-mentioned shrimp. Personally, I try to keep half a dozen or more opportunities going at any one time. That way I never put pressure on my writing to deliver a Lotto check that precise second, and I rarely feel the sting that comes from having all my *huevos* in one basket.

Why You Should Have Your Own Agenda at Any Meeting

Make sure you have a goal or objective for every pitch. Why are you seeing this particular person? What do you want to happen as a result of this meeting? Is there a way to close this transaction right here and now? Usually there isn't. So, at the very least, you should be looking to establish a time line. Ask yourself what tangible thing you will have when you walk out that door. Recently I posed this last question to another writer. "Tell the story, I guess. See how it goes. I don't know much about these guys," was his answer. Remember that producers and execs get paid to take meetings (often referred to as "face time"); sadly, you don't. The other side of the desk takes meetings regardless of whether they're able to buy anything or not.

Your Agenda for a Meeting

1. Find out if the producers or studio executives are interested in purchasing your work. If not:
2. Are they considering you for a specific project, and what are the details? If not:
3. What do the producers or executives like about your work?
4. What kinds of projects might the company be interested in purchasing right now?
5. Are there upcoming projects you might be brought back in to pitch for?
6. What kind of material and budget level does the exec or producer consider his or her specialty?

Having an objective for every meeting forces you to do your research. To that end, invaluable sites like inHollywood.com, imgb. com, and 4lists.com list *loglines* (one-sentence capsules of projects) while tracking projects in development of every Hollywood exec you could meet. Use this tool to make every meeting more productive. Bottom line: Meetings and face time can be important, but don't let them become an endless merry-go-round that leaves you no time to write. If you can't see the immediate strategic objective of taking the meeting, then don't go. And make every meeting as productive as it can be.

How Not to Mistake the Sizzle for the Steak

If momentum on an immediate project and steps that build your career is the steak, then sizzle is the hype of posturing, gossip, etc.— aka things that can cause you to lose focus. Creative and monetary rewards are intimately entwined. The resulting pressure can be intense. Add to the mix the collaborative nature of film and Hollywood can seem to be only about personalities. Hundreds of movies still must actually get made each year, however. Egos jostling each other around like bumper cars is just a reality of this town where the politics are often brutal. And in such cases we writers rarely win. That's another reality. So avoid ego collisions at all costs. I was once on a project where the director had an in with the head of the studio and used it to cut the legs of the producer out from under him. This same director used me, the writer, as a blunt instrument to humble the studio exec in charge of production. He demanded revision after revision to a project that had already been green-lighted. Many things can happen with such a torrid dynamic, but the realization of a masterpiece usually isn't one of them. In this case the wheels came off, and the project came to a grinding halt. Throughout, my main objective remained to just hold on, so when we resumed, I was still part of the mix.

Infighting clouds perspective. More important, it wastes time. As sacred keeper of the story's spine, it is the screenwriter's job to rise above the situation. If you do get bucked from the horse—and sometimes you will, despite all your efforts—live to fight another day. Stick to making your script the juiciest steak it can be—that is your only real goal.

Pitch Story

"I'm loaded for bear but I'm also really nervous. I don't know which of my ideas to go with first because I don't know what they want." The writer was just an hour away from his pitch meeting with one of the top comedy actors in the business when he called me. The actor's team had already heard the pitch but a deal wouldn't happen unless the writer could find a way to tailor the project for this star. "It's counter intuitive, but, at least initially, I think you're there to listen," I said. "Get a sense of what they already liked about the pitch and what kind of movie the star wants to make before you say anything from your side." The writer called back a few hours later, ecstatic. The strategy had worked and he had sold his project for six figures. "Man, if I'd just charged in there, I would have blown the deal," the screenwriter told me.

Listening. It works.

TYPICAL RESPONSES YOU WILL RECEIVE FROM THE STUDIO

You can meet hundreds of different execs or producers on dozens of projects over the course of your career, but 99.9 percent of their responses can be logged into the following convenient categories. Note that it helps to know what the answer you're receiving means in real time, rather than wait for a Navajo code talker to become available days later.

A Firm Yes or a Firm No. "We're prepared to make a *preemptive offer* [an offer ahead of the script being taken out into the market for competing bids] today." Or "We would never make a movie from a script this terrible!" Both responses are rare. You must be seated before a true green-lighter for the "yes," or before someone who prides himself on his bluntness for the "no." Since nobody really knows who may come up with a million-dollar idea tomorrow, or, worse, who is mentally unbalanced, even moguls shy away from the blunt negative answer. Meanwhile, executives who are too enthusiastic about going to bat for a particular project can get fired.

Action for a Firm Yes: Don't get hung up on dollar amounts. Instruct your agent and lawyer to nail down contract terms as quickly as possible, while continuing to apply pressure by requesting status information and details on the negotiations. Many deals have died in business-affairs limbo simply because regimes changed and a contract wasn't signed. A deal isn't a certainty until the contracts are signed and the check has cleared.

Remember—this is your deal. While an agent may be most concerned with dollar amounts, it is you who will have to live with the contract you sign. Tickets to the premiere, participation during production, including on-set rights or at least visitation, a guaranteed number of copies of your movies on video and DVD, right of consultation concerning creative issues—if any of these issues are important to you, now is the time to get them locked down in a contract. The industry is replete with stories of writers locked out of the Hollywood premieres of their own movies. A friend of mine who wrote one of the top blockbusters of 2002 found himself purchasing the DVD at an electronics store simply because he hadn't stipulated anything in the contract. Arguably, he could have called his management to pursue the matter, but is that really the best use for high-powered management?

Action for a Firm No: Move on. Quickly. Be glad that you can move on without waiting. If there's a reason given for the pass, see if you can use the information to improve your project, but don't dwell on the result.

The Firm Maybe. "I love this so much I'm gonna run it by Stan [VP, head of production] this afternoon!" The exec is genuinely excited, but must get the rest of his team on board. You can build something tangible from this. Establishing a timetable for progress is a good place to start, as is receiving substantive notes to address issues and strengthen the project while waiting for the rest of the studio to get on board. Many writers refuse to act on such notes. They feel that they're close to their goal, so doing "free work" signifies weakness or desperation on their part. Such an attitude is a huge mistake. For starters, a lot of Hollywood is playing the "hurry and wait—now GO!" game. True desperation comes from a writer who has been idle for a couple of weeks waiting on a response, which comes back, "Congrats. You got the gig. You can make the changes we discussed as well as new ones by the end of next week?" Even when the Firm Maybe fades away to a Soft No, and many will, a writer who has received and executed notes (aka "free development") is in a strong position to submit the strengthened material to a competitor.

Action Plan: Your agent should be your listening post while waiting for the decision. Check in with your agent often via phone and e-mail; they should in turn be talking regularly with the producer and/or executive.

The Soft Yes. This is "I love it. Now, we don't have a discretionary fund [money a studio-based prodco has in reserve to buy or option projects without studio approval], but do these changes and come back in four months and let's talk."

Action Plan: Do the changes if you agree with them, knowing that maybe you'll be back in four months and maybe you won't.

Your chances of doing business together will be stronger if the production company has a proven track record of getting movies made.

The Soft No and the Soft Maybe. "This project isn't 100 percent right for us right now. But things could change and I'd like to stay in touch and possibly revisit this discussion at a later date." Or "This is a very intelligent script. You certainly got it down on the page. I would love to make a prestige film like this." Both responses are a "no," but sound like "Wahoo! Maybe!" Both are designed to get you out of the room without bruising your ego or elevating your blood pressure. Depending on the skill of the user and the circumstances, the answer is time-released and recognition ranges from the elevator lobby directly following the meeting to two weeks later, when your calls are no longer being acknowledged.

Action Plan: Congratulate yourself on getting in the door, even if for a pass. Send a thank-you note in appreciation of the decision-maker's time. Express how much you value his or her expert opinions, along with your wish that, in the future, you hope to work together. Your objective is to make a good impression by showing your willingness to handle rejection and to work on improving your writing even as you cultivate this new relationship. To this end, add the decision-maker to your contact list, tracking their progress in the trades and sending congrats whenever something noteworthy occurs.

You and your craft are always works in progress. Thus every interaction—even the most cryptic ones—are steppingstones to building the kind of career you want. To that end, always try to project the following qualities in every meeting. You are:

1. smart
2. fun
3. enthusiastic
4. easy to work with
5. dedicated to improving your craft

WHY SOME DEADLINES CAN BE APPARITIONS

Working writers soon discover that timeliness and proper story-telling are often at odds. That's because deadlines are crucial to transforming a script to the screen; however, for the writer, it's more imperative to get the script *locked down* with compelling and logical story lines and fleshed-out characters who have *arcs* (show personal growth as a result of their experiences). Most of us writers need the discipline of deadlines. But often you will rush to meet an arbitrary deadline like the weekend read to finish a draft that sometimes no one will read for weeks. The solution is to write every day, but always keep in mind that you survive by learning to pace yourself. Failure to heed this truth can lead to no life outside of the business; the cumulative effect is death of a thousand cuts to your career via loss of perspective and resulting disillusionment.

Good Writer . . .
- has no problem with rewrites
- is available for last-minute punch-up work on the set
- makes his or her deadlines without fanfare

Bad Writer . . .
- has a cynical attitude
- is "unavailable" when the studio needs a rewrite in a hurry, but suddenly becomes "available" when the studio offers a substantial amount of cash; earns the enmity of the exec and director
- misses deadlines and has his or her agent deal with the resulting situation

The start of the spec season in September signals renewed hope and vigor for the development season ahead. But we all know that this is a tough town with a tough agenda, analogous to turning an aircraft carrier in the middle of the ocean, as a seasoned director once said. In the face of such difficulty, the best of us see ourselves as students of the process. We always remember that the incubation process for ideas into film can be long, and isn't one that any of us has any control over. All we can do is put pen to paper, fingers to keyboard. While thinking we have control over Hollywood is illusory, we can stay alert to potential patterns and the objectives of others. Then our job is to correctly read and make the most of the opportunities with which we are presented.

-7-

A verbal contract isn't worth the paper it's written on.
—SAMUEL GOLDWYN

Screenwriters delight in spinning words into unforgettable images. Telling stories is our particular passion. And passion is what agents, producers, and executives look for in writers. It is a powerful ally in choosing the kind of projects you want to do, and the kind of career you want to have. Passion is the manna of inspiration from heaven—a currency passed from writer to producer to executive, then to director and actor, down the line to the promotions department and, ultimately, to the viewing audience. And therein lies the rub. As we have discussed, film is a convergence of art, industry, and entertainment like no other creative medium. As a result, our work occurs in the context of business and law. So, whether option or outright spec script sale, pitch or assignment, we screenwriters must temper our enthusiasm to create, unfettered by market realities, with a thorough understanding of the sometimes arduous dealmaking process leading to the development of our projects.

Many writers steer clear of the legal aspects of their work. At first glance, the reason is apparent: Most contracts are written in the passive voice and filled with inscrutable jargon. It's like looking for online porn and stumbling upon a Klingon chat group. But do enough contracts and you begin to cut through the clutter, and the legal aspect of writing becomes not only tolerable but downright interesting, as all things do that are the province of writers.

HOW TO REGISTER WITH THE WGA TO PROTECT YOUR WORK

Taking care of bid-ness starts with registering your work with the Writers Guild of America at www.wga.net. Serving both members and nonmembers, the Guild helps writers protect their rights to their material against plagiarism or copyright infringement. Writers can file concepts, treatments, and scripts intended for film and television—anything short of pop-up books—prior to circulating them to others in the industry. For a modest fee, the Guild will secure the material for a period of five years and testify on the writer's behalf to the possession of the material on the date of the registration, which is legally effective in helping to assert a writer's rights in literary material. Note that when you write an original script, you own the copyright by virtue of having created the script. So deals are not about bringing rain to your parched bank account so much as about the transference of your copyright ownership to a production company. Thus, when an original script is sold, the writer usually transfers the copyright as part of the sale. Conversely, when you are hired to write a script under an employment contract, you are creating a *work for hire*, which, under U.S. copyright law, vests the initial copyright with the employer. This is true whether the script is original or is based upon material assigned by the employer. Ownership of the script copyright, whether by acquisition or under the work-for-hire doctrine, is the practical means by which the companies preserve their rights to exploit the scripts they pay for.

In practical terms, ownership means that writers can restrict prospective producing entities (i.e., producers) from shopping the material to third parties (i.e., studios, bigger producers, directors). Many writers are so eager to land a deal that they allow would-be producers to send scripts to whomever they wish. However, when a producer fails to land third-party involvement, the script is effectively dead around town, taking a year of the writer's life down with it. Such writers are truly living on the career edge, and are sure to be that "bitter guy" at parties and family functions. Landing a deal is hard enough without also going swimming with rocks in your pockets. You should always restrict the circulation of your work to a list of mutually agreed-upon parties. A track record of active development deals, distribution deals, or production or financing deals should be the main criteria for your agreeing to allow your work to be sent out.

WHAT IS THE MINIMUM BASIC AGREEMENT?

All deals in Hollywood stand on the meaty shoulders of the Writers Guild Minimum Basic Agreement (MBA), which stipulates a foundation of creative protections and financial incentives for your intellectual property. It helps to think of the MBA as a kind of writers' minimum wage and working conditions arrangement with producers and studios. It is broken down into the major categories of Fees, Arbitration Procedures, and Residuals. Before commencing to negotiate your own personal contract, you should familiarize yourself with the MBA, available on the WGA website at www.wga.org, endeavoring to go beyond it to negotiate even better individual provisions. The right to stick around during production and postproduction, and the right to share (meaningfully) in ancillary and sequel profit participation are up for grabs. Since the MBA offers a wide umbrella of various payment minimums and contractual protections for your resulting work, rarely is it in your best interest to undercut the MBA. If you do, via non-Guild work, you should go in with your eyes open, since such contracts will always be weighted in favor of the producer, with few protections for the writer. Worse, the WGA will be unwilling to mediate such a contract in the case of a dispute.

UNDERSTANDING THE SPEC-SALE CONTRACT

In Hollywood, nothing is covered in more hype and glory than the spec sale. Writers relish the concept of a Cinderella scribe toiling away in obscurity—believing in himself or herself enough to write many hours for free, long before there's even the thought of a buyer—and winning the lottery. It happens. However, the reality falls somewhat short of that ideal, since humongous, seven-figure spec sales are but a tiny, tiny portion of the actual deals made each week. What follows here is an overview of four types of deals that writers typically encounter. In discussing merits and shortcomings of the resulting contracts, and ways a writer must give "the process" its due, let me state at the outset that I am not a lawyer. Many film schools offer excellent curriculum and adult education courses in entertainment law that are well worth your time. In addition, Stephen Breimer's *Clause by Clause*, Mark Litwak's *Dealmaking in the Film and Television Industry*, and *The Writer Got Screwed (But Didn't Have To)* by Brooke Wharton are all palatable, must-read legal guides for any writer serious about his or her craft. Read any of these books and you will be ready to discuss the salient points of what you want from your prospective deal. For myself, I always look for a guarantee of first opportunity for rewrite, polish, and corresponding fees after the initial purchase terms. That includes assignment contracts, and the issue is often a deal-breaker for me. Logically, I want to hold on to the project as long as possible to make my mark.

1. **Purchase contract for a spec script.** A studio or production company purchases all rights to your script outright for a negotiated price, along with additional monies if the project is actually produced (remember that only one in twelve actually is). The terms of such a contract are too complicated for the purposes of this section, but the bottom line is this: if a spec sale happens to you, forget Cousin Vinny and get to a Hollywood firm specializing in entertainment law ASAP.

Like the compression of synthetic coal into the diamondoids sold on the Home Shopping Network, major spec sales occur when there is intense "heat" coming from inside the industry, in the form of trackers whose job it is to keep tabs on new and interesting projects coming to market. As stated, such specs are but a fraction of the actual business of Hollywood. It's important to keep in mind that only certain producers involve themselves in this high-stakes market. Many others forgo the market entirely, preferring to adapt best-selling books to film, or meeting with established writers for sit-downs to flesh out interesting concepts.

2. **Option agreement for a spec script.** Given that a single producer may be developing as many as fifty scripts at one time, a production company will rarely purchase a script outright since it would go broke very quickly. Instead, for a contractually specified time period, producers will rent or *option* the right to develop the project and attract interest from a studio, a notable director, movie star, or all of the above. When the contract period ends, the producer may seek to extend the option with additional payments to the writer. If no extension is offered, then the producer is essentially abandoning his or her involvement in the project, in which case, all rights revert back to the writer, who has the right to *shop* or look for a new producer.

What's important here is *price* (how much will be paid) and *time* (how long the option period will last). Options normally range from $1 up to $20,000, with $2,500 to $5,000 paid to the writer for an option period of twelve months being most typical. Note that even if your contract is for one dollar, you should pay a lawyer a few hundred dollars to run through it for you, since the cost will be a write-off on your taxes, and the healthy development of your career is the true objective. The whys and wherefores of options will be discussed in greater detail further on, but note here that producers typically use the option contract when attempting to package the project with director or talent elements. Time is a crucial consideration, since your script will be off limits to competitors while the option holder tries to develop the project.

Remember that you must live with the terms you set during the initial eager-puppy excitement. It's also important to believe your purchaser has the ability to get your script produced. If you're desperate, but have a nagging suspicion you're dealing with someone who couldn't sell sandwiches to the Donner Party, don't short-sheet yourself on price, or extend the option time period to what will seem like a death sentence for your project.

3. **Deal memo for a writing assignment.** On the high end, writing assignments fall into the highly lucrative areas of rewrites for projects in studio development, and script doctoring for projects in preproduction that are in need of a quick punching up. Remember that assignments tend to go to established writers because they're easier to pitch to the studio, where politics are an integral part of the deal-making process. Sometimes a producer with a studio deal who wants to give a new scribe a shot can circumvent the popularity contest by using a discretionary fund to hire the writer. In the workaday world of most writers on smaller-budget or direct-to-video projects, a deal memo agreement is typical for a modest four- or five-figure fee writing assignment that doesn't necessitate lengthy negotiation (translation: lawyers). A deal memo lays out specific terms of the project: you will write x project or x scenes by x date for x amount of dollars (partial payment up front upon commencement and remaining amount upon completion

and delivery is typical). Purchaser retains rights to *x* in exchange for *x* credit (if applicable). Usually, it's that simple.

Much of the writing in Hollywood is commissioned via deal memos. The prospective purchaser may ask you to submit an outline or sample scene for the project on spec before agreeing to hire you. Sometimes the terms are worked out earlier. In one of my own cases, a deal memo was presented to me by the producer at a pitch meeting after I had been brought on board by the director. We discussed the listed terms, and made changes by marking up the memo right there. I signed it, accepted a check, and started working that day.

Writers who have landed studio and production company assignments often ask about structuring the deal. The payment terms for an assignment contract may occur as percentages of the overall contract, as per the following step form:

1. Treatment (an outline the writer provides for the work they will do): 10 pecent of the overall contract.
2. Commencement of draft (beginning to write or complete the script after you have approved the treatment): 25 percent.
3. Completion of draft (paid upon delivery of the script): 25 percent.
4. Commencement of rewrite (based upon your notes for changes): 20 percent.
5. Completion of rewrite (paid upon delivery of the rewritten script): 20 percent.
6. Polish (final revisions of the script based upon your final notes): an *additional* amount that is usually 10–15 percent of steps 1–5.

Be aware that a smart producer will negotiate all of these steps even if he or she plans on only using steps 1–3. The advantage of such a contract for the producer is enormous, since he or she can exit at any time—in other words, fire the writer after treatment (usually occurring on Christmas Day or during the funeral of the writer's loved one). Meanwhile, the not-yet-fired writer cannot hold the producer hostage later on. Say, for example, only steps 1–3 have been agreed upon, but then a director, star, or studio becomes interested in the project *if* certain changes to the script are made. The writer would be in a good position to ask for double or triple the earlier amount, while the penny-pinching producer will be faced with either ponying up the dough or starting over with another writer. Writers opting for security of employment over the gamble of a big payday later on will seek a deal that addresses all steps of the process.

> **4. Oral contract.** Producers use such handshake arrangements to take a project from point A (the producer) to point B (the potential developing partner or studio). Oral contracts are used for setting such specific goals, and are an important part of producers' development process where the intention with the oral contract is always very clear and supported by letters back and forth communicating what the intent is. As stated above, it is crucial for the writer to limit a project's exposure to the industry—particularly when no money has changed hands.

Some advice: for a writer who has made an oral agreement, paper trails are the *essential* footprints in the sand. Therefore, if the prospect of marching into Producer X's office and demanding a contract seems particularly daunting (it often is), you should state during the meeting that it's your understanding you are there for the purposes of developing your project for purchase by this producer at some point. If Producer X doesn't agree that this is the case, leave. *Now.* If Producer X does agree (most will), follow up with a letter stating that it was a pleasure to speak with him regarding your project (be sure to include the title), then repeat your understanding regarding eventual purchase. Such a step will ensure that you have legal recourse should things go awry.

Personal experience: Back in the early days, I had more than a dozen oral agreements. None resulted in a deal. However, I was also never "burned" (had my script or its concepts or story line stolen) in the manner that many writers fear. Instead, I learned that at the very least, long after the "handshake agreement" expired, I still had someone to nod to in restaurants or just before screenings. More important, I earned the right to submit additional projects, whenever I created them, to those with whom I had oral agreements.

Many writers believe in the infectious powers of their passion, and like to build the writer-producer relationship by working together first and then making a deal. In fact, established producers like opportunities to work with new writers from time to time because they're eager to prove themselves. Producers like discovering new writers and helping to shape their careers. Remember that in all contract cases, it is important that your would-be producer has such a track record and is well regarded in deal-making circles. Such track records are verifiable through the indispensable *Hollywood Creative Directory* (www.hcdonline.com) or via the *Producer Link* (www.producerlink.com). If the producing entity doesn't have a verifiable track record beyond his passion for your work, remember that you will never have as clean and unencumbered a relationship as you do right at the beginning. The time to agree to terms for option or oral contract is during that initial honeymoon period.

Writers often wonder why producers don't purchase their scripts outright. The explanation is that the amount the producer or studio has committed to a given project is referred to as being "on the hook." The logic is simple: The more on the hook the producer or studio is, the more they stand to lose if they don't make your script into a film. In practical terms, since many producers have as many as thirty projects in development at a given time, they cannot afford to be on the hook financially or time-wise for more than a few of those projects. Your own long-term objective is to develop the script and give the project a lineage, while building the relationships that will ideally move you up on the producer's priority list. True contractually verifiable lineage is of great importance, since the next interested party will look at a script that was optioned for one dollar from a known entity with much more interest than they'll listen to the sordid tale of "some big-time guys who were once very interested, but all I got was this T-shirt."

FINAL THOUGHTS

There is a value → no value → value evolutionary quality to the business side of screenwriting. During its evolution, a finished script represents great achievement and therefore great value for the writer. In the marketing process that follows, it may seem as though all the cards are held by producers or the studio and the newly minted script is little more than a drink coaster for some would-be producer. Writers may be tempted to cede their entire position just to make something happen. They shouldn't. The simple truth is that the industry is dependent upon the art. Everything else—the deal-making, the casting, the producing, and the marketing—is in service to the writer's story. Without the story, all the other elements are hollow. Meanwhile, with every experience a writer learns something vital that propels him to a new level. Like a lobster who must shed its old shell, the writer is for a time soft, vulnerable, and untested. Hardening of the shell comes quickly when the writer takes responsibility for his or her own career. Having the passion to write and take chances, while pushing for the contract or agreement with inherent legal steps to protect yourself, is the best way to ensure that "the process" works for you.

PART THREE

The Hollywood Game and Its Players

-8-

Which is the most reasonable, and does his duty best: he who stands aloof from the struggle of life, calmly contemplating it, or he who descends to the ground, and takes his part in the contest?

—Thackeray, *Pendennis*

A Crash Course in the Studio Development Process

Let's jump right into the cool stuff first. Say you've completed your script, which you describe as "*Gone With the Wind* in outer space," and your agent LOVES it. What can you anticipate happening next? Well, your spec (or the *property*) is sent by the agent to prospective production companies. Even if the producers are as enthusiastic as your agent, they may or may not feel that additional changes are necessary to prepare your script for the marketplace, in which case you sit down to hear their *take* (notes), then huddle with your agent to see if you agree that going back to the keyboard is warranted. But let's assume no changes are requested right now. Depending on where relationships are strongest, producers at prodcos fan out to the various studios, called *territories*, to submit the property.

Producers will first go where they have their *first-look studio deal* (a type of deal a prodco may have, which I'll explain in the next section), then move on to places where they've heard that a particular executive is looking to acquire a certain kind of movie, or one that can be made for a particular budget. Obviously, if your would-be producer already has the proper relationships in place, the process is streamlined enormously. If more than one studio exec at competing studios responds "Wahoo!" to the material, you've hit the jackpot and a bidding war will ensue that will be orchestrated by the writer's agent.

Once they have acquired it, the studio sets out to develop the material. This is the time you will go in to meet the development or creative executive in charge of developing the project. After a few pleasantries whereby the lead exec (and perhaps members of his team) congratulates you on your success and expresses his enthusiasm for the project, the exec usually collects himself and wades into the substance of the meeting. Notes, usually lots and lots of notes, are the real reason for this sit-down. Notes are changes the studio deems necessary for the transition from page to screen.

The Trail of Development from Script to Screen

Writer → Agent → Producer → Studio Exec → Director → Movie Star → Editor → Distribution → Marketing Dept. → Movie Theater

THE FIRST-LOOK DEAL

There are many ways studios structure their deals with independent production companies, but the one you most often come across is called a *first-look deal.* Here the studio covers the upkeep of maintaining an office, employee salaries, rent, utilities, etc., in exchange for a first-look opportunity at any material the production company may choose to develop into a movie. If the studio execs decide that they are interested in a particular project, they have the opportunity to finance and distribute the resulting film. If not, then the prodco is free to shop other studios for financing and distribution. Generally, first-look deals are reserved for producers, directors with proven track records, and movie stars who want to develop projects tailored to their personal strengths or aesthetics. In order to land a first-look offer, a screenwriter must be a hybrid of writer/director like Todd Phillips (*Old School, Starsky and Hutch*) or writer/producer like John Hughes (*Home Alone, Ferris Bueller's Day Off*).

WHAT KINDS OF PROJECTS DO STUDIOS LIKE?

New material not derived from prior source material is an unknown quantity. Figuring out its potential is like descending into the basement of a spooky old house. Studios and their executives love projects with track records, proven appeal, well-known actors or directors attached and notable source material. Movies adapted from other successful material generally guarantee built-in audience awareness. Realize that when someone sniffs that "the film wasn't as good as the book," it usually means that they paid to see the movie, which is really all that the studio cares about. Producers who choose adaptation projects must also secure rights to the original material; these are called the *underlying rights.*

Because producers may have as many as thirty or forty projects in development at any given time, they are loath to commit much money to any one given property. Thus it's paramount for them to find well-known projects (with built-in audience awareness) where the underlying rights can be secured for free. Copyright regulations and length vary from country to country, but here in the U.S., copyright protections of books last for seventy-five years. Books older than seventy-five years are said to be in the *public domain* and can be used as material for movies without payment to anyone. Adaptations of Shakespeare and the Bible are good examples. In other words, you, the writer, can borrow situations and characters and owe the original writer—in this example, Shakespeare or God—nothing. Recent examples of such movies are *Clueless* (based on Jane Austen's *Emma*), *Romeo and Juliet*, *Hamlet*, and *Little Women*.

STUDIO DEVELOPMENT BUZZWORDS

Many of the terms that studios use to describe various phases of the development can sound a bit like inside baseball and take some getting used to. You should familiarize yourself with the following :

1. **Coverage.** Because few people really have time to read every script and book that is submitted, the entire film industry runs on a type of Cliff Notes called *coverage*. The form coverage takes is standard:

   Logline: a one- or two-sentence description of the concept of a script, book, or idea.

   Description: Usually one to three pages, this section summarizes the basic plot of the script.

   Comments: A one-page evaluation of the strengths and weakness of the work.

Note that on the lower portion of the front page is a checklist with the terms Highly Recommend, Recommend or Consider, and Pass. One of these three terms will be checked. More than 90 percent of the material that arrives at the studio or production company inboxes garners a Pass. Usually that's the end of that.

2. **Turnaround.** Projects that are purchased by the studio and then abandoned, usually following a period of unproductive development,

are said to be in "turnaround." Multiple drafts of a script that don't resolve issues or problems a studio may have, or fail to attract elements—a name director or movie star committed to work on or appear in the movie—will result in turnaround. Such projects can be acquired by a competing studio for *development costs* (overhead charges including rewrite, interest, and studio overhead), along with vested or *rooting interest* in the project. Such interest usually means 2–5 percent of net profits from the theatrical release, DVD, video, and cable sales, etc.

3. **Unsolicited Material.** These are screenplays submitted to the studio that it did not request. All are returned to the sender unopened and unread, because the threat of a nuisance lawsuit, or a lawsuit because the similarity of material already in studio development is too great. For example, when the movie *Twister* came out, the studio was sued by dozens of people claiming that they were first to have the idea to make a movie about tornados. Of course, tornados aren't particularly novel as subject matter; it's the execution that matters. For just this reason, all movie productions carry special *errors and omissions insurance,* or E&O. Basically this insurance covers both the studio and the produced work from claims of idea or person similarity, or copyright infringement. Given that many movies are seen by millions of people, there are bound to be a few dozen people with varying degrees of plausibility who believe "that's my life story up on the screen," or "Gee, I wrote a story about a boxer. Stallone must have stolen it." E&O insurance covers the cost up to a specified amount (usually $1 million for each occurrence) for defending against such copyright infringement lawsuits.

4. **Decoding Script Colors.** Script pages are changed out as a script is developed. Learn the colors, and you can tell at a glance how far along they are into the development process.

> original draft—white pages
> second draft—blue
> third draft—pink
> fourth draft—green
> fifth draft—yellow
> sixth draft—goldenrod
> seventh draft—buff

5. Hook. The hook is your premise or concept in a nutshell. In short, why a mass audience would want to see this movie. What's so unique or exciting about it? Why would an actor like, say, Tom Cruise, want to play the lead? Studios like to make movies with bankable elements to hedge against the uncertainties of the market. A killer hook is something that can make an executive take notice. It's something he can sell to his or her boss.

STUDIO NOTES: WHAT THEY ARE AND HOW TO HANDLE THEM

There are two types of project developers: Those who don't presume to know how to write, so they don't try, and those who do, and leave it to others to deal with the results. You should know that most studio and production company notes come in sandwich form—that is, a top sliver of praise for elements of the project that stand out; two pounds of corned-beef "serious concerns" criticism; and a bottom-line wrap-up of the exciting possibilities of the project as a whole, once you make the necessary changes. Learn to recognize this concoction, and only fear the breadless sandwich. When the notes don't make sense, don't panic. If you have a clear idea of what and why you're doing something, stick with that. The 120-page script format demands that the story be told in concise fashion. You can't wander in the wilderness for twenty pages, as you could with a novel, for example, and expect to keep your audience.

The Secret About Notes

Many writers feel that *everybody* at the studio has an opinion that they feel inclined to share about what's wrong with your project and how to make it better. For all those notes that execs hand out like parking tickets at a monster truck convention, they actually don't like doing substantial development on projects. One exec told me that *Memento* sprang directly from the draft submitted by the writer onto the screen with virtually no notes. Scripts with great premises or subject matter but that require a lot of fixing go into what Hollywood refers to as "development hell." It's called hell because developing draft after draft saps everyone's patience and enthusiasm for the project.

Many writers get confused and disoriented by notes, because in a sense they are being asked to dismantle an engine that in their mind works, even if inefficiently. Story elements, problems, and solutions can feel like dozens of parts disassembled and spread out all over the shop floor. Now they're being asked to make a spaceship out of a dune buggy. To avoid panic and disorientation, it's crucial to have a visually logical system for organizing notes in place. When I receive studio or production company notes, the first thing I do is make a copy. On the duplicate I proceed to highlight every "positive" comment with a yellow marker. Then I go back through and highlight every concern or problem in orange. Related notes on a particular issue, say "characterization" and the "protagonist's arc," I circle in red and connect together with arrows. Any problem or solution that I've discovered on my own, or that occurs to me while reading the notes, I write along the margins in pen. I post the notes across my bulletin board, highlighting in pink every issue I've completely addressed, as I complete them in the rewrite. When I come to a problem or potential solution that needs discussion, either by running it by my manager or by calling the producer, I write the item out on a Post-it that also goes on the page. The predominant color on the studio notes will be walls of pink marker when I'm finished.

Sometimes a producer or, less often, a studio exec will mark up the physical draft of the script. When that happens, I fold lengthwise and tuck in any pages where no *notes* have been given, leaving only pages with script notes sticking out. Again, I use a pen-and-marker system to record my reactions to the notes, along with problems and solutions I foresee. When a particular issue has been addressed, I tuck in those pertinent pages, too. Ultimately the script rewrite is not complete until I have folded and tucked in the entire screenplay. The importance of the above steps is giving yourself tools and a system for attacking the rewrite, while mollifying any frustration and/or panic you may feel about having to jump back in within days or weeks of having completed the previous draft.

-9-

Never judge a book by its movie.

—J. W. EAGAN

WHO ARE STUDIO EXECUTIVES?

Development executives and creative executives, aka DEs and CEs, are the studio gatekeepers and note-givers just below the vice-presidents and well above assistants. A common trait of solid DEs or CEs is cat-like, rapid-fire mental agility. Since the average exec probably hears and reads more stories in a month than you will pitch during your entire professional career, they are particularly adept at mixing and matching elements from all parts of the cosmos. Meanwhile, most writers focus on making a single story work in a complete and coherent fashion. DEs and CEs do the heavy lifting required to move projects forward in Hollywood. These people are in their twenties and thirties and work frenetically cruel schedules six and seven days a week. They are fueled by adrenaline and fear. The adrenaline that fuels them comes from having power to put a multimillion-dollar movie into production. As Art Linson points out in *What Just Happened,* the fear comes from having green-lighted a project, forcing the studio's checkbook open, and then watching the gaining momentum that will propel it out of the executives' control.

Executive Code Talkers

Execs who are about to pass on or reject material will use euphemisms like "intelligent" because the designation appeals to a writer's vanity. However, the experienced screenwriter quickly learns that "intelligent" is a kiss of death because it implies limited audience appeal and a tough sell.

Likewise, writers who are complemented on the "gritty realism" of a script's ending, can bet that the studio's first note will be for something that's "a little more upbeat." To wit: The endings of *L.A. Confidential* and *Fatal Attraction.* Execs often "flip" for material they find "fabulous," but these are generic compliments and hold no stock unless more substantive comments are also given.

WHAT DOES IT TAKE TO BE A STUDIO EXECUTIVE?

Many writers have reactive intelligence, that is, they observe something and react to it with detached perspective. It's a protracted, slow-moving way to process information, and it requires a great deal of concentration. In contrast, studio executives are passionate workaholics who cook with heat. By this I mean that there are two things you need to know: First, Hollywood execs are ambitious; and, second, they worry constantly about getting fired. Those two goals are diametrically opposed. Execs' desire not to stick their necks out too much for any given project gives way to a rugby scrum for credit when it's clear that a film is going to perform well. So a good exec must stand out from the pack even as he or she remains mindful of studio politics, where many, many people vie for the credit on relatively few successes, and flee from a minefield of failed, often expensive projects.

Most execs work so hard that over time they develop an internal sense of what works and what appeals to a particular target audience. For them, the ideal group to captivate usually consists of young males aged fourteen to twenty-eight. When you pitch to a CE or DE, they will look for stories with such elements and hooks as a particularly interesting protagonist (i.e., a conflicted, no-name anti-hero with both a personal agenda and a conscience) or an inventive time constraint (i.e., a bomb on a bus set to detonate if the bus goes slower than fifty-five miles an hour).

Executive Skills

1. rapid-fire intelligence
2. internal story sense
3. knack for pinpointing script problems
4. passion
5. workaholism
6. skill at office politics

Past box-office grosses, famous names, and present politics are an exec's only candle in the darkness. Whereas familiar concepts presented in tried-and-true three-act structure give execs tangible security and a steady reference point, a radically new idea represents the unknown—an end product whose result is unforeseeable. New ideas are that mysterious fiery-eel gumbo studio execs once tried while trekking through the Amazon. Meanwhile, it's safer to say no to hundreds of projects than to say yes to just one. And when an exec does like something, it's better to have safety in numbers, in the form of more execs on board. Decisions by committee are a vastly safer bet. To wit: A few years ago, a rising-star producer/manager newly ensconced at a top production company gave a self-aggrandizing "wonder of me" cover story interview in the local paper. The industry buzz was that his employers didn't appreciate being overshadowed, and in fact, within eight weeks, the producer was fired.

Early in my career, a CE at Disney took a liking to a big genre script I had started in grad school. The exec was so enthusiastic that he offered to help me shape the script during the rewrite process, with the goal of setting up the script at Disney. The executive was also extremely diligent—often our story meetings were over the phone late on Sunday nights, which was the only "free time" the exec had. Six months of hard work later, I had a promising draft in hand. However, by then, the executive championing my project had been fired, presumably for not seeing eye-to-eye with his boss on developing the exec's slate of projects, or perhaps for showing a penchant for going it alone. Despite possessing the prerequisite tools of work ethic and passion, the exec apparently lacked stomach for the riptide of studio politics, and quickly threw in the industry towel to enter law school. Of course, the exec's replacement showed little enthusiasm upon hearing about my project.

Tale from the Front

I was brought in to pitch the new senior VP of a well-known production company specializing in big-budget monster movies. We really clicked, and the VP loved my project. He said he was taking it directly to the head of the company that very afternoon. A tense week of silence passed before I heard that the company president wouldn't commit off a pitch. So I began to write out my existing treatment into a script as fast as I could. Ten weeks later I had a rough draft that needed some cleaning up. When I asked my manager whether I should send over the script for comments before starting the rewrite, he said, "I don't know if [the VP] is going to make it." Two weeks later and less than four months after he started, the new VP was fired.

How to Think Like an Executive

As the above anecdote illustrates, the world of the executive is all about risk management, production cost, and profit analysis. "How much will it cost, and what will it earn?" Most execs start their day by *tracking,* or dialing up all their contacts for the latest buzz on a hot prospect, for example a highly anticipated spec delivered by a well-known writer. The exec is always looking for ways to cut through the standard shop talk and discover any true secrets that a colleague may let slip, such as how much another competitor may be willing to pay for the aforementioned hot property. A writer can benefit from such impulses by staying informed about the industry beyond his or her own projects via the trades, screenings, Internet boards, and industry gatherings. Sometimes a writer can glean and pass along a bit of information that will be of benefit to an exec with whom they are solidifying a relationship. For example, I was once at a screening hosted by Clint Eastwood. I asked him if there were any projects he was interested in but had been unable to make for whatever reason. He considered the question thoughtfully and then said, "Yeah. I've always wanted to find a way into *Golf in the Kingdom.*" Later I mentioned this to a director of development with whom I was meeting. He shrugged, indicating no awareness of the book, and simply said, "Interesting," before moving on to my work. As I was leaving, however, I overheard the exec asking his assistant to track down a copy of *Golf In the Kingdom.* A few days later the exec messengered over a newly purchased spec script of the book with a note that read, "Thought you'd be interested in checking this out. Love to hear what you think." It was a quid-pro-quo thanks.

-10-

Work like you don't need the money, love like you've never been hurt, and dance like you do when nobody's watching.
                                        —SATCHEL PAIGE

WHO ARE PRODUCERS?

Producers develop movies from such source material as screenplays, books, theatrical plays, songs, and newspaper and magazine articles. Subjects may include historical or fictional events or characters, as well as first-person experiences; any combination of these elements can become a story. Producers look for projects that make their pulses pound and get their brains exploding with ideas. This last part is crucial, because it falls to the producer to stay enthusiastic for the marathon of preproduction, production, and postproduction ahead, since he or she must still be there to market the finished project long after the actors, director, and writer have moved on to other movies. For example, Sal Zaentz pursued the making of *At Play in the Fields of the Lord* for two decades, and Joel Silver believed in the potential of *The Matrix* at a time when the conventional wisdom of Hollywood was that audiences had no interest in cybermovies, based on the high-profile box-office failures of *Johnny Mnemonic* and *Strange Days*.

"What is a producer?" Actually, that's a pretty tough question, since just about anybody with access to a cell phone and trendy sunglasses can claim to be a producer. As you may be thinking right now, defining what constitutes a producer can be a slippery task. Much danger lies in the fact many sleazy stowaways take advantage of the situation via go-nowhere deals that waste weeks or months of a writer's time, and, of course, there's the legendary casting couch. Thus the title of producer sometimes takes on a diminished or sordid connotation in the industry pecking order. A proven track record of credits on completed films is your best gauge of a producer's rank.

Tip on Producers

"Wow. That's a good story!" is the reaction you want when pitching a producer. However, many producers juggle anywhere from twenty-five to seventy-five projects at one time, so they often adopt an air that is vague and distant, since often they can't remember what they said to you yesterday. Pauses on their side of a phone conversation usually indicate the producer reading notes on a computer screen compiled by an assistant. The writer's job is to be clear and direct enough to cut through the producer's distractions and get his or her undivided attention.

WHAT ARE THE DIFFERENT KINDS OF PRODUCERS?

By strict definition, producers are responsible for the creation, development, packaging, and financing of a movie. They can specialize in one or all of these tasks. For this reason, good producers should be flexible, persistent, and hardworking. They are used to being told "no" a lot. They can be money guys who are able to secure financing, or relationship guys who have the necessary access to studio decision-makers or certain coveted talent and directors. A producer can be a *financier* adept at procuring money, *dealmaker* skilled at bringing money, talent and director to the negotiating table to close the deal, or *moviemaker* able to take a project from script to screen. The moviemaker title implies more creativity, since such a producer relies mainly on his or her instinct for a good story. Producers can also be *line producers* adept at squeezing out a finished film from an extremely convoluted production process, a kind of grease monkey who handles the budgeting, scheduling, and hiring of the film crew. Line producers should not be mistaken for full producers.

HOW PRODUCERS STAY IN BUSINESS

Many producers are former studio executives. And like many executives, producers are aggressive. Their motto is "Eat someone else's lunch before they have the chance to eat yours." Producers can have as many as seventy-five projects in development at any given time. As you no doubt realize by now, movies are difficult to get made. Producers are more immersed in the wrestling in canned corn that it takes to get a film into production than anyone else. So they hedge their bets by not relying on any one project to keep them in business. The producer who only develops a couple of projects at a time runs the risk of starving on Sunset Boulevard. Likewise, this profession is at the mercy of an unspoken "three strikes and you're out" rule. That is, produce three movies that fail commercially, and you're out of the business for all intents and purposes. (When a movie is truly awful, it is said to "fall off the screen.") Because of the three-strikes rule, producers try to bolster their position on any given project by *attaching* (securing contractually) recognizable names. Attaching famous names like Julia Roberts and Brad Pitt are called *elements*. Elements help producers push their projects through studio development and get them made.

PRODUCERS AND CRITICISM OF YOUR WORK

Here's an old Hollywood maxim that still applies: "When you get a 'yes' for an answer, cut the meeting short and then leave as quickly as possible, because 'yes' can quickly become 'no' if you say the wrong thing and the producer starts having doubts that you and he are on the same page. Writers should also become adept at reading between the lines when dealing with a producer. "I loved it. But I didn't LOVE! it," a producer once said to me after I pitched him on my spec. That meant that he liked many elements of the story, but didn't feel that fire in the gut required to shepherd a script to the screen.

Get Hollywood Coverage for $50

You can get professional coverage of your work for as little as $50. Simply call any literary agency like CAA, ICM, William Morris, UTA, Endeavor, etc. and tell that you are a producer looking for freelance readers. Ninety-five percent of all professional readers in Hollywood are freelance and competition for this work is fierce, so extra work is always welcome. Upon request, you will be given a list of names and contact info. Be sure to use a fictitious writer name and script title when submitting the project. Note that professional readers are known for their brutal honesty. However, should you receive glowing coverage, you can submit the coverage to the agency where the reader works and solicit their interest in the project which they have essentially already "covered."

It's crucial to be honest with yourself about any professional criticism you *do* get from a producer on your script. Kind, polite words delivered like a verbal fortune cookie are not the same thing as detailed, specific comments or notes. Contrary to popular belief, most decision-makers are nonconfrontational. As a very general rule, people in Hollywood hate to be overly critical because they never know when their comments will come back to bite their back-sides. Producer and former studio head Paul Lazarus III tells the story of granting a courtesy meeting to a bedraggled but earnestly passionate young man who had cobbled together a scruffy, unfor-matted story about a boxer. The man in question was Sylvester Stal-lone, and the script was an early version of *Rocky*. Years later, when Stallone was STALLONE, he reappeared, smiling, at Lazarus's office. Paul's kindness and not the rejection he had delivered was what was recalled. "Nicely written. Unfortunately this isn't what we are looking for at the present time. Please keep us in mind for your next project." This is a common response from a producer to a director's reel or a writer's script. Again, if a producer or exec "responds" to your work, they will be crystal clear about specific elements they liked.

PRODUCERS AND THEIR RELATIONSHIP TO STUDIOS

At the top of the food chain are producers who function pretty much like studios: Joel Silver, Rob Reiner, Brian Grazer and Jerry Bruckheimer. These are producers with long-standing deals with a studio. Next, are producers who bring promising projects they dis-cover to the studio for purchase, and these are jointly developed into a film. The producer will give input and sometimes have crucial relationships (with financing, talent, or a notable director) to offer, but final decisions are ultimately made by the studio.

Producers can be freelance, i.e., in business for themselves, or they can have development deals or commitments with a studio. There are two major types of development deals with studios: *exclusive* and *first look*. *Exclusive* means that a production company or individual devel-ops material exclusively for one studio; *first look* is an arrangement that either a production company or, in some cases, an individual producer has with a studio, in which they must allow the studio the first right of refusal on purchasing a project the individual or company is interested in. If the studio passes, the project can then be shopped around to other interested parties. A third studio group, independent producers, develops projects outside of the Hollywood system, usually for movies with budgets far less than anything made by the studio.

Writers looking to sign on with a producer should be looking for the following elements:

Access. This is the necessary momentum to get a script moving along the development process. A good producer must have access to the studios, in the form of ongoing projects or recently concluded projects. In addition to or in lieu of studio connections, a producer must have sources for financing or casting (i.e., a relationship with a coveted actor or casting agent), or a director willing to attach or join the producer's prospective project.

Enthusiasm. There are many bumps in the development road. You should seek out the producer who is bound and determined, burning with passion to see your project realized on the Big Screen. All producers pay lip service to this quality, but the knowledgeable writer can read between the lines. Did the producer offer at least $500 to $1,000 for the option, or were you given take-it-or-leave-it terms for a free option? Did the producer read your work within three weeks and contact you promptly to set up a meeting? A producer may have considerable clout, but if meetings don't occur for months at a time, it's hard for a project to gain any kind of traction. Finally, does the producer respond to your questions, comments, or suggestions? Succinct e-mail or phone messages from you that go unreturned are a strong indicator of where a producer's priorities lie, and where your project stands on his or her development slate.

Tales from the Producer's Trench

During preproduction and production of the upcoming film *Hard Scrambled,* which I co-produced, everything that could go wrong did go wrong. Problems ranged from last-minute scrambles for financing, locations becoming unavailable days before shooting, and actors having conflicting schedules. In one case, a star who wanted to appear in the movie was unavailable in Canada at the last minute because his movie production there was two weeks behind schedule. All battle-hardened producers know that these situations are more the norm than the exception.

On the same film, final changes to the script's third act needed to be made in a matter of days. However, writer/director David Hay was already well into rehearsal with actors, preparing his shot lists and shooting schedule with the director of photography, and approving last-minute art department details on the four major locations used for the film. We producers huddled through the night to give bullet-point suggestions for the necessary script revisions. We then ran interference for David while he was sequestered away on the rewrite during a very tense sixteen-hour schedule. It was a lot to ask of our writer/director. However, we rewarded him with a ninety-nine-seat theater just off Sunset Boulevard as his rehearsal space, instead of the usual office space or sound stage (David Hay comes from a theater background, and all actors, even movie stars, love the "feel" of a stage). We then made the space off limits to all of us producers. End result: Although exhausted and preoccupied, David bulled his way through the rewrite so that he could get back to the beloved theater where his actors were so comfortable that they stayed extra hours to nail down the changed pages of the script.

A FINAL WORD

If creatives like the writer and director guard the artistic integrity of the work, and studio execs, often referred to as "suits," guard the budget and bottom line, then producers straddle the middle space, oscillating between the two camps. The producer is usually looking for ways to cut costs while fighting to give the director more time and money to make the best possible movie. Sometimes the producer is accused of favoring one side over the other, and has to do a spider's dance to earn both camps' trust. That's because a director who doesn't trust a producer can shut him or her out of the creative process. Remember that the project has already been green-lighted, so money is flowing. In this case, despite the studio's apparent affinity with the producer who is leaning toward their camp, the studio will almost always side with the director. Changing directors is expensive and gives out the industry perception that the project is in trouble. For these reasons, it's almost never done. Usually it's the producer who gets canned if tensions impede production schedules. It's just easier. If the studio smells out that a producer is too "tight" with a director, they will bypass that producer in favor of dealing directly with the director.

Finally, tact, passion, and persuasiveness are hallmarks of the best producers. They must recognize the merit of your work, then put a logical battle plan in place. The best producers are often natural storytellers who beguile others into involvement by selling the merits of the project, all the while exhorting you to do your best work in the rewrites. And like the very best salesmen, they don't take no for an answer, which is where their reputation as sharks comes from. They turn negatives into positives ("Less money for the production? That means we can beef some of those character-driven scenes I love so much in the second act!"). The best producers are always looking for ways to squeeze every dollar and get it onto the screen, all the while protecting the "vision" that drew everyone to the project in the first place. Like a championship-winning coach, these producers push their team past their endurance to create something that may be beyond any single individual's ability.

-11-

Extra Credit Reading:

I think too many screenwriters try to be commercial as opposed to being accessible. Find that material which speaks to you and has a certain truth. Forget about whether it's commercial. "Dracula" took me fifteen years. "Hook" took me ten years.

—Jim Hart (Hook, Bram Stoker's Dracula, Mary Shelley's Frankenstein)

Who Are Directors?

A movie script is essentially a two-dimensional chess game without players. You have the flat board, which is the plot structure, and then the chess pieces, which are the words that form characters, dialogue, and themes. A lot of people refer to screenplays as blueprints, with directors as the architects. Most writers find this model constricting, not to mention inaccurate, but that doesn't seem to stop Hollywood auteurs from talking about the Pygmalion-like process of "shaping the material." Since the mid-fifties, film has been a director's medium. Why? To truly understand just how pivotal the role of the director is, it's important to consider the flow of power that accompanies a script's journey to the screen.

A writer controls a script until the day he or she submits it to the producer. The producer will give a writer notes for changes to be made until such time as the producer deems the project ready for studio executives. In turn, the studio will give more notes in the quest to attract a suitable director. When the studio sends out the word that a project has reached a certain level of development (i.e., when CEs and VPs deem that it feels like more of a movie and less of simply a good concept), various directors are then brought in to offer their *take* on the project. The take is a director's vision of how the movie might look and feel. They may also discuss various aspects of the story, such as characters and dialogue that work particularly well or may require more attention. Producers may have input concerning choice of a director, but it is the studio that has ultimate power. In fact, a studio will sometimes hire a director over the producer's objections.

When a director does comes on board, the flow of power and direction of the movie flows to him or, less often, her.

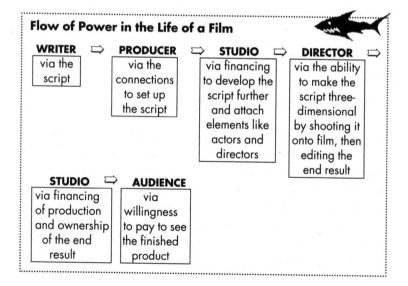

Flow of Power in the Life of a Film

WRITER ⇨	PRODUCER ⇨	STUDIO ⇨	DIRECTOR ⇨
via the script	via the connections to set up the script	via financing to develop the script further and attach elements like actors and directors	via the ability to make the script three-dimensional by shooting it onto film, then editing the end result

STUDIO ⇨	AUDIENCE
via financing of production and ownership of the end result	via willingness to pay to see the finished product

Sometimes a movie star of sufficient stature may vie for control of the project. Such a battle can be highly contentious, with the project often losing valuable heat shields along the way that protect it through the development process. Several years ago, John Travolta clashed with auteur-director Roman Polanski on the set of *The Double*. Production screeched to a halt, lawsuits were threatened, and when the studio couldn't resolve the situation, despite having already spent millions of dollars, the project was abandoned.

Good directors inspire confidence. They command not only the actors and raw equipment of filmmaking, but also the entire vision of the project. Good directors have gone to acting classes and have tried their hands at writing scripts. In other words, they understand creative processes other than their own, and recognize the fluid and collaborative nature of production. Good directors understand that large egos are sometimes part of the process, but they never allow personality issues to derail completion of the project. Sometimes such give-and-take gets the most out of the writer/director development process. Finally, *good directors use the producer as a buffer* between the movie they are making and the studio, which is often more concerned about the cost than the result. Successful checkmate of the movie comes when the director or "king" uses all the pieces in an orchestrated fashion.

THE RELATIONSHIP BETWEEN DIRECTORS AND WRITERS

To be sure, short of a finished film, working with a director is the most valuable experience of all for a screenwriter. The process doesn't get any more real until you yourself become a director. In the best of all possible worlds, you will add important elements to your writing through working with a director. For example, most writers will come into a scene in linear fashion, that is, master shot, followed by inserts. Meanwhile, directors are unencumbered by the process of making words into images. Instead they search for visual metaphors to lock the scene in place. Say you write a scene involving a fire, as I did on a Miramax Studios project titled *The Hellseeker.* My scene was written in master shot to convey the main action. However, the director saw an exploding furnace reflecting off the hero flame-jumper's visor. He then spun the camera to the shell-shocked man next to the hero. Suddenly the scene, which was initially pro forma, jumped with immediacy and style. Often the director will reveal to the writer how he intends to get that magical shot. While you don't want to go overboard and start directing your own script as you write it, by adding just a touch of such elements, a scene can really feel "in the moment," while enhancing the overall point of view.

If you're dealing with a director, then your project is already pretty far along the development track. Depending on circumstances, your focus on the script will shift from striving to "get it right" to the pressure not to "screw it up." First-time meetings with a director, usually taking place in a producer or studio exec's office or conference room, are crucial in that regard. You should be enthusiastic, even though advance word coming from your agent may make you feel otherwise, as in, "I heard from the studio that Director X thinks the whole second act needs to be rethought, along with the love story." Suddenly, four months of your work may be up for grabs, but you must still arrive open-minded, ready to generate the

---

Five Keys to Working Successfully with a Director

1. Show mutual respect. Appreciate what strengths the director brings to the project.
2. Demonstrate informed understanding of the director's visual priorities.
3. Be a good listener.
4. Be as detached as possible from your work, and thus open to new ideas.
5. Express enthusiasm. Look for ways to end every conversation or meeting on a high note.

necessary energy to get everybody excited about the project, and to warrant your continued involvement.

A director who is good at development uses the writer and the development process to clarify the story. A bad director is like a barber armed with a blowtorch and a Weedwacker pillaging scene after scene. Early on, expect a full read of your script using professional actors. If one isn't offered, ask for it. The reason for the full read has to do with notes, which can be delineated as either arbitrary or constructive. Arbitrary notes come from the "perfect movie" floating around in the director's mind's eye. Such notes from the director will have little to do with the movie you've actually written, but a full read might stop a director from trying to superimpose one over the other. You want the director to be aware of what the script is before he begins to strip it for parts to build his own vision.

DEALING WITH DIRECTOR'S NOTES

Development with directors inevitably results in notes. That's normal, but when addressing any rewrite, the physician's ancient injunction, "First do no harm," always applies. Unfortunately, our craft has developed in inverse proportion to development notes and the development process. The closer you get to production, the more the notes. While you and the director *must* be on the same page about the theme of the script and the spine of the story, all else is negotiable. During story meetings, where you hear many ideas kicked around, use this simple guideline: Do these suggestions clarify the story line and increase the emotional resonance of the characters? If not, then they're outside of the box, and it's your unspoken job to get back into the structure already laid out in the script.

Good directors respect impassioned and informed arguments from writers on the major issues of the script. But usually they react to challenges on little disagreements with the W.C. Fields edict, "Get away, kid, you bother me!" In general, don't count on the studio for help, since it will side with the director approximately 85 percent of the time. The studio or producers can end any disagreement simply by saying something like "The director writes," or "The director has a writer he's comfortable with." This nuclear-winter scenario means that if you don't pony up with the desired changes, the director can send you to the showers at any second. Someone else will come in for the pass while your seat is still warm. So choose your battles carefully. Most of the little ones aren't worth fighting. If you don't feel comfortable with your writer-director relationship but want to keep the gig, sometimes the best strategy for dealing with arbitrary comments is simply to ignore them. Smile, say something like, "That's an excellent idea. I'm going to address it ASAP." Satisfied, everyone in the room will move on. Nine times out of ten they will go away between the time the note is taken and when it is executed. If you're cornered during a story meeting with a director note like, "So what do you think about the native girl befriending a telepathic monkey?" simply look out of the window or off into the distance and imagine whooping cranes taking flight in the Himalayas. "Yes . . . yes!" you should respond brightly. "Exactly!" Weeks later, if pressed on the matter, you can mumble something about the monkey interfering with the big love scene, and you will be let off the hook. Of course, I'm kidding here, but you get the point.

While engaged in the rewrite, expect to be put through more paces and positions than the Kama Sutra. Again, this is what is called Development Hell. During heated debates, you may feel the overwhelming desire to blurt out, "I'm not a stenographer!" Stifle it. Such an unburdening will only invite others to sit around waiting for you to exit the project. Copping an attitude works fine for auteurs and stars, but will only hasten a writer's return to sandwich making at Blimpie's.

A FINAL WORD

By its very nature, developing a script entails the sometimes painful process of going from personal project to commercial enterprise. Directors are the most crucial part of the equation. You should realize your frustrations are usually process-related. Everyone is trying to make the best film according to his or her abilities. It's just that few agree on what that film should be. For that reason, no matter what you do, it will be hard to meet all expectations and agendas. Your goal is to survive. Be the defender of the story's spine, and don't get embroiled in the politics of power and personalities. Leave actual execution of the movie to the director and producer(s). In football, this is called "staying in your lane." Despite the many challenges you will face when passions and egos enter the picture, you can tunnel through the process like Clint Eastwood in *Escape From Alcatraz*, so that you may live to fight another day.

-12-

Keep away from people who try to belittle your ambitions. Small people always do that, but the really great ones make you feel that you too, can become great. —MARK TWAIN

Good scripts attract good directors. Good directors attract actors. Actors are literally the face and breath of a film. Movies cannot be made without them. In an age of CGI special effects, there can be a tendency to treat actors as props—just one more set element. To see your script go from page to scene, you may have to watch actors who are instructed to move from scene to scene like stick figures. Such a method may have worked for Alfred Hitchcock or John Ford, but few of us are of that level of genius or stature. Nothing is more rewarding than watching a fine actor make your words his or her own.

HOW ACTORS FIND WORK

Actors find auditions via trade publications like *Drama-Logue*, *Casting Call* and *Backstage*, which is the best way to contact them.

They submit their equivalent of business cards, *head shots*. These are eight-by-ten photos of the actor. Usually actors have a few variations of these head shots, to show their dramatic and comedic sides. A tiny ad for auditions or readers placed in the trades will net you hundreds and sometimes thousands of head shots a week later. Actors have a tough row to hoe because supply always exceeds demand, and because relatively few are college-educated, so they have limited career options to fall back on, although that is changing. Lack of higher education means that actors have very little to fall back on financially. They wait tables and do all of the other stereotypical things, like retail and telemarketing, to earn money.

Like writers, actors must get used to rejection. On my recent film *Hard Scrambled,* we received some 2,000 head-shot and less often videotape submissions, resulting in about 100 auditions. In other words, the selection process is both highly selective and idiosyncratic. I saw many good performances, and many actors who were extremely dedicated to their craft. Often it came down to a gut feeling that the director and we producers had.

**How to Sort Actor Head Shots
(aka Type Casting)**

1. Appropriate by type.
2. Appropriate by age group.
3. Inappropriate but interesting.
4. Totally inappropriate and destined for the wastebasket. Seventy-five to ninety percent of the submissions you receive will fall into this category, so, to paraphrase Roy Scheider in *Jaws,* you're going to need a bigger wastebasket.

ATTACHING ACTORS TO YOUR SCRIPT

Aside from a lucrative paycheck, actors are motivated by good scripts and good directors, as well as the chance to work with esteemed fellow actors. It's important to keep in mind these motivations when you approach an actor about your project. Actors are at the mercy of the director's vision. A good director allows an actor to experiment and give *colors* (delivering dialogue in different ways and allowing different takes of the material, varying tone, speed of delivery, and facial expressions). An actor who only delivers a single color isn't going to give a director much to work with in the editing room, and isn't going to make your script come alive, either.

Many writers who have settled in to Hollywood will move into producing their scripts by attempting to attach to their work actors they've met. Likewise, that actor living just down the hall from you will be thinking about how he or she might circumvent the audition process and get in on the ground level of a promising project. As important as an actor's ability is his name recognition. Attaching talented but unknown actors to your script will impede its chances in the marketplace. That's because a good producer may wish to attach a "name" in order to set it up. For example, maybe he or she knows of a financier willing to fund a Vin Diesel movie. The only thing missing is the script—your script—which may be unnecessarily encumbered by an actor whose best credit is a Zest commercial. Remember that actors will wish to work with actors of similar (or higher) caliber and "stardom." Before contractually attaching your karate instructor-turned-actor to your *White Belt Fury* script, ask yourself how the relationship will benefit the marketing of your work.

MOVIE STARS AND ACTORS

Actors with marquee status come in two categories: Those who are intimately involved in the development process of every project that comes their way, and those whose major concern is the money behind the deal. When pitching to an actor's production company, it's crucial to know whether the actor is doing legitimate development or merely *housekeeping*, meaning maintaining an office on the studio lot mainly so that he or she has a private place to go for lunch. These actors sometimes use discretionary monies given to them by the studio to option material with a vague notion of developing it. However, the purchase is mainly intended to keep loyal staffers busy in between lunches. This latter arrangement is known as a *vanity deal* and can needlessly tie up your project for a year or longer because the lack of a true development process means your project is predetermined to gather dust on a shelf. Writers concerned about such a scenario should make inquiries with the actor's director of development regarding what projects they have in development and what movies they have produced in the past twenty-four months. Actors who are heavily involved in the development of projects they appear in have a strong sense of aesthetic. For example, it's hard to imagine an actor like Dustin Hoffman or Sean Penn just showing up for principal photography to utter the lines they've been given. Such actors gravitate toward character-driven as opposed to action-driven material, then mold it to fit their on-screen personae.

Writer's Tip

Many writers specifically write small, personal stories, hoping to target an actor they admire. However, almost always, the nicely told story of "How Mom Survived Cancer" will be considered too soft for development and a very tough sell unless it's woven into a bigger story. Think *Terms of Endearment* or *Lorenzo's Oil*. In the latter instance, a true-life family's anguish led them to defy established medical opinion in search of a cure for cancer. It's easy to see how such emotional tours de force would garner passionate commitment from actors.

QUERYING AN ACTOR

Approach an actor or his development executive the same way you would an agent, a producer, or an executive. On a single sheet of paper or in a three-minute phone call, state who you are (brief sum-mary of your credits), the project you have, and why you think the actor would be right for the part. If you have an agent or manager, consult with them about making the pitch for you. Your representation will also discuss with you the merits and viability of approaching the proposed actor.

My Foray into Acting School

An actor friend asked me if I was interested in tagging along to his class at a legendary acting school in New York. He assured me that I could just hang out and watch the proceedings. My friend lied. Before I knew it, I was alone on a tiny stage telling twenty or so strangers "a little about myself." A toothpick was the only thing that saved me from having to fake heat stroke to escape. The toothpick was in my front pants pocket, and I fidgeted with it so much that about thirty seconds into my "monologue," it pushed through and was free-floating around somewhere inside my boxer shorts. The threat of an imminent "kebabbing" distracted me so much that I finished the exercise without trouble, then walked very carefully back to my seat. Since then I've sat in with several groups. I often am inspired and humbled by the talent of actors.

-13-

I have called this principle, by which each slight variation, if useful, is preserved, by the term Natural Selection.

—CHARLES DARWIN

WHO ARE AGENTS?

Each year, thousands of Hollywood hopefuls plunk down hundreds of dollars each, trying to unlock the mysteries of one topic: Agents.

With that in mind, I will take a little extra time with this complex subject.

Hollywood agents come from a variety of backgrounds. Some are ex-lawyers and some never went to college. Almost all started out in talent agency mail rooms where they sorted mail and delivered packages and learned who is who in the industry. Following about six months of long days of tedious work for little pay, a select few are invited into the agency's training program, where they work as assistants to agents. This rigorous *landing-at-a-desk* training period features even longer hours and more stress, and can last up to about two years. Following that time period, either the assistant will be fired to make way for the next crop of trainees, or if lucky, he will be invited to become a junior agent in the firm. An assistant who feels that she won't be offered a junior agent position will preempt the process by finding an agent vacancy at a smaller firm than where she trained. Small agencies employing fewer than twenty agents are called *boutiques.* They offer clients greater personal attention in exchange for the decreased standing they hold in the industry. Agents may also create their own firms and work alone. Such agencies are referred to as *one-man bands.* Usually, such an agent must have at least one star client in order to be worth your time.

The business side of Hollywood is a volatile mix of high-octane deals and combustible personalities. The agent profession in particular seems to attract type-A personalities. For agents, the pressures to land the best client and make the deal happen are enormous. Thus all agents share certain characteristics. Usually they are young and aggressive and come fully equipped with the famous killer instinct that barely needs mentioning. They are dealmakers and sale-closers. Agents prowl the Hollywood waters for promising material they can sell with a minimal expenditure of energy. Agents must sell projects in order to survive. Until a decade ago (ancient history in Tinseltown time), agents were seen as cultivators of talent and sounding boards for both creative and personal issues. Many had literary backgrounds and were prolific readers. They cared about all aspects of the client's life and were good hand-holders who might even loan you a few bucks when times were tight. However, the increasing corporatization of the entertainment industry has made such "caring and sharing" obsolete. For instance, my previous agent didn't even know I was married. It just never came up.

Good and Bad Agents

Good Agent . . .
- has a passion for the deal
- is detail-oriented
- remembers the little things
- remains in constant contact
- follows up by calling around for feedback after you take a meeting

Bad Agent . . .
- doesn't return calls
- loses submissions
- is dishonest
- promises the moon but can't deliver the cheese
- is unprepared for meetings, then tries to fake his or her way through discussions of your work

---

Success for an agent is determined by the number of projects they sell. The writing, directing, and other creative input they leave to you. For this reason, few agents speak in terms of whether a particular property is "good" or "bad," but rather address whether or not they feel they can sell it immediately. Until you are an earning client, most agents are bad about returning calls, reading material, or answering e-mail. The best thing you can do is not take any of it personally. Agents read hundreds of mostly bad scripts in a given year, which is more than enough to darken even the most sunny agent's disposition.

> **Let's Do Lunch . . .**
>
> If you want to see what agents look like and how they sound and smell, go to Kate Mantilini's industry haunt at lunchtime. You'll pay exorbitant prices for glorified diner food, but will also glean invaluable reconnaissance. Kate's is located on Wilshire Boulevard, a stone's throw from *uber* agency ICM. I recommend that you bring your best hearing aid and go eat lunch there every day for a week. The experience will be very enlightening. Of course, if an agent offers to take you out to lunch, you can expect them to pick up the check. The same goes for a producer.

The Agent Roster

The average agent may have a dozen or so working writers at the midlevel, who command low to high five figures per project. Most writers who persevere reach this next level in about two to five years. When a writer sells a high-profile spec or consistently strings together enough midlevel assignments, that writer is said to be pulling his or her weight. Unless the agency is a powerhouse, most agents are lucky to have more than one writer of this caliber. Such writers command the undivided attention of the agent. I once saw a client list at a midsized agency where some agents were handling thirty-five writers. You can bet that only about five of those writers are working at any given time, and only one was A-list.

TIP: Never take a meeting with a prospective agent without knowing who his or her key clients are. You can locate such information on the website whoRepresents.com or via a Google search.

Meeting an Agent

Many writers are apprehensive about how they should behave when meeting with an agent, particularly in the initial phases of the relationship. First, be sure to dress casually. Don't try too hard to impress via your wardrobe. Jeans and a shirt are enough, while a suit will have you competing with your intended rep. It sounds superficial, but Hollywood expects screenwriters to look like they were typing away or more likely, goofing off ten minutes prior to the sit-down. The agent will assume you sleep in your clothes, anyway. During the meeting, anticipate a general consensus on the direction and marketability of your work, or what those business types call a "market overview." Knowing *exactly* what expectations you have is critical going in. What is the agent's perspective of your work? This one's crucial, since an agent's best asset is his or her judgment. How many writers does the agent rep? Ten to twelve working writers is ideal, with a couple of high-powered names thrown into the mix. The writer-to-agent ratio indicates the likelihood that the agent will work aggressively for you.

Is there synergy between you and the prospective agent? Some agent types have a habit of rephrasing tough questions into something they'd rather answer. Ideally, the actual meeting should be held in a conference room where you won't be interrupted. Look for signs that calls are being held. Fifteen minutes is reasonable to expect. Any conversation that ends with "What are you, some kinda freak?" probably doesn't bode well for the relationship. Realistic expectations are important, and one unspoken expectation by an agent is that you'll continue to aggressively market your own career. Simply writing and providing an address where to send the Big Giant Checks, while leaving the business end up to your representation, is a sure way to jeopardize your career.

The follow-up after a first meeting provides key information for the writer. Is the agent aggressive in contacting you afterwards? Does he or she return each new round of calls promptly? For your part, send a thank-you note that includes an elaboration or reference to something memorable from the meeting. Then watch to see if the agent acknowledges receiving your thank-you, script, or other follow-up mailed materials.

FIVE WAYS TO IMPRESS YOUR AGENT

Many writers go to great lengths to procure an agent, only to let their promising relationship slip away through lack of due diligence. Usually this occurs when a beginning writer assumes that all his or her hard work on the business side is over, and now the agent will be 100 percent responsible for generating opportunities and deals. Problems can arise when the same writer then turns in a new spec that's less than a home run, then sits at home and waits for the phone to ring, berating the agent when it doesn't. A healthy client/ management relationship evolves and matures over time following the initial honeymoon period, and a good client stays involved in helping to shape his or her career. Here are five ways to ensure that your relationship stays positive and continues to grow:

1. Be knowledgeable but not pushy about the industry. Not long ago I had a script going *out wide* (sent to dozens of potential buyers). I submitted the following list to my agent:
   - 20 producers who I felt might welcome the submission
   - 6 execs who were fans of my work
   - 10 directors whom I considered right for the material, several of whom had active production companies
   - 5 actors who developed their own material and might be willing to buy my spec

   Result: My agent was impressed that I had taken the time to research the market and compile the list.

2. Be productive and prolific. Agents love self-starters who don't need to be cajoled into finishing and polishing their work.

3. Always write on the side. Even if you are a writer with a lucrative studio assignment, you are still essentially a gun for hire. Agents like to be surprised with spec scripts that capture your true ability and aesthetic.

4. Be professional. Follow up introductory meetings with a thank-you note. Send a copy to your agent of any correspondence going to the studio or production company. Don't force your agent to clean up your messes. For example, I know of a writer/producer who didn't like the amount of money the studio was offering for last-

minute changes on her green-lighted project. The writer instructed her agent to demand a certain amount of money, then hopped on a plane for Las Vegas. Careers were on the line, so the studio execs caved, but the writer earned the enmity of many people who vowed never to work with her again.

5. Be a good listener and don't tell tales out of school. *Schadenfreude* is a sport in Hollywood. To paraphrase Oscar Wilde, it's not enough for you to succeed but your friends have to fail in the process. Agents are excellent at sizing people up, so will quickly note whether or not you, too, have this tendency. If you do, the agent will automatically devalue in their minds whatever comes out of your mouth regarding the business.

HOW TO BECOME A CLIENT

Most agents have an entire spectrum of clients ranging from new to very experienced. At the bottom rung, most agents have as many as a couple of dozen "pocket clients" for whom they expend minimal energy. Such clients are beginning writers who have no track record but who show promise, often in the form of a gritty, compelling screenplay that is tough to market. Becoming a pocket client is relatively easy: Place well (quarter finalist or better) in a major competition, and an agent will be inclined to read your work. Plow through the *Hollywood Agents & Managers Directory* (www.hcdonline.com), and then cast your net wide enough, and you will make a connection. Querying an up-and-coming entertainment lawyer is another way to go. Spec sale news in trade publications like *Variety* and *The Hollywood Reporter* usually include the lawyers who brokered the deal. Lawyers of a certain level are looking to build their client base, and so will develop and matchmake relationships with both writers and agents. Any fledgling producer with some standing in the business, or a low-level exec you tricked into reading your work, can also provide an entrée to an agent (provided they like your work). Simply ask if they can recommend an agent they like. Most will gladly offer this in lieu of actually giving you work. Still another way is via your writing community. Put six writers in a room and one of them is bound to have a line on an agent. If all of these scenarios fail you, no writer should be without K. Callan's book, *The Script Is Finished, Now What Do I Do?* which interviews, evaluates, and gives access to hundreds of agents at dozens of agencies. The key to all of these scenarios is to submit work that is solid. One agent I talked with put it succinctly: "Write something we can sell."

BEING A POCKET CLIENT AND RISING ABOVE THAT STATUS

To that end, an agent will expend some energy during the pocket-client honeymoon period, which typically lasts from thirty days to six months. Said energy comes in the form of notes on a draft, returned phone calls, and maybe a few submissions sent out to strategically targeted production companies. During this special time, the writer feels a tremendous rush that comes from a bit of security. You have an agent. All is right with the world. However, you should be aware of the insidious, Dorian Gray time element that quickly creeps into this arrangement. If a pocket client writes an undeniably marketable script, sells a project, or lands an assignment (tough but not impossible to do), he or she becomes a full-fledged client entitled to more of the agent's time and attention. If not, there's a remote-control-operated trapdoor under the chair for writers like you. In my own case, the agent in question was a husky-voiced, chain-smoking femme fatale who, in six months, went from "Work with me and I will be relentless for you" to quoting Public Enemy lyrics, as in, "I can't do nothin' for you, man. No-thing." Boy, did it ever hurt when I fell off that particular teacup ride. Agents are notorious for going from "can't miss" to "can't rep" in a matter of weeks. As said, acquiring an agent is relatively easy, but keeping one is hard. In agents' defense, developing careers for beginning writers requires a tremendous amount of time and effort. "Like pulling an engine up from the bottom of the ocean," is how an agent once described the process. Therefore, most established agents opt out of this heavy lifting. "Love your work; catch you at the next level," they say. It will then hit you that responsibility for jump-starting a career rests squarely on your shoulders. This is a painful admission, but really right where things should be. So expect to change agent partners often during the early period of your career.

Generally, you must option a spec or get an assignment somewhere to survive the pocket-client gauntlet. Remember that agents are good at promising the moon, but they only get 10 percent of the cheese. Keep working and you'll discover that the balance between high expectations and cruel reality shifts over the course of your career. That's where what you can expect from your agent also changes. When the commission checks you write to an agency start paying their rent or for their Dead Sea salt body-scrub spa fees for an entire month, they'd better pay attention to you—or you need a new agent. Writers at this middle level have more cushion than their pocket brethren, but these scribes are vulnerable if they hit a dry patch—like a pair of specs that fail to find a home, or being fired from an assignment or two.

THE ROLE OF QUERY LETTERS AND QUERY CALLS

One-page query letters are the way to approach agents and producers about the project(s) you have to offer: "I wrote X—would you like to read it?" A writer will gain the necessary contact information, usually from the *Hollywood Creative Directory,* then "query" the target. Sometimes this tactic works out fine; however, Hollywood is a phone and face culture. By that I mean that most business is conducted on the fly via telephone and in face-to-face meetings around town. In fact, many agents make it a point to visit every studio in town on a weekly basis. Although the industry is built on paper in the form of scripts, few people have time to read anything unless they absolutely have to, which is why I'm not a big fan of traditional query letters. Borrowing the logic of *What Color Is Your Parachute?,* most query letters are too impersonal and too random and too many people send them, making the odds for success very remote. Too few agents (and producers) feel obligated to respond, so most query letters pile up like snowdrifts on a desk and never get past the assistant. What follows are some other options for the traditional query letter.

E-mail. Because e-mail can be read and responded to on the fly in a more informal manner, written queries sent via the Internet garner better results than postal mail, particularly among younger agents. While even a form letter response requires a signature, stationery and printing, envelope and stamp, an exec can simply respond to an e-mail with "Send it." or "Not for us. Thanks." The key to calling attention is a compelling subject line like "Jim Smith, Disney, Referral," "Chesterfield Script Competition Finalist," or "New Teen Horror Spec."

Phone queries. If you do enough research to target the correct company and individual, phone queries have a much higher success rate than most written queries. Use your *Hollywood Agents and Managers Directory,* and simply call the agent on the phone. Most agents will take note of the initiative involved, while the voice-to-voice interaction will allow you to take advantage of the famous Hollywood aversion for confrontation.

FORM FOR ALL QUERIES

The major rule of thumb for good query calls and letters is to avoid gimmicks. You may think it's the height of cleverness to mail your screenplay along with a shoe and a punchline about "getting a foot in the door," but such a package will attract more attention from the security department than from an executive. Likewise, being too "cute" will miss the bus for most agents, who only have about ten seconds to figure out the essence of what you want from them. Besides the fact that all agents have very little free time, the very nature of screenwriting means that you must master the task of telling a complete story in a predetermined time limit of usually 110 to 120 minutes. So it's imperative to avoid telling your life story and the details of your difficult birth in a query. Get to the point and be straightforward. Limit your query to one project per letter or call at a time. Listing all fourteen projects you have going will overwhelm and confuse the agent, while raising the question, "If you're so gifted and prolific, why haven't I heard of you?"

Your query should follow the form below:

1. Why are you contacting this agent?
2. What material do you have for consideration?
3. Your credits or qualifications as a writer.
4. Your contact information.

SAMPLE QUERY

Lee Knight
2673 Ellis Lane
San Diego, CA
(619) 555-1234

January 7, 2003

Steve Frost
Agent
X-Factor Writers & Artists
8442 Wilshire Boulevard
Beverly Hills, CA 90212

Dear Mr. Frost:

I have just completed a teen romantic comedy called *Prom Date.* Per your most recent spec sale of Jenna Tandy's *Gym Class* discussed in last month's *Variety,* I believe that my script may be right for your representation.

Three high school couples anticipate the perfect prom, but all three relationships break up just days before the big night. A mad scramble to mend fences or find a new date ensues.

If interested, I will be happy to sign your standard release form and submit *Prom Date* for your perusal. In advance, thanks very much for your time and consideration.

Best regards,

Lee Knight
Lee Knight

KEEPING AN AGENT

Keeping agents is the single biggest issue on many screenwriters' minds. That's because agents are fundamental to moving up the creative ladder since they can give you access to bigger players and better projects in the industry. An agent hopes that with perseverance and luck, inevitably a prospective client will find the right relationship. The key is strategic planning and taking responsibility for your own career, with the help of your agent. New writers are consumed with how best to get this year's top spec seller at ICM to sign them (generally, you can't). Midlevel scriptors worry that their agency isn't 100 percent behind their latest work, or haven't pushed hard enough for that high-profile studio assignment. For them, someone else's agent is always working harder for writers who are clearly less talented. And upper-echelon screenwriters? This group is consumed with cigars and floral arrangements—as in which bouquet or burlwood humidor to send that agent who is "terrific at the little things and more like a close friend." The irony here is that the agents involved in each scenario may be one and the same person. In other words, depending on a writer's place in the pecking order, the same agent can be unattainable, not diligent enough, and a conscientious career partner who can change your life. So where does the discrepancy of performance come from? A key factor is the client roster, of course, and the vibe you get from the agent. A guy outside the loop has to hustle ten times as much. You should talk to existing clients, find out what projects they're doing, how much money they've made, and how long they've been with the agent.

HOW TO AVOID STICKING WITH A BAD AGENT

Working writers worry less about relationships with *any* agents than about having the *right* relationship. So what should you look for in an agent? In a word, access. In addition to the ability to recognize talent, a good agent is "plugged in." Before signing, make sure the agent has key relationships within your potential market. Find out by requesting to talk to current clients. Most will feel an overpowering compulsion to unburden themselves and give you the straight scoop. Prior to signing with my present agency, I talked with three clients. Once satisfied, I signed. That relationship lasted more than three years. That's a long time in the agent world. In addition to access, a good agent or manager should also recognize talent. You'd think that quality is a given, but you'd be surprised.

Telltale signs that you may have a bad agent. Do you hear about calls made by the agent berating the execs involved with your project? Is there an inordinate amount of he-said-she-said regarding the conversations you have with others regarding the progress of the project, and what the agent tells you they said to him or her? Is the agent abusive to assistants, waiters, support people, etc., in front of you? These are warning signs that you may have a bad agent.

When you're doing a deal or on assignment with the studio or production company, the agent will be in direct contact with producers and executives, often on a daily basis. There's an unspoken rule of thumb that creatives are to be left alone as much as possible at certain times in the process—for instance, while writers are completing a script or directors are completing a *rough cut* (the director's initial assemblage of the movie). So those on the other side of the desk will be relying on your agent to communicate the studio's wants and needs. I know of an instance where, because of an agent's corrosive behavior, a production company passed on a project that they had initially wanted. Said the senior production VP, "This guy is a mess. And although we liked the project and the client, in the end we decided he wasn't worth the trouble." I cannot overemphasize that an agent with a personality problem can derail your career. Similarly, you can do similar damage by copping a caustic attitude regarding constructive discussions of your work.

While some agents give story notes (as I said before, fewer and fewer do), most just sell. Newer writers tend to need notes. However, if necessary, leave the notes to your trusted readers and colleagues, since experience, aggressiveness, and enthusiasm are more important traits for you to seek out in an agent. It's relatively easy to be an agent in a bull market, but only an experienced agent will have a sound strategy for a tough sale in a lean period. To that end, a good agent is a pit bull with a pot roast on your behalf. A key indicator here is how aggressive the agent is in signing you. Many writers ignore the danger signs of a lukewarm initial effort—only to prolong the inevitably disastrous results. Sometimes having *no* agent is better than having a lousy agent.

Part of a writer's lot is incurring lots of war wounds in the form of lost creative battles and unsold or shelved projects. Your agent's eternal optimism is the right salve for such contusions. I once had an agent who tore me a new one about various elements in my just-completed draft. Later I learned from her assistant that the agent was working off four pages of coverage and hadn't actually read the script. In fact, most of the coverage was positive. Needless to say, her use of negative reinforcement, coupled with one too many fibs, soon had us tearfully parting ways. Conversely, is the agent waxing poetic about your script, but you suspect he or she hasn't even read it? This astral phenomenon is known as "shining the client." In many ways, such a carrot-and-cinnamon-stick approach is even more destructive to a writer's psyche than the aforementioned full frontal assault on the ego. The right agent will also share your vision for the future. Here, the short game of short-term work to earn money and the long game of career should be in sync.

What is the reputation of your targeted agent? Ask around. You should also learn about the agency where your agent works. Again, ask around. Yes, agencies have reputations, too. In fact, any experienced script reader will tell you which agency sends quality and which sends X-rated pop-up books as submissions. And is there any potential to package you with in-house directors or talent? Ask.

The Agent Assistant

Once in a while, an agency really rolls out the red carpet for prospective clients. I attended an intimate group breakfast at a Big Five agency (CAA, ICM, WMA, UTA, or Endeavor), which was hosted by a legendary agent. His assistant had the air of a grad student in literature, which she was. This senior assistant was a good listener who was smart, well-read, and funny in a self-deprecating way. Although she had been at the agency two years, it occurred to me that she seemed better suited for the book publishing world. In fact, moments after I had this thought, the agent announced that he wanted us to meet "a real comer." Next, a young woman blew into the room with the air of a shark thrashing about inside of a power suit. Her eyes flicked across the room before coming to rest on the senior agent, as if to say, "I'm doing this for you, Senior Agent X, otherwise I wouldn't have time for this nonsense." In fact, she was a newly minted junior agent who had risen up the ranks in half the time of the other female assistant in the room. For the next two minutes or so, the junior agent delivered machine-gun-style some prepackaged remarks about how "you gotta be the best of the best if you want to impress [me]." Then she answered exactly one question and was gone. In her wake, the senior agent smiled and winked. "She's something, ain't she?" he said. The message was clear: The saying "There's no 'I' in team" doesn't apply in Hollywood. Writers should take that into consideration when choosing representation. As one veteran writer once told me, "My agent is an asshole so that I don't have to be." At the same time, that agent is your emissary in the industry. If he or she's mindlessly aggressive or unscrupulous, that too will hurt your career. Unfortunately, there's no easy answer here.

DECIDING WHETHER TO LEAVE YOUR AGENT

The standard length of a representation contract is two years. However, you can formally withdraw from an agent-client relationship if the agent hasn't procured work for you in ninety days. Most scriptors would rather take their chances in Thunderdome than be without an agent. However, bad representation gives the writer a false sense of insecurity. By this I mean that writers often misdirect their efforts and frustrations on a single individual who they believe is keeping them from perpetual employment and untold riches. These writers spend their waking hours trying to find ways to motivate their representation to better do their bidding. *For the love of God, please take the spec out wide, or at least set up the meeting with Jody Foster's people.* Better to take a page from the Richard III School of

Screenwriting and act upon your winter of discontent. If you fear that your agent is using your latest screenplay to paper-train his iguana, it's time to move on.

Agents are of little value if they have no access, or are unwilling to expend their access on your work. Without these qualities, agents are like lion tamers without whips or chairs. An agent who takes two weeks to return your call is not looking out for your career. I once had an agent who would leave tormenting messages on my machine like "Michael, they passed on the script. They said the protagonist wasn't ironic enough. I'm leaving for New York for five days, so I'll try to find out more when I get back and then we'll touch base." I finally got up enough courage to leave this agent and strike out on my own. Contrary to popular belief, I had little trouble getting producers and directors to examine my work without an agent. I simply made my pitch and when the potentially interested party said the inevitable, "Have your agent submit the script to us," I would answer that I was changing agents so would instruct my lawyer to send the materials. An attorney friend who is not even in the entertainment field had given me a set of form letters on his letterhead. I simply inserted the name and address, and out the package went. At other times I simply requested to sign a standard release form, which many companies maintain for considering material submitted directly by the writer. These forms can be e-mailed, faxed, or snail mailed. The point is there are ways to work around the system if you are temporarily without an agent.

MARKETING YOUR SCRIPT WITHOUT AN AGENT

Welcome to "Why you can't have a career or even a life . . . without an agent." Wait, that's not right. As I've noted, the primary reasons for having an agent are for access, information, and enthusiasm. An agent has information and key contacts that are useful in the marketplace. They're also a professional person in the industry who is an enthusiastic sounding board. An agent is basically a salesman. Ideally, you churn out magic—your agent runs out and sells it for gazillions. Once in a while it works just that way. If an agent doesn't give you access, information, or enthusiasm, then you're better off without him. You can move your career forward even without an agent. With a little practice you can do all those marketing things yourself, but first, relax and focus on being a writer. Here's how.

1. PREPARE THE SCRIPT TO BE ALL THAT IT CAN BE

Having judged four screenplay competitions to date, I can tell you that 95 percent of the scripts sent out aren't ready for the market. Basic story elements aren't locked down like a compelling protagonist, central question, or integrated subplots. Make sure you give your project a good title that's either mysterious like *The Matrix*, or hints at the nature of the story—*Touch of Evil*, for instance. Or something suggestive like *Raging Bull*. Next, read your finished opus aloud. Or better: Have someone read it to you. Typically, my drafts change about thirty percent following the full read. Bad dialogue and passive voice will all be exposed. At the end of the sequence, ask your reader or yourself questions. Is the dilemma clear? What are the subplots? Does the protagonist have clear needs and goals?

Five Trusted Readers

Don't even think of sending out a script until you pass it through a gauntlet of five colleagues, teachers, or instructors and other people whose opinion you respect. Ask your readers questions about the project. Remember, this process isn't about propping up a threadbare ego—it's about making your script all it can be.

2. PREPARE THE PITCH

Before you rush for the Hollywood Creative Directory, prepare a beat sheet: a three-page synopsis conveying the main action of the story. Don't get hung up talking about subtext, as in "Jane wants to go to St. Louis but fears intimacy because of unresolved issues with Mom." Despite the fact that many writers enjoy discussing the tiniest twists and turns, such minutia is confusing for the listener.

Logline

What is your story about in two sentences? Sounds basic but many writers will spend months writing a script, then stammer when asked to describe their project in a nutshell. Tip: Check out the VideoHound's *Video Retriever* for a sense of how to boil down your story to its most basic premise. Write out your logline onto index cards and stick it out your board, wall or computer. Get used to seeing it so that the premise becomes second nature.

Research Your Target

Read the trades. Arm yourself with the *Hollywood Creative Directory*. Google search any producer you're about to query to find out what he's currently working on. Right way: "I read in today's Hollywood Reporter that you're looking for a scifi comedy in the spirit of *Galaxy Quest*." The wrong way to go is to shoot from the hip. "Hi, is producer Don Simpson in? No? Well, guess I can speak to his partner."

3. PRACTICE YOUR PITCH

I use a tape recorder and a stop watch. The idea is to get it down so that it sounds natural.

4. APPROACHING YOUR TARGET

The most enlightened way to approach your target is to call direct. And stand up when you phone. I'm serious. You will have both better energy and more force when you stand versus compressed lungs while sitting. For more authority and control of the situation, create a mental picture of the listener sitting while you are standing. Next, you should request a specific producer or executive and when he answers you say, "I'm Lynwood Bangs. I have a project that's perfect for you." Usually, he or she will say ask for the logline, to which you would reply, "It's about a girl who sees extra-terrestrials, but no one else can. They're trying to communicate with her, and she's scared to death." "Uh-huh" is the response you'll get, which means he's listening. So you say quickly, "It's *Sixth Sense* meets *E.T.*" Congratulations.

You just made a pitch. Of course, the producer knows that it's all in the execution. What you've said so far isn't outright garbage, it might be something and it might not be. The point is that you've approached him in a confident, professional manner. So he says one of the following:

A. "Send it." BAMM! You're in.
B. "Have your agent send it over."

You say, "I'm in the middle of changing agents, will my lawyer do?" Ninety-five percent of the time he will say, "Fine," and you get your cousin the tax attorney to send it over. Five percent of the time he will say, "Who's your agent?" Without missing a beat, you answer, "I'd rather not say." Now's there's a pregnant pause. You don't have an agent, you have *never* had an agent, so you do the one thing we writers are fantastic at, you *panic*. You hem and haw, then blurt out about your difficult time with puberty, the ICM agent who stole your lunch money. Guess what? The exec was playing gotcha, and you just blinked. You're not a pro, you'll never be in his league, and no, he does not want to read your crappy little script. Let's rewind. Let's say you have an agent, but are thinking about leaving this agent because you feel he isn't being aggressive enough—very normal writer complaints. Let's say you're already talking to a new agent but nothing has been finalized. Let's say you want the new agent to commit so you can leave what's his face who won't return your calls. So you decide to get pro active, do a little digging on your own. You approach a producer you think is perfect for your project and pitch yourself, because it feels liberating to take charge of your career and make things happen. Which is exactly the same place you are right now *without* a crappy agent you have to hide. So when the producer says, "Oh, who's your agent?" you say what is logical, which is, "I'd rather not say." Now there's an awkward pause. No, not because the producer can smell fear wafting over the phone lines—but because he has breached good business sense. He was unprofessional. After all, it was you who brought the project of potentially great value to him. And because you have the good manners not to call him on his faux paus, you invoke your Zen-like power of silence, allowing that pregnant pause to continue. Now the producer quickly fills it with something like, "Fine. Send the script."

C. The third option to your phone query might be, "Sorry, we don't do kid's movies." This option is unlikely since you should have researched the producer to know whether this is his genre. If he still says no, you still win, because you just cut three weeks out of the waiting game, and your answer was free.

By the way, 99 percent of the time, no response to your submission means no interest. When you send something and don't get an answer back, your first instinct should be to move on. Finally, don't sabotage your chances by giving into the impulse to get off the phone as quickly as possible. When acting as your own agent, it's important to keep in mind:

1. No one owes you a spec sale or development deal. It's hard work and you're responsible for the end result.
2. The more times you cast your net, the better you'll get at it, the greater your chances will be. It's a numbers game.
3. Seek out people who have succeeded at what you are attempting via phone, in person, emails or a well-crafted letter.
4. Be professional, pleasantly persistent.
5. Don't go after what's available. Go after what you really want the most.

Follow the above strategy, and you can create your own access, strategically plan and take responsibility for your career.

THE BENEFITS OF A GOOD AGENT

You will eventually want to secure a solid agency representation to enhance your legitimacy as a professional writer, as well as to increase the number of opportunities from which you may benefit. Agents scour the town looking for assignments and other opportunities, and most writers aren't nearly as well connected. Further, agents provide a minimum-quality-control standard for the industry, since agents who continually submit substandard work will soon find doors closed all around town. How you find new agentry leads us back to building a community: Put six creatives in a room and one of them is bound to have a line on an agent. By the way, remember that guy who threw the best all-night parties in school and then peeked over your shoulder during Film Theory finals? He probably became an agent. It's time to dust off those suspiciously identical test results and give him a call.

Response Time

Agents take from 3–8 weeks to read material from prospective clients, so be patient. Call the agent's assistant a week after submitting your script to verify that the package arrived and has been logged into the computer. Do not request a status report or to speak with the agent until at least 2½ weeks have elapsed.

Agents are fundamental to moving up the career ladder. They give a client a certain level of credibility. With perseverance and luck, you will inevitably find the right relationship. Once again, the key is strategic planning and taking responsibility for your own career. Finding the right relationship is not easy, so if at first you don't succeed, try, try again. If you've never had representation, the agent list (wga.org) of agencies willing to look at material from new writers is a good place to start.

-14-

I had to be my own best salesman. I had to know everything that was going on in Hollywood, who might or might not be interested in my piece, and guide my agent in those directions, even if he disagreed.

—TOM SCHULMAN (*DEAD POETS SOCIETY*)

WHAT IS A MANAGER?

A colleague once commented that since I already had an agent, he couldn't understand why I also needed the manager with whom I had recently signed. "Managers are there to see that the creative [me] who wakes from a fever dream doesn't get hit by a bus," I said. In other words, managers are the creative's buffer between the artistic process and the harsh business realities of the industry. "But that's what agents are for," my colleague replied. "That's what they *used* to be for," I answered. While managers routinely work for talent, the idea of management is still a concept that attracts curiosity and skepticism.

THE DIFFERENCE BETWEEN MANAGERS AND AGENTS

Agents *used* to be sounding boards for developing material, and some still are; however, as stated earlier, nowadays they are mainly about the art of the deal and not much else.

Today's agents don't so much develop talent as acknowledge success. As a case in point, while in graduate school, I wrote a script that won a contest and landed me a development executive at Touchstone, who agreed to be on my thesis committee and "help bring the project along." At the same time, a senior Big Three agent offered to work in tandem with the exec and take me on as a pocket client. I graduated just as the rewrite was coming together, and needing a stake to set up shop in Hollywood, I was thrilled to receive $5,000 up front against a total $45,000 contract from a Florida producer. The assignment was writing the true story of Dr. Ben Becker, a former Jack Dempsey sparring partner who became the head coach of the U.S. Boxing Team for three Olympics. Becker had been Muhammad Ali and Sugar Ray Leonard's corner man at the 1960 and 1976 games. When I called my agent with the good news, I was told that the deal "fell below her radar," but that she wished me well. You can imagine my shock at hearing those words.

It often falls to the manager not only to build a career incrementally, but also to bridge the chasm between the writer's often cloistered environment and the realties of a push-push business. A good manager can be the go-between who interprets the market while building a bridge to a strong agent-client relationship. They concern themselves with the general maintenance of your career.

HOW DO YOU KNOW IF YOU NEED A MANAGER?

Most working writers avoid hiring a manager for as long as possible because of the additional 10 percent they will have to pay out. However, if you've made some inroads in your career, such as signing with an agent, optioning some of your work, or landing some cable movie or low-budget assignments, you may begin wondering how to increase your visibility. After all, your agent is most likely only sending you on pitch meetings for projects you can land right now—in other words, projects at your current level. You may feel that more vision and future-mapping are needed in your strategic career arsenal. Or maybe you wonder if you'd benefit from a weekly rap session to discuss the marketability and progress of your latest spec before and during the writing process. If you're asking these kinds of questions, it may be time to consider a management service.

Most managers are ex-agents. Some have gone on to production roles at the studio. Such people then make the next logical leap of combining both backgrounds to become—tuh-dah!—managers. The key job of a manager is to keep you productive while trying to generate some traction or industry awareness for your career. This is the person who makes sure you work on your projects every day, gets you introductory meetings, and leaves you inspirational messages on your answering machine and in your e-mail box, particularly when you're feeling frustrated or blocked. To wit:

Manager's Message No. 1, delivered Tuesday, 8:47 a.m.: "I think the new third act is brilliant. I think it will be even more brilliant when you make it bigger. I can't wait to see it. When will that be? How about next Wednesday? You can give me the script and then we can go for breakfast. Call me."

Manager's Message No. 2, delivered Tuesday, 9:01 a.m.: "I told Benny Jacobs about you. He's the new VP at Fox. He says they're looking for a romantic comedy, and I said I had the perfect script, which I will when you hurry up and finish it. Let me know about Wednesday . . . unless you think you might be done by this Friday, in which case we can slip the script to Benny in time for his weekend read. That would be great. Let me know about lunch this Friday. Are you out of town or something? Call me, call me, call me." (Applying pressure to speed up delivery dates is the manager's "friendly noose strategy." If the tactic fills you with anxiety and fear, that's good.)

Because today's breed of agent is more inundated than ever, the one-on-one relationship with the writer is critical. Since teamwork to close a deal is essential for an agent, good agents are mindful that managers are there to help them prepare a client's work for market. Managers are integrally involved in the process—the development of an individual script. For that reason, managers will sometimes read a script a dozen times, trying to find ways to make it better. Traditionally, managers work with a very select client list. Whereas a top agent will service some thirty-odd clients, most managers work with fewer than half that number.

Managers are sometimes referred to as "agents with smaller client lists." This is a misconception, since creative input isn't necessarily a prerequisite to be a good agent. Having a nose for the deal is. In contrast, managers work at getting the material ready with creative input, and then implementing a strategy that will give the writer visibility and exposure in the marketplace. Managers also keep the lines of communication open between the writer and the agent, the producer, the studio, etc., while a project is going through the script-to-screen process.

AVOIDING BAD MANAGERS AND FINDING GOOD ONES

Good managers work in tandem with your agent to create a cohesive strategy for building your career.

Bad managers are abusive; not team players, they cause rifts between you and your agent. Ideally, managers can be "a writer's silent partner." You should expect both good advice on specific projects and long-term strategic planning from the relationship. Further, a good manager should be able to roll up his sleeves to pull together a script or make a deal happen. Other keys to look for in a manager are diplomacy, careful honesty, compassion, a good background in psychology, intelligence, and taste.

DOUBLE-DIPPING

There are certain trade-offs between the roles of agents and managers. For example, agents can legally negotiate deals, but managers can't. Managers, on the other hand, can attach themselves as producers to the projects created by their clients. Agents don't. Such a role entitles the manager to not only 10 percent of the client's earnings, but also to a negotiated fee as producer. This sum can be hundreds of thousands of dollars. In fact, managers who attach themselves as producers to all of a client's projects (sometimes referred to as *double-dipping*) is a legitimate concern when the credit is inappropriate. That's because a manager/producer who offers little more than the ability to deliver a coveted project can add hundreds of thousands of dollars of additional expense to a project, since a legitimate producer must still be procured for the project. Producers I know have been forced to pass on a coveted project simply because the acquisition cost was too great—and this usually comes from double-dipping. There is no set rule for dealing with this issue. In fact, the pros and cons of manager/producers are currently a topic of much spirited debate in Hollywood. Bottom line, discuss the situation with your peers and your lawyer. Make sure you go forward with eyes wide open.

-15-

SCRIPT READERS

Every studio and every major production company has a story department that *covers* (reads and evaluates) material submitted to executives. The task of analyzing thousands of script submissions is handled by mainly freelance readers who are independent contractors paid approximately fifty to sixty dollars per script. While a few union reader positions do exist, these positions pay very well and have greater job security, and so are highly coveted. The only way to become a union reader is to fill a vacancy when someone leaves the union. One well-connected friend I know waited nearly three years for his spot.

Writers arriving in L.A. will find that freelance reading positions are relatively easy to obtain, mainly because the pay is modest and the reader must read a *lot* of scripts in order to make a living. Readers who are adept at the task can cover from six to ten scripts per week. Most new readers get their position by querying the story departments they find in the *Hollywood Creative Directory*, then submitting sample coverage. This coverage can be done on a friend's screenplay, and is mainly to show a story editor at the studio that you know correct format for coverage. Most readers spend their day covering unsolicited submissions—aka crushing the hopes and dreams of their screenwriting brethren. Usually, unsolicited material is the poorest in terms of quality, and new readers can expect to read the worst of the worst, initially, until they have proven themselves. Coverage consists of two pages of synopsis and one page of comment, followed by a recommendation to "consider" or "pass." One writer-turned-reader whom I know did not give more than one "consider" during his first four months.

Initially, it's difficult to read a script of a potentially unfamiliar genre, then analyze what works and what doesn't and write it all out in fewer than four pages. Such a task may take an entire day, which will leave you feeling like David Copperfield when you get that tiny, tiny check. However, the huge trade-off is that you're learning about writing and writers, what works and who doesn't. Such experience can be invaluable in terms of your own work. Needless to say, you won't retire to Maui on such an income. But the flexibility of schedule is an important benefit, since you're working at home and can still take a phone call or make a meeting.

What follows is a list of twelve elements I use in my own writing to impress a reader:

Twelve Ways to Impress a Reader

1. Make sure the script is properly formatted. Do not use cheap covers or tin or plastic brads (solid brass are best).
2. Have more white space than black (typing). White space means that the writer has focused only on the essential details.
3. Your script should ideally run 108–115 pages, but no more than the industry standard maximum of 120. More than that number of pages indicates a poor understanding of what constitutes a professional script.
4. Create a major story or action beat (key moment) on page 1 of the script.
5. Establish the central theme by page 3.
6. Establish the protagonist's universe by page 10.
7. Select key details and description that pop off the page, and discard others for a lean look.
8. Do not overuse adverbs. Avoid passive voice.
9. Make the reader feel he or she is there by using stage directions that are "intense" and "in the moment."
10. Give the protagonist an Achilles' heel, a potentially fatal flaw. Give him or her one big speech (what I refer to as the Oscar clip moment) that lays bare motivations and themes.
11. Give supporting characters distinguishing quirks. For example, Ted Danson is a DA who happens to tap dance in *Body Heat.*
12. Figure out each character's private agenda for each scene, to play off conflicting agendas and the disparity between what is said and what is meant.

SCRIPT CONSULTANTS

Every two years the industry magazine *Creative Screenwriting* spends more than $10,000 to go undercover and rate and review the leading script consultants in the industry. That this review is a cover-story feature is an indication of the size of this cottage industry. A good analyst should provide you with the following:

- The equivalent of studio coverage
- What's right and what's wrong with your script
- Suggestions for fixing script problems

Basically, script consultants should be able to point out strengths (e.g., a promising premise) and flaws in your script (e.g., weak dialogue or a reactive protagonist) with an expert's eye. There are so many different story elements to juggle when writing a script that even expert writers will overlook a few. That's why it's good to have another set of eyes. Unfortunately, 90 percent of emerging screenwriters hope that potential buyers and agents will be those eyes—a poor option, given the dictates of the market. Remember, you want your project to be as perfect as possible *the first time* a producer reads it, since few will have the time or inclination to show you how to fix it. Personally, I use a consultant to evaluate my work, and I highly recommend the investment.

Script consultants are not cheap, with a price range of $100–$1,000, $400 being the norm. The best have development backgrounds at the studio or production company level. The consultant that I use understands all facets of the script-to-screen process because he has the following credits: director of development at a well-known production company; producer of a feature film; director of a feature film; writer of six screenplays; part-time college instructor; and professional consultant for more than six years. Again, such expertise does not come cheap, but the cost is tax-deductible, and far less than ruining a potential sale by submitting a "green" draft.

Here are some basic qualifications for a good script consultant:

- has studio or production company development experience
- is willing to provide samples of prior critiques particularly in the same genre of your project
- has references available upon request
- is available for a follow-up consultation within a prescribed time period for limited additional cost
- works within the framework of your script to help you write the story you intended, as opposed to some other story the consultant envisions
- offers to turn around a script within two weeks

If you are primarily right-brain functioning (instinct- and imagination-oriented), try to find a consultant whose comments are left-brain (logic- and detail-oriented), and vice versa. Such a pairing will use distinctly different criteria to point out inconsistencies or weaknesses in your story.

Finally, consider consultant services only after you have submitted your script to your Five Trusted Readers and you feel that the project is the best it can be. Remember, rewriting is the essence of screenwriting, so the consultant is one of many strategic steps en route to the screen.

ASSISTANTS

All producers, executives, agents, managers, and successful directors, and some writers, have assistants who handle all the secretarial and non-secretarial functions of the office, ranging from typing letters and answering phones to reading scripts and picking up dry cleaning. Assistants in Hollywood work long hours, often six or seven days a week. They are like an army of seemingly invisible gnomes who wield connections and information for their bosses, and often for themselves in pursuit of their own career aspirations. A big faux pas to avoid is making reference to someone's "secretary." For one thing, most assistants aspire to have their boss's job or a comparable one at some point, so few aspire to be secretaries. While true career secretaries do exist in Hollywood, they earn much more than assistants, and are usually reserved for senior executives.

Assistants are sometimes referred to pejoratively as "phone monkeys," because they must effortlessly handle hundreds of phone calls each day. For example, imagine that Julia Roberts and Mel Gibson call at exactly the same time. Knowing that Hollywood is the most insecure place on the planet, where saying "Mel, Todd will call you right back" may be grounds for the star to move to another agency, whose call do you put through first and whom do you put on hold? Depending on circumstances, putting Julia's call through, while shamelessly flirting with Mr. Gibson for the thirty seconds it takes for the agent to deal with Julia and then pick up the second, may be an assistant's course of action. All the stories you've heard about assistants taking a lot of abuse are true. For example, one powerful agent has a complete collection of pro football helmets from all the teams. This agent is well known for hurling the helmets down the hall at his assistants whenever he's in a tirade. However, while such dysfunction was rewarded in the past with a "tough, but gets it done" rep, such boorish behavior is becoming increasingly archaic in the corporate culture of modern-day Hollywood.

As a writer, you must get to know and place in your Industry Rolodex every assistant you encounter, for three reasons:

1. Not only do assistants have access to contact information for every player in the industry, and sometimes use their own discretion in passing along information, but they can provide or deny access to the specific exec, producer, or agent you've targeted. Assistants hold the keys for every decision-maker.
2. Assistants are usually first to see and judge any material coming into the office.
3. Assistants may only be weeks or months from becoming decision-makers themselves. When they do, the former assistants will need their own contacts. You may be the first one they call.

Note that assistants can move around a lot from office to office and exec to exec, as they try to find the optimal fit that will allow them to jump up into the decision-making ranks. You'll need to update your Rolodex regularly to keep track of all of their movements.

PART FOUR

Ways Into the Hollywood System As a Screenwriter

Ways Into the Hollywood System as a Screenwriter

-16-

THE POWER OF NETWORKING

Whether or not you come to live in Hollywood, you should get used to traveling in packs. Writing, in particular, is a solitary pursuit, but that doesn't mean you have to become Travis Bickel from *Taxi Driver*. Building relationships with other "creatives" is crucial because of the interactive nature of the filmmaking enterprise. There is a logarithmic progression of the number of people involved as a movie travels down the development path. The benefits of building a creative community, or at least a marauding hoard of like-minded individuals, are immeasurable and will enhance your opportunities in this business. Commit the following to memory: Community is crucial and coveting kills careers. Many in Hollywood believe that since the money used to buy scripts and make them into movies is finite, someone else's failure is their success. However, I have always believed that the success of a colleague validates the strength of my group, and people remember who offered a hand during a difficult time.

In film school, it was five of us sharing lunch every Wednesday for story meetings. Nowadays it's a Friday-morning breakfast at the worst dive we can find, along with an every-other-Thursday poker game. The second Monday of each month is dinner with still another group. At these occasions, projects are discussed and information is shared, while strategies and contacts are offered. Think of your own group as not only an opportunity for interaction but also a web of support. For example, while in grad school, I used a connection to submit my best spec to the undisputed biggest agency on the planet at that time. Three weeks later, a three-quarters-of-an-inch thick package slithered back into my mailbox. Inside was my screenplay, along with an unsigned form letter pass. I soon discovered that my script had undergone a disturbing metamorphosis during its time away. For starters, someone had used a red marker to write "Dream on!" on page 12, then "Why do you keep directing this fucking script????" on page 17, apparently in response to an overzealous stage direction. The size-9 shoe prints imbedded into page 21, accompanying a helpful suggestion to "Learn to write!!!!" did little to prepare me for pages 26 and 27, which were stuck together with a substance that I will forever give the benefit of the doubt as spit.

My reactions ran the gamut from incredulous laughter to an impulse to murder, to an overpowering urge to take a swim with cinderblocks in my khaki short pockets. However, my group of fellow student writers quickly closed ranks to bolster my sagging ego with contact offers, tales of bitter recrimination, and jokes about diminutive agents. Within days I was able to go back to my writing, while wishing my anonymous, saliva-control-challenged friend the very best of luck with all those pesky inner demons. Then, two weeks later, the same version of the trampled spec garnered an offer of representation at mega-agency ICM. Such scenarios play out dozens and dozens of times during the course of a creative career in Hollywood. Having a group with whom to commiserate keeps the wax on your Icarus wings.

WHERE TO GO TO SEE AND BE SEEN

Dedication to one's craft is certainly admirable, but there's certainly no reason to risk contracting rickets by spending hour after sun-deprived hour working without coming up for air. You should have *your* ritual that gets you out of the abode and away from all those phone calls that you hope will come today, but often don't. Beyond my home office, I alternate different venues for my workspace. These include libraries and coffeehouses. Many writers like to mark up scripts or work on their laptops at a favorite bean grind where they can nod to a few other creatives and hold court at a place where everybody seems to know their names. In fact, coffeehouses are perfect places to observe all kinds of human interactions between bosses and subordinates, friends, dates, customers and staff, etc. These places are conducive for certain aspects of the creative process, like bringing authenticity to your work. However, sometimes it can get kinda noisy with the frappaccino machines going and people discussing the character flaws of loved ones. Such a place can be especially distracting when you're trying to nail down a problematic scene. That's where the library comes in handy, too. Besides being a quiet space for research, libraries are good for feeling like you're part of the human race, even if it means not hearing the human race.

Some Well-Known Places Where Writers and Filmmakers Hang Out

Samuel French Booksellers in Hollywood and Universal City
Book Soup in West Hollywood
Mel's Diner on Sunset
Best Western Hotel Diner on Franklin
The Beverly Hills Library
The House of Pies in Los Feliz
Farmers Market on Fairfax
WGA Screenings at the Writers Guild in Beverly Hills
DGA Screenings at the Directors Guild in West Hollywood
Writers Block Lecture Series in Beverly Hills
UCLA Extension courses in Westwood
The Writers Computer Store in Sherman Oaks
Jerry's Deli in Beverly Hills and Studio City

Bring Your Laptop, Get a Latte—Coffeehouses Where Writers Work

Bourgeois Pig on Franklin Avenue in Los Angeles
Stir Crazy on Melrose Avenue in Los Angeles
Lulu's Blue Plate on Sawtelle in Los Angeles
The Coffee Table on Rowena in Silver Lake
Patrick's Café on San Fernando in Glendale and Patrick's on Wilshire
    Boulevard
The Coffee Bean (locations throughout Los Angeles)
Insomnia Café in Santa Monica
Seattle's Best Coffee on Montana Avenue in Santa Monica
The Novel Café on Pier Avenue in Santa Monica
The Office on 26th Street in Santa Monica
Psychobabble on North Vermont in Los Feliz

WRITING GROUPS

In Hollywood, both writing groups and social groups for creatives are plentiful. Check the Web postings for long-established groups like the Screenwriters Organization of California and the Alameda Writers Group. With so many from which to choose, the question becomes

"Which one is best for me?" The answer is the one that comprises peers at your own career level (i.e., those who have finished at least one short film or feature-film script) and one level above (i.e., those who have optioned a project). For example, my own group includes mainly writers who have received studio assignments or have written for television shows, as well as directors who have completed feature films—small feature movies for a studio or for cable companies, or independent films. The group speaks with a lexicon formed from common experience, so the potential synergy is obvious and effortless. Conversely, I once sat in with an older group of writers who had all done series television work in the seventies and eighties. We knew none of the same people and had none of the same priorities in terms of our careers. While educational to listen to, the group's cynical perspective was potentially damaging for me, a young plebe, to take to heart.

I was also part of a group where five of the writers involved were basically neophytes in terms of their writing skills, while three were professionals like myself, earning their keep via their craft. As such, there was more than one level separating the two factions. It soon became clear that we three professionals chafed at having to read five scripts that always had many basic errors, and at struggling to explain the problems in a way the five beginners could understand. Meanwhile, the five beginners struggled and often failed to give constructive criticism to works submitted by the three pros. For example, one writer brought pages from his assignment. The five kept attempting to reinvent the wheel by offering ways to completely rework the entire existing project, for which the writer was already under contract. Unfortunately, the group was divided by a schism of experience and soon disbanded. So a good rule of thumb is to stick with people on your level, whom you can relate to, and people one step above, who are where you want to be and have recent experience with the level you're at now.

COLLABORATING WITH WRITING PARTNERS

Working with the *right* partner who complements your style and whose strengths compensate for your weaknesses (and vice versa) can be amazingly time-effective. Conversely, two writers with conflicting styles or who both struggle with writing on deadline can be problematic. Potential partners can be found in shared film courses and workshops, writers' groups, and in online chat rooms like the Done Deal Message Board at http://pub130.ezboard.com/bdonedeal. The caveat here is to choose wisely. You don't want to encumber the future as well as ownership rights of a promising project by splitting up as a team scant months after commencing your partnership. To that end, draft a partnership memo that stipulates a process for resolving disputes should any arise. For example, the WGA offers mediation services, the guidelines for which are available at www. wga.org. Litigation should be avoided at all costs, since a trial may tie up rights to a project for months or even years, and the results may please no one.

The main benefits of collaborating are that two heads are better than one and that output is much faster. The downsides are creative differences that may arise and splitting income. Obviously, you want a writing partner who writes in the same genre, as well as complementing your skills and work ethic. Two writers who can nail *Terminator*-sized action set pieces but have no flair for story development or dialogue—or one writer who churns out pages in days, with the speed of a wood-chipper, while the other ruminates for months before writing a single line—such pairings aren't going to have much success. So focus on your strengths and weaknesses *before* choosing someone with whom to join forces. Are you left-brain analytical or a right-brain conceptual thinker? Left-brainers will be stronger at making sure that every scene and action makes logical sense. Right-brainers come up with the killer concept and imaginative set pieces.

Left Brain	Right Brain
logical	random
sequential	intuitive

rational	holistic
analytical	synthesizing
objective	subjective
sees pieces of the puzzle	sees the Big Picture

Again, try to find a collaborator who will help you realize your full potential as a writer. To that end, I highly recommend taking the Jungian-based Myers-Briggs Typology test (PersonalityType.com) to find out more about your personality and how you process information. According to C. G. Jung, all people can be classified using three set of polarities: extroversion or introversion; sensing or intuition; thinking or feeling. Isabel Briggs Myers added a fourth set: judging or perceiving. Understanding typology is a good tool for anticipating potential personality conflicts with potential partners. It's also a good tool for a writer as an observer of human nature. What's important here is that you have some sort of objective criteria for establishing a long-term relationship.

SCREENINGS

Screenings are where you can go for advance peeks at the current crops of student films, cutting-edge indie films, and a studio's soon-to-be-released movies. Often the filmmakers themselves will discuss their works following the screenings. There may also be opportunities for questions and answers, along with meaningful discourse and interaction. At such events I have met legendary writers like Richard LaGravenese (*The Fisher King*) and novelist Elmore Leonard (*Get Shorty*), as well as directors like Clint Eastwood and Ridley Scott. You can get on film screening lists via UCLA Extension, USC, and AFI, as well as via publications like *Film Threat, Movieline,* and *Premiere.* There are also many, many news groups on the Web, like AintItCool.com, that post such events. Try to work into your schedule at least one screening a month.

JOIE DE VIVRE

My Writing Schedule

6:25–7:45 a.m.	Run/swim/box/gym, and/or take dogs on hike.
8:00–9:30 a.m.	Read *New York Times,* industry trades. Send out and answer e-mail.
9:30–10:00 a.m.	Make phone calls to set up meetings.
10:15 a.m.–12:00 p.m.	Do prose writing (magazine writing, etc.).
12:00–12:30 p.m.	Lunch. Check messages and return phone calls.
1:00–2:00 p.m.	Revise or complete day's prose writing.
2:15–4:00 p.m.	Screenwriting.
4:10–5:00 p.m.	Afternoon hike with dogs. Bring notebook to finish thoughts.
6:30–8:00 p.m.	Read, respond to e-mail, do research for next day's effort.
11:00–11:30 p.m.	Read day's snail mail and/or periodicals.

Whether you write alone or with a partner, here in Los Angeles or somewhere far from the Hollywood lights, is your decision. However, you can enhance your chances for success by plugging into your writing community. Write at a coffeehouse where other writers congregate, attend film festivals and screenings. Join a writers' group in person or on the Web. Remember that the best part of the writer's life is the lifestyle. Writers don't have to wear fancy clothes to meetings—tennis shoes, T-shirts, and sometimes pants are de rigueur for most meetings. We also drink as much coffee as we like, and it doesn't stunt our career growth. In fact, simply saying to a Starbucks employee who is trying to reclaim the table you've camped out at for six hours on a $2.76 purchase, "It's okay. I'm a screenwriter," will be like waving a badge and muttering "Homicide" at a crime scene. We are creators and visionaries whose work is seen by thousands and sometimes millions. You don't have to have a mega spec sale to lead this rewarding life. Most working writers never do.

The Story of Manny, Moe, and Jack

In 1998, Erik Bauer, publisher of *Creative Screenwriting* magazine, approached me about hosting an industry poker game. I had never really played before, but knew that games like the one hosted by the late director John Huston were the stuff of legend. So I said, "What the hell." I went out and bought *The Idiot's Guide to Gambling,* and a week later, six strangers and Erik arrived at my apartment. I put out a spread of sandwiches based on what I had gleaned from an *Odd Couple* rerun, and we started to play. An hour later I was cleaned out both financially and in the kitchen. "Well, I'll never do *that* again," I thought. However, lasting friendships were formed, a house game called Manny, Moe, and Jack was established, and two weeks later, somehow I was hosting yet another game. A feature film and a spec sale are just two of the tangible results from what has remained a regular game. The every-other-Thursday event is kept fresh by the more than thirty guest players to date, who have ranged from hit series television show runners (writer/producers who "run" a sitcom or series) to lawyers working on some of the biggest film deals in Hollywood. In 2002, the group sent me and two other players to represent us in the World Series of Poker tournament held in Las Vegas.

The main point of this section is that you gotta be in it to win it, and Hollywood is a tough place to succeed all by yourself. Whether you collaborate or not, join an organization or attend screenings, you still must work on your projects. Every day. Whether you're inspired or not. That's how the process works. Remember how you wanted to be a writer because you liked it, and you had something to say?

-17-

I don't know if other writers experience this, but when I sit down in front of the computer, all of a sudden cleaning the refrigerator becomes incredibly attractive.

—ALAN BALL, AUTHOR OF *AMERICAN BEAUTY*

WRITER'S BLOCK

I'm not going to tell you how or what to write, or which movie to make, because I don't know. Filmmaking is a highly individualized process where no two methods are alike. However, I do know something about writer's block, aka procrastination, aka extreme pain and suffering. First off, I highly recommend that you check out Dennis Palumbo's book *Writing From the Inside Out*, which I believe is the definitive resource on this topic. For a long time I started my day by rereading certain chapters. I think I read the book cover to cover four times over the course of one year.

Several events can bring about a creative tailspin leading to a block: the pressure of facing the blank page; an impending deadline; not knowing where to start on a rewrite; coming back from being taken off a project.

                        Inner Voice
    Golly, that sure is a lot of Web surfing you're doing today.

                            Me
            I know. I can't help it. I'm blocked.

                        Inner Voice
      Say, won't that nice producer be calling later today?

                            Me
              I'm tapped out. The well is dry.

                        Inner Voice
        "Breach of contract" is such an ugly term.

                            Me
                    Help! Help! Help!

                        Inner Voice
                    (à la *The Shining*)
              Red rum! Red rum! Red rum!

Except when it's done poorly, filmmaking isn't much like laying bricks, so a certain amount of angst is a normal part of the process. I suspect that procrastination comes from being judgmental about one's human condition and place in the universe. Fear of failure is really about handicapping and betting on the chances of success. We creatives judge the outcome even before we've started, which, of course, is nonsense because so much of the material we create changes during the process. Realize that the project in your mind has limitless potential that cannot be judged until it is finished. It is what it is. What is important here is to figure out the underlying reasons why you are struggling with your craft, and then address those issues. That inner voice has a thousand murmurs ranging from "It won't be any good" to "This workspace is inadequate" to "The task is enormous, and I just don't have enough time to really get anything done." The solution is simple: Give yourself firm deadlines, then work every day on things you truly care about—even when the end result is crap. Bad work is part of the process on the road to good work. Only by setting a consistent schedule on material worthy of your dedication can you become more confident about your abilities and more established with your routine. Meeting these deadlines will help a lot later on when the due dates are imposed by producers or the studio. That's the very best solution to writer's block.

Ten Methods for Avoiding or Relieving Your Writer's Block

1. Relax. Many creatives tend to build up the complexity of the task before them. Define your goals for the session, as in x number of pages in the next three hours, or a certain number of scenes edited or completed minutes of film organized.
2. Leave off a day's work in mid-thought. You'll roll right into your work tomorrow just by completing the previous day's thought.
3. Edit your previous day's work, but set a time limit of *one hour*. Again, the idea is to stay in a groove and build upon the previous day's solid production. Warning: Limit the amount of time you spend rewriting at this point, or you may risk overwriting and obsessing over existing work.
4. Keep a clean workspace. For most people, clutter on the desk causes clutter in the mind. Conversely, don't use the clean-up as a way to avoid working. Now is not the time to install a new computer cataloging system for your paper clips and Post-it notes. Simply stack books, papers, research materials, and congealed pizza, setting all aside for later.
5. Eliminate extraneous noise. Shut off televisions, turn off your phone's ringer and allow messages to go to the machine.
6. Take thirty-minute breaks every two hours to stay fresh. Periodically stepping away from your writing will give you microbursts of detachment that will energize your body and brain when you sit back down again.
7. If you don't know what to write, try imagining what the characters would say back to you if they could, about themselves and about the

scene. Then set a stopwatch or cooking timer for thirty minutes. Do stream-of-consciousness writing as fast as you can. Don't stop. Just keep going. Often, the very next day, you'll discover a few diamonds in the rubble. This is a game you play with yourself to make the process feel less one-dimensional.

8. Establish performance-enhancing goals. Twenty-five pages in three hours. Believe it or not, it can be done. Stream-of-consciousness writing doesn't care what comes out—you just WRITE. My all-time record was thirty-seven pages in three hours.

9. Have work rituals. Hemingway used to stand at his bedroom dresser and write at 5:30 a.m. every day. Theologian Martin Luther did his best thinking during epic bouts on the commode. Find the ritual, however unconventional, that gets you going creatively.

10. Reward yourself for a job well done. Treat yourself to that twelve-year-old single-malt Scotch you've been saving up for, go out for your favorite messy hamburger, or take your dogs on that particularly pristine hike that overlooks the ocean. Whatever works for you.

AGEISM

"Can our lawyer be closer to twenty-one? Because twenty-seven just seems . . . *old.*" These words trampolined out of the forty-something-year-old producer's mouth in the midst of our story meeting. Even as my writing partner and I explained that given the time required to finish law school, to become a former hotshot criminal defense attorney turned ambulance chaser, and to take a few chin shots in career and life, twenty-seven was definitely pushing it, I could see the producer tensing up around the gills. So I took a deep breath and then heard myself say, "But sure, he can be a little younger." "Absolutely!" my partner exclaimed, as if his lithium patch had just kicked in. Cash money was on the line, and we all knew which way the wind blew. Internal rationalizations shot around like a leaf blower in my brain. *There must be hundreds of "Cody Banks/Doogie Howser with a libido" types running district attorney offices all over America. Hundreds of them. So let's move on.*

Five Ways to Combat Ageism

1. Work with themes that pertain to your level of life experience. In other words, the quest to authenticate the vernacular of sixteen-year-olds is far more difficult when you're forty-five than when you're actually sixteen.
2. Seek out producers who make the kind of movies you admire.
3. Do not allow yourself to feel entitled to a certain level or type of treatment from agents or producers.
4. Seek out agents who represent writers and directors the same age as you.
5. Conduct yourself with the utmost professionalism in person, on the phone, and on the page. Be sure every sample you send out is industry standard.

Several years ago, when the producers of *Felicity* discovered that what they thought was a fetus-in-pigtails staff writer named Riley Weston was actually a sixty-seven-year-old actress named Kimberly Kramer (okay, she was just thirty-two pretending to be nineteen), many in Hollywood said, "Good. Serves them right." If you were close to thirty years old or older, you knew exactly what was meant by that. Most producers and execs in Hollywood are all about target audience, and fourteen-to-eighteen-year-old teens are the prime targets they seek. So, while in real life the vast majority of nuclear physicists up for Nobel Prizes who are also hotties and under twenty-five are pretty rare, in Movie/TV Land they abound. For screenwriters, too, therein lies the rub. Producers desire the worldliness and the mastery of craft of a forty-year-old channeled into an eighteen-year-old voice. Since gifted-beyond-their-years phenom writers are few and far between, the result becomes that nineteen-year-old Next Big Thing Riley Weston gets a staff spot on a heavily hyped TV show, along with a lucrative six-figure contract with Disney, and a place on *Entertainment Weekly's* "It List" of the "100 Most Creative People in Entertainment." Meanwhile, thirty-two-year-old Kimberly Kramer is deemed dangerously close to menopausal, so she gets a one-way rickshaw ride to a retirement community in Florida. And everybody wins except screenwriters. We face a limited shelf life where only about eighteen percent of the WGA's working writers are over age fifty. Somehow, important movies with strong messages can still get made, but in a lean year, some superficial shared experience and raw emotion without perspective is the best we can hope for in feature films.

Admittedly, I have yet to be personally affected by this bias. Although screenwriting is a tough business no matter what age you are, I suppose I have even benefited from being a fairly young, pasty white guy. However, a reality of American youth culture is that it's easy to feel old even if you're young. (For the record, I, too, am nineteen. Honest). Just visit the production offices of a TV series, and often you will witness the strange phenomenon in which twenty-something-year-old show runners are surrounded by forty-something-year-old below-the-line people—production managers and DPs, etc. "The kids," as they sometimes refer to themselves, are often referred to by others as the "fresh idea people," whereas the veterans are the studio's "security" so that the end result will actually look professional and be within the budget. Recalling that *Twilight Zone: The Movie* scene where a snotnosed ten-year-old rules the world and drives it to ruin, you'd think such a dynamic would be chaotic. Mostly you'd be wrong. As stated earlier, at twenty-six or so, it's pretty hard to have the level of polish, craft, and life experience to justify a world stage for your work. So young writers tend to leaven familiar plot lines and structures gleaned from recent adolescent viewing, with the latest jargon and fashions of their peers. For example, I often note key scenes from *The Graduate* reworked into contemporary stories, but the "homages" lack any underlying meaning. Such an end-product suits the studios just fine. Not only do they plug into the financially lucrative latest trends (trends = money) that those damn oldster writers are probably missing, but the execs get neophyte scribes who are still not quite formed and are thus far more malleable than their battle-seasoned counterparts.

Does ageism exist in Hollywood? Absolutely. The upper mid-levels of Hollywood are chockablock with twenty- and thirty-somethings. Is it fair? Of course not. It's not even healthy for the art form. Will the practice end anytime soon? Probably not. Should you let it strip-mine your hopes and ambitions? Hell, no. What's to be done about it? Good question. Personally, what I keep coming back to is that challenging yourself to write well must be the cornerstone of your career. But ask me again in ten years. Writers like Bill Goldman, Larry Gelbart, Bo Goldman, and Larry McMurtry, who have managed to climb on top of the tiger and continue to write into their fifth or sixth decades, have left few clues to their longevity beyond the familiar platitude "Write quality and the world will beat a path to your door," and playing the political game of screenwriting successfully. Unfortunately, no one is ever quite sure how "quality" is defined in today's Hollywood. At a Writer's Block symposium to discuss excerpts from a book titled *The First Time I Got Paid for It . . .* (containing excellent first-person accounts of the fledgling writing gigs of more than fifty Hollywood writers), I had a chance to talk with Ed Solomon (*Men In Black, What Planet Are You From?*) about the topic of ageism. He said simply, "The business side never gets better, only your craft does. Other than that, there's no easy answer. But if you're meant to write, then that's what you gotta do." Further elaborating on this point, panelist Michael Tolkin (*Deep Impact, The Player, Deep Cover*) recalled once having given his students the following test: Write the ten best films in history on one side of a page, and your ten favorite films of all time on the other. Ideally, the two lists should contain the same ten films. Only a few in the class understood without prompting what Tolkin's point was. If their favorite movie in the whole wide world is *Birth of a Nation,* then, unless someone was paying them, they shouldn't be writing *Hungry, Hungry Hippos: The Movie.* Beginning writers continue to churn out mediocre fare because the biggest misconception about a screenwriting career in Hollywood is that it is a linear *a*-to-*b*-to-*c* progression to succeed. It isn't. Instead, imagine a Rubik's Cube whose parts are constantly moving. At the Writer's Block symposium, Ed Solomon reminded the audience that "what's certain is that the rules of the game keep changing, and what it means to be a screenwriter keeps changing, so you can't always be so result-oriented."

I could advise you to take solace in the fact that the ol' lazy Susan of karma goes round and round—that today's twenty-somethings will be told one day that they're too old for a coveted job, if they haven't been already. But I won't tell you that. Movies and TV series are tremendously hard to get made, so cynicism is of dubious value—kind of a lose-lose proposition. Yes, here, like everywhere else in America, youth is served. What I will tell you is that in Hollywood *everyone* gets opportunities, and a producer or exec needs things to work out as much as you do. And it's what writers make of these opportunities that counts. Mature writers write mature work. In the end, if you know the odds, and writing still bubbles and burns in your soul, then it's better to just go for it! Your unyielding optimism and willingness to improve your craft will be your primary weapons to counter the vicissitudes of the industry.

Mantras for Avoiding Cynicism About the Industry

1. The past doesn't equal the present or the future. Just because disappointment always seems to be part of the Hollywood landscape doesn't mean it always happens.
2. It's just what happened. Don't attach value to a result beyond what positive insights may be gleaned from the experience.
3. The cumulative effect of Hollywood equals not failure, but experience.

"PEOPLE WHO NEED PAPER" BY SONIA LENT

Here's a section created expressly for you to share with a loved one, a family member, or a friend. A little while back, I received an e-mail from a concerned friend of a writer. This friend had witnessed first-hand the hard-fought birth of a screenplay, followed by the giddy excitement of producer interest that suddenly became apocalyptic depression when the deal crashed and burned and the producer evaporated like snow in Tallahassee. Now the friend was desperate to get the ego-shattered writer back on his feet. What triage might I suggest? Certainly, support is crucial to a writer's development, so, before responding, I consulted with the one person who could commiserate most. My wife, Sonia, is the keystone in my own arch of creative being. As such, she has nearly a decade's worth of experience on the subject of partner support of a screenwriter. What follows are Sonia's battle-tested observations written in her own words.

—*Michael Lent*

Michael and I had just moved in together, and one day it was my turn for cleaning patrol of our teeny, tiny, overpriced apartment. With my trusty no-name vacuum attachment in hand, I happened upon a very strange phenomenon—someone had scribbled hieroglyphics all over gum wrappers, snippets of magazine lap cards, torn Post-it Notes, even a section of two-ply bathroom tissue!. My generic Hoover sucked them up by the dozens. Lesson No. 1 was learned that evening somewhere just after midnight as we Dumpster-dived with flashlights clenched in our teeth for the shreds of "inspiration and material written in code" that Michael had painstakingly "saved" under the bed, on windowsills, and in pants pockets in preparation for an upcoming project. Nowadays, when I find snippets of genius that read "A mnky bcms t/ prsdnt!" I leave them alone. Beyond being a testimonial that writers are very odd people and inspiration strikes at strange times in even stranger places, the moral of the story is that there are definitely guidelines to being a partner of and supporting the writer in your life. Believe me, I'm an expert. If you are a writer's mate, you may want to cut out and tape to the fridge my hard-earned advice.

THE JOURNEY OF A THOUSAND MILES
BEGINS WITH BASKETS OF EGGS

Witnessing the evolution of half an idea into a polished piece of work is pretty cool, as is having a front-row seat at the development of a creative career. Way back when, I don't think either of us was prepared for the long journey ahead, and the level of commitment required. Maybe that's a good thing. Writers are passionate people, but they get a lot of rejection. A lot. But you already know that. So they can be some of the crankiest people on the planet. They get "blocked" and into "funks." They need loads of support and encouragement. You've got to understand their plight. You have to be positive, no matter the circumstances. Writers will even beat themselves up over things out of their control, so there's no point in piling on more negativity. Staying involved is the most important part of being a partner. Sometimes that's easier said than done.

Writers work autonomously, sometimes with little or no human contact for hours or days at a time. Their partner becomes their link to the outside world, the person off whom they bounce their ideas. Again, easier said than done. Writers can be protective about their ideas—especially when they're still in the drawing-board phase. Suggestion: Offer to full-read the day's pages. You read; they listen . . . they mark up their work as you hand it back to them. They hug you and thank you profusely. I've learned that besides having a glass of water at the ready, there is a certain level of skill required for this out-loud task. Reading in an emotionless monotone will make the pages drag and depress the writer. They say things like, "Oh God, it sucks. I'm so screwed!" However, being "in character," especially when you're not a trained actor, will make even a horror script sound like an after-school special. Instead, I've learned that punching nouns and verbs with the hushed tone of a thrilling bedtime story works best. You get into it. They get into it. Everybody wins, and if you're lucky, nobody gets sleepy. Michael and I have utilized this technique with all of his scripts, and I take a small amount of personal satisfaction when a producer or exec notes how well the pages and dialogue flow.

Screenwriters tend to focus on just one thing. Did I just write "focus"? I'm sorry, I meant "obsess." Usually the current script is the object of their fixation. A partner helps a writer stay grounded by encouraging him or her to have more than one basket with lots of eggs in those baskets. For example, in Year One following grad school, Michael wrote seven days a week and did little else beyond maintaining basic personal hygiene. It was the textbook example of obsession. The end result was a studio spec sale, a production company three-assignment deal, and an independent film . . . that all *fell apart*. All of them. Michael began to refer to his workspace as the "losertorium," while showing sudden interest in the exciting career potential of stuffing envelopes at home. Beyond the pep rally, I realized that in the face of a film industry that had the spine of a Slinky, Michael's short-term ego and long-term career depended on finding some kind of structure. Fast. He needed to receive paychecks with a couple of zeros after them. Whether the money came from writing or not didn't matter. We had a talk. We made a plan. Five years in Hollywood would be our commitment and benchmark. If sufficient progress in the form of a spec sale or studio assignment hadn't occurred by then, we would start Plan B (teaching at the college level, or the above-mentioned envelope stuffing). Michael made a list of things he could do to cut down the odds a bit (many of the items on the original list are discussed in this book). In the meantime he got a job doing research writing, and later worked as a weekend manager of a real estate office. I brought breakfast to the office on Sunday mornings to boost our quality time. Soon money began to flow in, which took the pressure off the many small production-company assignments Michael chased and sometimes landed. When your writer begrudges the time spent on a job-job—and trust me, they will—remind them that all peripheral experiences impact the writer's development. Sarcasm and snarling may be the initial response you receive to this truth, but you can write out the IOU that's sure to follow when the lean days are over.

9 TO 5 . . . A.M.

You want to play; they have to work. You go to sleep; they're still working. It's important to realize that writing is time- and schedule-intensive. A project can result from one meeting and hit like a hurricane, without warning. A partner learns quickly that while there are no true deadlines and no real certainties to when and if movies get made, all writers are constantly on deadline. Given this paradox, writers and their partners should strike a balance that keeps both of their lives on the same page. Work hard and play hard. One example: We had finally booked our first vacation in a long while. Suddenly, Michael's Miramax deal came through with a deadline for delivery of Act One that coincided exactly with our big Hawaiian getaway. I was already committed to taking the vacation time away from work, and the nonrefundable tickets had been paid for long ago. What to do? We came up with a schedule whereby Michael got up each morning at 5:00 a.m., went for a predawn swim in the ocean to get the juices flowing, then wrote intensely, hunched over his laptop on the balcony, from about 5:30 until 10:00 a.m. The rest of the time was ours until bedtime back at the hotel, when we read the morning's pages in preparation for the next day's effort. Michael made his deadline with half a day to spare, and we had a working vacation that worked well for both of us.

CALL FOR BACKUP

A partner plays a key part in the writer's success by under-standing the complexity of this difficult but rewarding endeavor. Theirs is a chancy business, so taking chances is a fundamental part of the process. Beyond encouragement and protection, you are there to give insight, offer a critical eye, and restore passion in the face of frustration. "Patience!" is your constant theme. You're there to remind your writer to breathe when the disappointment seems unbearable. You always remember that the writer's life is not without its frustrations. Early in our relationship, I remember being at a dinner and mentioning that my new boyfriend was an aspiring screenwriter. "A writer?" a lady with poofy blue hair boomed, while clutching her anchor's worth of pearls. "Then you better get used to being poor!" If this were a do-over world, I would eagerly go back just to say, "A life with a writer is rich in passion, hopes and dreams . . . and many of them are attainable!" I could tell her that firsthand.

-18-

WRITERS AND THE INDEPENDENT FILM SCENE IN HOLLYWOOD

There are many, many books available on the subject of independent filmmaking, but this section deals specifically with how writers can use the independent film to create opportunities in the studio system. After tearing out your beard over your inability to find a home in Hollywood for your manifesto, you may decide it's high time you took the bull by the something and go the independent route. Here's what you need to know.

Ten Rules for Successful Independent Filmmaking

1. Have a completed screenplay that is camera-ready (a polished shooting script).
2. Use "recognizable faces" when you can (actors that your audience will recognize even if they don't know the names, as in "Hey! Isn't that the guy from the Depends commercial?").
3. Try to get the script to a few people working in the industry, to elicit their reactions.
4. Determine who your intended audience might be. In other words, you may want to rethink your claymation Falkland Islands War docudrama that's shot in French but intended for American audiences.
5. The finished film must be at least seventy-six minutes long in order to qualify as a feature film. Anything less is considered a short film. The market for short films is very, very limited.
6. Before commencing principle photography, make sure you have *all* of the necessary funding to complete production.
7. Do not run up credit cards or plunge yourself hopelessly in debt in order to make your movie.
8. Unless you are a veteran filmmaker, avoid shooting in tough locations or during inclement weather (i.e., outside of a train station during a rainstorm).
9. Avoid elaborate props that may malfunction.
10. Avoid working with animals and children, because they are prone to noncooperation under pressure.

Just as in the Hollywood scene, pitfalls abound in indie filmmaking. First off, it will most likely be your money on the line in the form of misappropriated student loan funds, Uncle Oscar's retirement account, or some incarnation of a bank loan or hastily organized investment consortium. In such scenarios you may find help in Rick Schmidt's *Feature Film Making at Used Car Prices* (the book Kevin Smith used to make *Clerks*). This primer provides step-by-step instructions for making movies on a shoestring. And just so that everything will be legit and you won't end up on *Judge Judy*, Schmidt's book, along with Mark Litwak's *Contracts for the Film and Television Industry*, also includes boilerplate legal contracts for everything ranging from partnership agreements (deals with producers and investors) to day-player contracts (actors) to distribution agreements (contracts for putting your film in theaters). A word of caution: Thousands of aspiring independent filmmakers take the "build it and they will come" approach. However, only a teeny, tiny handful (fewer than 1 percent) ever recoup their investment monies. That's because making a film without business or marketing plans is analogous to setting your pants ablaze and counting on the fire department to show up before any real damage is done. You want your movie to be more than just a time capsule of ego and naïveté.

CREATIVE CONTROL IN THE INDIE SCENE

Because screenwriting is only one piece of a complex filmmaking puzzle, many scriptors long for total control over their work. The major creative appeal of independent filmmaking is analogous to the old *Saturday Night Live* commercial for the Bass-O-Matic 5000: You catch the bass; you kill it; you puree it; you eat the *whole bass*. In other words, it seems an incredible opportunity for personal accolade and vision. Writing, directing, and producing your own short or feature can be a good way to get out into the market and make some noise for yourself, especially if you have no previous credits or track record. Much of the excitement and many of the advances propelling modern cinema come from independent film. Unfortunately, the flip side is a very public opportunity to fall on your own sword. If you've ever been pummeled and jeered by angry friends and loved ones turned investors during the unveiling of the "director's cut," you know what I mean. Grandma Sadie may not have her own teeth, but she can still leave a mark. However, in either scenario, making your own flick puts you smack-dab in the middle of the game. Just remember: It's your bass on the line.

MY OWN EXPERIENCE AS AN INDEPENDENT FILM PRODUCER

Screenwriters are supposed to chain themselves to their keyboards, crank out a magical, flawless script to give to their agents or producers, then wait patiently for the phone to ring with news of a spec sale or an opportunity to pitch on an assignment. Sometimes a bit more initiative is in order. In the riptide that is a Hollywood career, there is merit to barrel-riding a tsunami any way you can. Producing a movie is an incredible odyssey, a real test of will and dedication. Let me rewind to 2000, when I volunteered my time, giving notes on a play turned first draft of a screenplay that had just won a competition called the New Visions Fellowship. Note that many "earning" writers avoid reading others' work unless there's a direct monetary benefit for them. That calls in bad karma, in my opinion. In any case, *Hard Scrambled*, written by Chicago playwright David Scott Hay, was a produced stage play with a gritty, character-driven, Mametesque feel. Think *House of Games* set in a dead-end diner. Principal work, during the two years following the New Visions Fellowship award and option, entailed adapting the emotional power and subtext of the stage work into the visual language of cinema. I was lucky enough to come on board as co-producer on this project. During this development period, fellow producers James Mercurio and Erik Bauer did double duty, guiding David through multiple rewrites while simultaneously going out to find investors and then potential cast members.

I can tell you that the key to connecting with investors is a solid script. The same goes for attracting a good casting agent. David delivered a dynamite draft in early 2003, on the strength of which veteran actor Kurtwood Smith (*That 70's Show, Dead Poet's Society, Robocop*) committed within twenty-four hours of receiving the script. The only catch was that principal photography on the feature had to be completed during Kurtwood's summer hiatus from *That 70's Show*, so we producers had just a few months to cast the additional roles, raise the additional money needed for production, and shoot a movie.

BUT YOU'RE A SCREENWRITER . . .

"But you're a screenwriter, and producing a movie is really hard work. I don't see what's in it for you." That's what a director friend said to me when I was first approached by Jim and Erik to come on board, just before preproduction. I had just optioned a screenplay and was obligated to deliver a rewrite on that project. Meanwhile, I had never produced anything beyond my own student films back in grad school days. But counterweighted against my fear of the great unknown was the memory of a chance meeting with a veteran writer a few years previously. The writer had had a financially lucrative twenty-plus-year career, but had never received credit on a single produced project. Many times I have thought about him and have vowed, like Lex Luthor, that he wasn't going to be me. I decided to put my option on hold and roll the dice. As anyone who has seen *Lost in La Mancha* knows, preproduction in no way guarantees a successful result—or even that a movie will actually be shot. But the opportunity is great and the odds are manageable.

I quickly discovered that what I lacked in feature film production experience I made up for in writerly instinct. Don't let anybody kid you: We scribes have a secret weapons stockpile going for us that no one else in Hollywood has. For starters, we're research-, detail-, and deadline-oriented. We're used to pitching our most private or protected work to people we've just met five minutes ago. We filter information as we receive it, and are naturally inclined to organize and prioritize tasks. We bring less ego to the table, and are more inclined to be empathetic toward others. Because we tend to be low-key and good listeners, when the fit hits the shan on set and others are freaking out, we writers are still taking it all in, looking for ways to work outside of the box. "You say we shoot in one week and Tom Cruise's company just forked over five times our rate to buy our location out from under us? Hey, no problemo. There's a better locale up the road, anyway." Finally, screenwriters-turned-producers are sworn on the crucible to respect and make the script everything it can be.

INTO THE BREACH

At this point, I know what you're wondering: "So where'd the money come from?" It came from investors, barter dollars (trading ad space and professional services like script analysis for goods and services), courtesy of *Creative Screenwriting* magazine, innovative dealmaking, including guarantees that investors could visit the set and would be recompensated before anyone else received Dollar One. In short, we did whatever we had to do to claw our way into production. But first a bulletproof script was quietly crafted over two years. That's something that 90 percent of would-be producers fail to do—I can't tell you how many times I've heard stories about movies in production where everyone is aware that the script is weak. Even though we had a good script and director, an indie film dream cast, a gifted cinematographer in Matthew Heckerling, and money in the bank, it still wasn't easy. You know that old commercial about the army being the toughest job you'll ever love? That goes double for producing a movie. Catching ninja throwing-stars in your teeth is easier than overseeing staff and crew and equipment for several months. Shooting locations fall through *during* production, and Porta Potties on the set seem always about to blow. You're there on the set at 6:00 a.m., thirty minutes before the first crew members show up. And you're still there at 1:00 a.m., thirty minutes after the last crew person goes home. On the way home you're on the phone with the other producers, setting up for the next day, putting out all the little fires. Through it all, you're running on cold coffee and survival instincts.

I can tell you that producing is an epic endurance test and you'd better be in shape physically to withstand the rigors of days that last as long as eighteen hours. Preproduction meant lots of twelve-hour days—six weeks' worth, in my case. It seemed like I had 1,001 little tiny jobs, but my strength was in tracking down information, being an empathetic ear for below-line problems like wardrobe, hair and makeup, catering, locations logistics, etc., procuring corporate sponsorship by pitching "the story" of our movie, and turning "no" into "yes." Marketing the movie for items we needed in production became a pitch—the story of a ragtag band of misfits willing to risk all for the sake of a dream. Truth to tell, I made mistakes (one whopper was to comment about an actor's performance within earshot of another actor), owing mainly to nerves or inexperience. But I always corrected them and took ownership. For me, amending a mistake on set during production was no different from doing a rewrite.

Taking matters into your own hands isn't easy. Many times I wondered what the hell I had gotten myself into. But one day I was prepping for the move to our next big location in the San Fernando Valley, where it was routinely 107 degrees under the simmering July sun. In walked a location scout for director Michael Mann, who would be shooting at the very same site two months after us. We exchanged pleasantries and sniffed each other's projects. And I thought her eyes gleamed just a bit as I explained what we were trying to accomplish and the challenges we were up against. "Wow! You're doing it," she finally said. "How's that?" I asked. "Making this movie, *your* movie. You're living the dream," she said, shaking my hand and giving me her card. It all came about because a group of people, including me, were willing to take a chance and make something happen. Right now, six-person crews are putting movies together on free weekends, and producers are scouring the Web for shorts and feature scripts to shoot. My advice: Don't be afraid to get dirty in the trenches, because there's no greater teacher than experience. Word, especially good buzz about a project, travels fast. Within weeks of completing production on *Hard Scrambled,* I was engaged in talks to produce on three different feature film projects, all with budgets two and three times greater than the budget of *Hard Scrambled.* I've decided that, ideally, I'd like to divide my year by spending six months writing and six months producing a film, from my script or someone else's.

BUSINESS CONTROL IN THE INDIE SCENE

Funding for independent films comes from four main sources: art houses, exploitation, cable television, and the emerging realm of the

Internet. The following section illustrates a few of the strengths and pitfalls of each.

ART HOUSE

The current independent film movement emerged from the primal ooze of what was once referred to as "art house films." Subject matter for this group is often edgy and/or eclectic—perfect fare for niche audiences flocking to herbal-tea-and-velvet-curtain emporiums with names like Bijou Cinema and the Angelika Film Center. Companies that specialize in this milieu include MTV Films, Gramercy, October Films, Strand Releasing, and Artisan Entertainment. Many of these groups specialize in acquiring distribution rights to completed films that have already been financed (e.g., *The Blair Witch Project*). Occasionally, however, such companies finance projects themselves, as in the case of MTV and the film *Election*. The key here is attached elements, such as rights to a sought-after novel, a particularly hot director or an up-and-coming actor, or obtaining a critical cameo from an established actor, like Robert Duvall in *Sling Blade*. The upside to approaching art-house companies is greater access. Often the execs in these companies will take pitches right over the phone. Another important upside is that although these financiers buy a lot less product than does traditional Hollywood, the passion is much more real. If an art-house company buys your script, the chances are much greater that the company will go the distance to make the movie. The downside is that you can't expect the big bucks.

Somewhere between the studios and the art-house group are companies like Miramax Films and Fine Line Features. These are independent arms of major studios that operate with higher budgets and greater freedom than do their art-house brethren; however, writers working with such studios are faced with many of the same encumbrances confronted by big-bucks features—namely, Dantean levels of bureaucracy.

CABLE AND TV

If you've ever sat through an hour of a grown man interviewing a hand puppet on local access television at four-thirty in the morning, or seven broadcasts of *Free Willy* in three days, you know there is a plethora of channels dying for content, especially on cable. When it comes to films, you should be aware that the big cable companies and channels like HBO, Showtime, Cinemax, and Lifetime often buy the rights to existing stories, then hire experienced Guild scriptors to write a screenplay.

Writing for cable usually means pitching independent production companies that have access to executives at the aforementioned cable companies. Usually these companies have made movies for the cablers in the past and have a sense of what kinds of stories sell. The budgets are usually small, in the $1.5 to $50 million range. Compensation usually runs from $10,000 to $35,000. The main advantage for writers is that these production companies are more open to pitches from less established writers, and if they like an idea, you can find yourself in production within months of the initial pitch—unlike studio development, which routinely takes years. The downside of writing such projects is both the limited budgets and the ever-present contingency that you will still have to jump through the cable company's hoop. And if the production company fails at setting up your project at one place, your prospects are fairly limited elsewhere.

A few years ago a partner I had brought on board for a single, specific project and I were hired by an East Coast producer to write a legal thriller set in the world of rock and roll. Afterwards the producer was unable to set up the project. However, we had a connection with a production company that made many movies for a cable company that specialized in this exact genre. Our producer offered us a deal: Set up the movie with our contact and the cable company, and we could come on board as full partners and producers. That's a heck of a deal, considering we had already received $30,000 in compensation for what had been an assignment. The production company loved the synopsis sent via our agent, loved the script we submitted, and didn't have any problem with the three of us already attached as producers. In turn, their lead producer pitched, then sent over, the script to a development exec at the cabler, whose response was also enthusiastic. So we were brought in for a meeting to discuss story changes that would bring the script in line with the cable company's creative sensibilities as well as its budget. As a result, chase scenes were minimalized and localized, and the courtroom drama was downplayed in favor of more glimpses into the rock world. Turnaround for revisions was about four weeks, and we did the work uncompensated, since the production company still had to physically sell the project to the cable company. The development executive at the cable company felt the script was ready to submit to her senior vice-president, who gave final approval on all acquisitions. Our agent called to inform us that everyone was optimistic that we had a "done deal" that would be finalized after the weekend. On Monday my partner and I awoke to discover that the entire creative team at the cable company, including the senior vice-president, had been fired. The company announced that it was "going in a new direction." Our project was first in limbo and then later passed on by the new team. Meanwhile, the initial production company still believed in the project and had an in with a cable company specializing in legal dramas. Once again we did a free rewrite, this time playing up the legal aspects of the story over the music-world material. A few weeks later this cable company passed without giving a reason. With few other relationships and markets to turn to, the project remains in limbo. The above story illustrates the typical highs and lows of the cable world. As writers, my partner and I were really put through our paces, rewriting in weeks instead of months. Had the first cable company acquired our project, the chances it would get made, and quickly, were excellent. It's exhilarating to know that your work may be made into a film very soon after you complete it. My partner had completed two $4-million films just this way.

EXPLOITATION

Much like U.S. Supreme Court Justice Potter Stewart's 1964 definition of pornography, when it comes to the exploitation genre, the best definition for these guilty pleasures is the old "you know 'em when you see 'em." Often a film's name, like *Nazi Cheerleaders Do Compton,* is a strong clue. Such movies tend to be B-list genre films, action, horror, soft-core erotica (*Free Willy* has a whole different meaning to this crowd). They are targeting the straight-to-video or foreign sales market, or both. The trades (*Variety* and *The Hollywood Reporter*) and the *Hollywood Creative Directory* are useful for ferreting out these production companies. Meanwhile, the American Film Markets (AFM) convention held each fall in Santa Monica offers a chance to dress up in your favorite crime-fighter costume in order to pitch your project/product directly to producers and distributors. It's vaudeville and theater of the absurd wrapped into one, and not to be missed.

The straight-to-video market isn't as robust as it once was, perhaps as a result of piracy and downloading, which have made knock-offs of A-list films plentiful and cheap all over the world. There are still opportunities, however, for newer writers to build credits by writing genre movies in the $500,000–$1.5 million range, which is also a proving ground for new directors and producers. With script turnaround times of about a month and shooting schedules of twenty days or fewer (the average studio film is ten weeks), these projects are a trial by fire for all involved. As I mentioned earlier, a few years back I worked with a director specializing in these films. His approach to story development was simple: An explosion, gun battle, or sex scene every ten pages. Early on in my sojourn through Hollywood, one such producer stiffed me for completion-of-draft monies. The amount was a couple of thousand dollars, which gives an idea of the scope of these productions.

Three Keys to Creating a Successful Exploitation Script

1. Remember that the intended audience for these movies is fourteen-year-old boys. If the overseas market is the target, dialogue should be limited. That's why action and martial arts movies do well with both audiences.
2. Limit locations and CGI effects. The haunted-house approach works well if you can freshen it up with an interesting twist on the location.
3. Cheesy movies should be fun. That's why the tongue-in-cheek approach works so well with threadbare plots and sets, and marginal acting. Remember that you'll be hard pressed to create *War and Peace* on a budget of $500,000, so avoid being overly earnest in your writing.

MARKETING YOUR INDEPENDENT FILM

Yes, you should spend a lot of time devising a marketing strategy *before* you make a movie. Will you target low-budget film distributors via a special screening in Los Angeles, or maybe go the film festival route, trying to build word of mouth and catch a more upscale buyer there? If you decide to approach distributors directly, check out the *Hollywood Distributors Directory* (323) 308-3400 or (800) 815-0503 (outside of California), www.hcdonline.com. Everything you'll need to find distribution for your film is here, including contact info for more than 800 companies with 5,000 names and titles listed. Talk to these people, pitch your intended project, get a read on their level of enthusiasm. If you feel you may want to take your message directly to the people, at this writing, there are more than 600 film festivals worldwide. *The Ultimate Film Festival Guide,* by Chris Gore, is the bible for anyone interested in independent film. Many of the pitfalls of the process are covered there.

Don't let passion get in the way of practical business sense. You are trying to get noticed for your writing and filmmaking abilities, to show people that you have what it takes to earn a spot in Holly-wood while developing your contacts—always keep that objective in mind. It should be enough that you're directing and most likely producing your own script, so avoid also starring in it. Having name actors or at least professional regional actors in your film will enhance your marketing prospects by creating a more polished project. Many professional actors, particularly in areas outside of Los Angeles or New York, will jump at the chance to do a real live film. For example, not long ago, a friend held a casting call here in Los Angeles for principal acting parts paying fifteen dollars per day. He received more than 500 head shots and agent calls, including several recognizable faces from film, commercials, and series television. When we cast the feature film *Hard Scrambled,* we received head shots from more than 2,000 actors, including two who were Oscar nominees. Again, know that recognizable faces will greatly enhance your project's commercial viability. It's a rule of thumb that while most investors won't be able to distinguish a good script from the *Farmer's Almanac,* those same investors will instantly see the merit of having Gary Busey, James Caan, or Florence Henderson in a cameo in your film. You can often get such actors for one day or one week for very reasonable fees—particularly if those fees are in the form of cashier's checks. That's because a cash-in-hand offer shows that you are serious about making this movie right now. This last part is crucial, since to get things done in Hollywood you must create a time constraint—which is often tough to do. Getting a name actor to read your script may take months. That's the slow-boat-to-China route. Few actors read for themselves, however, and the chain of command is something like this: Producer or develop-ment exec takes three weeks to read and then gives to the actor's per-sonal manager, who takes another two weeks before passing it on to the actor's agent, who requires an additional twenty-one days. If all goes according to plan, the targeted actor then reads the script. An upset stomach from any of these people along the way will end your project. However, money behind a project helps speed up this process immensely. Having your casting agent say to an actor's agent, "We have a June start locked. We want your client for *x* role for *x* dollars and are willing to give you exclusive read on the script for three days before we go out to [name of rival actor]," will get things moving quickly. An agent is obligated to tell his or her client about all money offers, even if the agent feels that the offer is too low. In the case of the film *Hard Scrambled,* one veteran actor accepted our compensation terms over the objections of his agent, because he felt strongly about the part.

What you'll notice about all of the above is that going the independent route gets you, the writer, out from behind the keyboard and puts you into the middle of the filmmaking process and consequently in the driver's seat of your career. You're still writing, probably at a faster and more furious rate than you dreamed possible, but you're also expanding your skills, learning by experience how your writing connects to the overall process, as well as expanding your contacts throughout the industry. Case in point: Joe Carnahan wrote, directed, produced, and edited his ultra-low-budget film *Blood, Guts, Bullets and Octane.* A writing assignment for Harrison Ford, and a chance to write and direct the acclaimed cop drama *Narc,* with Jason Patric and Ray Liotta, soon followed. Likewise, the writer/director team of Owen C. Wilson and Wes Anderson (*Rushmore*) established their careers with *Bottle Rocket,* which was initially made as a thirteen-minute black-and-white short film that attracted both the Sundance Film Festival and veteran producer James L. Brooks (*Broadcast News*).

Few people really fail in Hollywood. More often they simply get frustrated with the system and quit. The resourceful creative learns that when the door is closed, it's time to go through the window. Sometimes you have to make your own opportunities. Even if you don't envision yourself as writer/producer or writer/director but are still frustrated with the system, you should try to expand your skills, or at least seek out someone wishing to collaborate on a limited budget project. Many such parties can be found on the Done Deal message board at http://pub130.ezboard.com/bdonedeal. In any case, the various avenues offered via well-planned independent film making can be your window of opportunity.

PART FIVE

Advanced Career Planning

Advanced Career Planning

-19-

There's one last thing that I know to be true about people who work in Hollywood: Very few of us, and this includes performers, dated the cheerleader. And then they became successful and did get the cheerleader—and that's almost worse, in a way.

—WILLIAM GOLDMAN

HOW TO MEET WITH AN EXECUTIVE OR PRODUCER

Despite all appearances to the contrary, meetings with producers and studio executives don't drop out of the sky. Today's version of the "Lana Turner discovered in a drug store" myth is that the next

Clerks or *Blair Witch Project* is ready to be discovered in some fourteen-year-old's home-video camera in Anchorage. Unfortunately, those odds are at least a million to one. You should aim for better odds in developing your Hollywood career. The gnawing reality is that most opportunities come via research and perseverence, with the ultimate goal of being face to face with a gatekeeper who can purchase your project. Meetings with the movers and shakers of the industry occur in these ways:

Contests and Competitions. A more elaborate discussion of this topic occurs later in this chapter, but know that if you win or place well in one of a dozen or more major scriptwriting competitions, the people in Hollywood will want to see what film you've made or script you've written. They'll contact you. It's that simple.

Set Up by Your Manager or Agent. You have an interesting short movie, student film, or spec script that is a tough sell on the open market. Nevertheless, your agent deems the work to be a worthy introduction to gatekeepers who might be interested in meeting you. The job of such gatekeepers is to learn about new talent like you. Thus, your creative interests and aspirations are important to know in the event that you *do* write something deemed market-worthy six months or six years from now.

Query Call or Letter. Meetings resulting from a query are pretty rare, since you'll need some sort of track record to gain even two minutes of time with anyone worth meeting. However, a snappy pitch in a query letter, followed by a worthy script submission, can open doors. The *Hollywood Creative Directory* (www.hcdonline.com) is basically the white-pages phone book of Hollywood. In it you'll find nearly 10,000 producers and studio and network executives representing more than 1,750 production companies, studios, and networks. The *HCD* includes addresses, phone and fax numbers, staff and titles, credits, and studio deals. Updated three times a year, the directory is expensive (about sixty-five bucks) but contains crucial contact information for tracking down the right people to receive your query.

Industry Referral. Someone who is well established in the industry may be willing to make a few phone calls on your behalf to various gatekeepers. In Hollywood this is known as "godfathering."

Such generosity is invaluable; however, you should always remember that the intended target is beholden not to you but to the godfather who initiated the meeting. Generally, that reality will be in the back of the mind of whomever you sit down with. While you'll be able to cut to the chase about possible job opportunities a bit more than someone off the street, always be respectful of the fact that you are mainly in the room because of the relationship someone else has with the person you're pitching. Complaining if the person you meet with doesn't follow up with you to the person who got you the meeting is an *uber* no-no in this case, and the surest way never again to get some of that sweet Hollywood love that is the godfather call.

Get into the habit of making circle-and-arrow diagrams of the people you call and when the call occurred, along with the person who referred you, with an arrow pointing to any result and follow-up, if necessary. Even if you're someone who is "naturally good with names," you'll be severely tested in Hollywood. Not only are there dozens and dozens of names to know over the course of a year, but I've discovered that a person's brain starts to specialize the longer he or she works here. That is, by concentrating your whole being on the highly visual endeavor of film, your brain will start to crowd out what it deems to be less important forms of processing, such as remembering names. Very quickly, you'll discover that while the name of the first president of our nation may suddenly escape you, you now have a knack for total recall of a line of dialogue from a Pauly Shore movie viewed in 1987. Luckily, you can fend off Alzheimer's by keeping your notebook handy for fast reference when the phone rings.

> ## Call Diagram
>
> 1/4/04 9:30 a.m. Called Producer (FRED WAGNER,) Liberty Films (310–555–1295) Re: Read of *Welcome Home, Mom*. Result: Left message on voice mail.
>
> Assistant (LARRY) called 10:03 a.m. to say that Fred would be calling cellular at 11:00 a.m.
>
> WAGNER 11:25 a.m. Response: "liked writing but not his genre" referred me to (JENNIFER LLOYD) (818–555–6592), producer at Cascade Pictures/Deal at Sony Pictures. Jennifer was former assistant to Fred. Note: Jennifer is expecting my call.
>
> 1:15 p.m. Call to Lloyd. Assistant is (PETER MARX.) Jennifer is on location in Toronto overseeing *Blood Feud* (must look up on net).
>
> 4:35 p.m. Voice mail msg. from Lloyd . . . Send script to L.A. office in time for her return Thursday and w/end read.

Because 90 percent of your interactions will be with a gatekeeper's assistant, be sure to write down the assistant's name, and work it into any conversation you have with said assistant, as well as any details you know about the gatekeeper's projects.

SETTING UP THE MEETING AT THE BEST TIME FOR THE BEST RESULT

Avoid Mondays and Fridays for setting up meetings, if you can. Try for Tuesday, Wednesday, or Thursday. On Monday, execs tend to be just getting into gear and back into the swing of things after the weekend or coming back from traveling to sometimes far-flung locations for movies in production and dealing with issues on the set that may still be vexing them. Execs will have departmental meetings to attend, lots of phone calls to return and e-mails to answer on Mondays. Meanwhile, Friday is gateway to travel, weekend fun time, as well as the release of the week's new films. Execs will be distracted, strategically looking for meetings they can bump (reschedule at a later date) in order to take off early. Sadly, unless you have a project with the company already in active development, chances are you'll be bumped a couple of times before the actual sit-down meeting occurs, regardless of what day your meeting is scheduled.

Ten-thirty a.m. is the perfect meeting time, plus or minus a half hour. This time period allows you to avoid the Hollywood rush-hour traffic. Try to get in before lunch, but not too close to that time. And not too early. To that end, avoid the 9:00 a.m. sit-down. My experience has been that execs often arrive a bit late and cranky from a long night of reading, braving L.A. freeway rush-hour traffic, a hurried breakfast, and often all of the above. Also avoid being the last meeting before lunch. Once I sat down with a CE for a noon appointment and thought she muttered something. "Sorry? I didn't catch that," I said, to which she replied, "Nothing. My stomach is grumbling." Many execs get queasy at having to admit that they are made of the same flesh and blood as you or I, so the admission threw both of us, and things sort of went downhill from there. For some reason, ending a meeting with "Sorry about your tummy" sounds better in one's head than when actually uttered.

Finally, know that meetings are scheduled very tightly together and usually run long. Thus a four-o'clock meeting can be forty-five minutes late because of all of the previous rollovers. Most likely you will be struck by the irony of waiting nearly an hour for what is designed to be a ten-minute meeting at best. But gently put aside your complaints, as you continue to patiently sip your exotic bottled water (Los Angeles is, in fact, a desert—for that reason, keeping you irrigated is chief among an assistant's duties).

How to Prep for a Knockout Meeting

Creatives neglect the business side of movies all too often, but such negligence can come at a terrible price. In Hollywood, daily industry newspapers like *Variety* and *The Hollywood Reporter* are referred to as "the trades." They are found in every reception room of every production company and studio in Southern California. (It's not a good sign when the trades in a Hollywood reception area are a few weeks old. Out-of-date status may indicate that they're probably bought sporadically or pilfered from other waiting rooms around town, which, in turn, may mean that the producer with whom you are about to sit down isn't quite as successful or plugged into the Hollywood juice as they would have you believe.)

Many libraries carry the trades, particularly in major urban areas. The media or film department at your local college or university may also make them available for students. Subscriptions to the trades are very expensive, but are a good write-off on your taxes. Note that the free online versions are basically just a marketing tool containing a few teaser headlines and not much else, so they aren't very useful.

I admit I'm not wild about reading the trades. However, I do subscribe to them, and in doing so I have discovered that the daily process of perusing them gets easier over time, like a bran muffin for fiber in your morning diet.

Tip: A friend maintains a massive professional Rolodex. Each morning he cuts out the photos of significant players and pastes them onto a card along with pertinent information gleaned from the accompanying article, as well as anything further that he has uncovered on the Internet. Screenings and trendy restaurants are always a veritable who's-who of the industry. My friend is genuinely affable, so he likes to walk up to these players and say, "Hey, Jim Sherman. Congrats on acquiring *No. 2 Pencil!*" The exec will invariably assume he has already met my friend, and they will begin to chat.

You should make use of the aforementioned trade publications as well as other print and online resources before your meeting. Additional resources are the *New York Times,* the *Los Angeles Times* print and online editions, *Fade In, Creative Screenwriting, Written By, DGA Magazine,* and *Script Magazine,* as well as other general interest film magazines like *Premiere* and *Movieline. Premiere* magazine, particularly its annual "Top 100 Hollywood Power Players" issue, is an important resource. I find it fascinating the way people move up and down, and sometimes abruptly appear on this list or vanish from it. The day you sit down with someone who is on the list is a particular thrill, akin to meeting the Wizard of Oz.

Two online sites that are helpful are the Done Deal message board *http://pub130.ezboard. com/bdondeal* and WhoRepresents.com. The key is to educate yourself about the industry and about people doing what you'd like to be doing. In prepping for your meeting, ask yourself questions like "What genre does the exec specialize in? What sort of material has the studio or production company recently acquired, and what might they be looking for?" Magazines and trades can tell you this. For example, a company that has recently made three low-budget hardware (guns-and-gadgets extravaganza) flicks probably won't be interested in your cerebral period drama. By making use of trade publications and other print and online resources, you can uncover the company's recent track record, as well as what is currently on its slate. Track down this info and ask yourself, "Do I have a sense that the company gravitates toward projects involving concepts, talent, or directors?" It's critical for you to know such things beforehand.

DEVELOPMENT SLATES

When a production company or studio acquires an intellectual property, a script, the company needs someone to manage the project on its journey to the big screen. A slate is the roster of projects in development for which a producer or studio executive is responsible. Usually, this task is handled by a VP of Development. A project in development is most likely still being rewritten at the script phase, whereas a project in preproduction has been out to directors and actors for consideration. The producer will also oversee a movie through is production and post-production (editing, sound, etc.) phases, right through to the actual test screening and marketing of the completed film. Via websites like Filmtracker.com, you can find out what a company is producing via development reports and studio production slates. Such information will include dates so you'll know how active a project is, as well as key elements attached like notable movie stars. Note that many of these sites charge a fee to obtain their information. However, most offer free trials or reduced rates for students or individuals.

Knowing what's on a gatekeeper's slate can give you an indication of budget levels (Jonny Depp as the lead versus Emilio Estevez), how active are both the producer/exec and his company since you can infer a lot about a company with no projects in production . . . or if the executive isn't assigned to them. You can also get a sense of the producer or exec's taste in material. I once took a meeting at a prodco specializing in big budget action films. An executive who had just come on board invited me in to discuss my action script. However, a check of the exec's track record indicated that he liked developing comedies. I guessed there might be extenuating circumstances for the hire. Sure enough, the meeting wasn't very fruitful (we spent the time discussing his theory of comedy) and the exec soon moved on.

THE MEETING ITSELF

Most meet-and-greets (introductory meetings) begin with very brief small talk about sports, your drive in to the studio, or what kind of weekend each of you had (theirs: Diving off Catalina Island; yours: Cataloging your collection of dryer lint), then up-shift to interesting tidbits usually gleaned from the trades that morning. While such topics may seem like a cliché, remember that the average executive works sixty hours a week or more, so preoccupation with what others are doing becomes second nature and part of one's survival skills for the industry. Small talk is also your way to gauge the temperature of the room a bit. So mention the new Brad Pitt comedy project and an exec will often give you a Ben & Jerry's–sized taste of the "inside scoop" behind the headline. In any case, the point of reading the trades is to send a clear signal to the creative exec or producer that you not only share reference points, but also understand his or her priorities. That makes you a potential project mate for the next six months.

The initial moments of the meeting are about gaining rapport and common interest. Do you know some of the same people? Do you see eye-to-eye on movies? Interestingly, the conversation will appear to be very casual and superficial but in fact it is full of subtext. To wit:

> Exec
> Sorry, I'm a little beat. Last night was the advance of
> *MTF [Mother Teresa: The Fury]*.

> You
> How was it?
> The exec waves his hand dismissively.

> Exec
> Let's put it this way, it won't be the *Thelma and Louise* tour
> de force Universal expected.

> [Notice that while the tone is gossip-laden, no actual names of
> people who could come back and chew the exec's butt later
> are used.]

> You
> Didn't they have like a dozen writers doing drafts?

> Exec
> (waves hand dismissively)
> Two words, "final cut." That film is fat easily fifteen minutes.

"Final cut" refers to the director's contractual right to make the final version of the movie. That means that no producer, movie star, or studio executive may step in to recut or rework the movie, no matter how disastrous the end result once the director has made his "final cut." Notice also that this exec doesn't see any problem in having a dozen versions of a movie created by a dozen different writers. At other times the same exec, trying to make a different point, will indicate that a dozen drafts by different writers was the death knell of a project. In any case, right now, your exec is establishing that his primary agenda is to run a tight ship. To that end, he doesn't put up with any artistic pretensions. Further, by passing along the above "insider info," the exec is indicating both that he's plugged in and that he's "a straight shooter." In reality, most execs dance to many tunes and shoot straight only when they can afford it.

Also apparent is the *Schadenfreude*. From an exec's point of view, 95 percent of the meetings they take are informational, as opposed to opportunities for dealmaking. Schmooze and gossip are big parts of an exec's day, akin to the amount of time we creatives spend trolling the Internet doing "research." In their case, the technical term for schmoozing is "tracking," which consists of dialing around to various friends in the industry for insider info, which can be a major means of furthering one's career. For this reason, information has platinum value. Hollywood info is fluid by nature and will eventually be known by all. Thus, terms for Mike Ovitz's firing at Disney and the golden parachute sum or production deal he was paid to go away quickly is known by everyone in town. In more practical terms, no exec wants to be caught plunking down hundreds of thousands or even millions of dollars on a project upon which the other studios have already passed.

In the Trenches

An exec told me about the sequel to a successful film that had become part of his development slate. I mentioned the name of a colleague of mine whose movie was about to come out, as a possible writer-for-hire for the assignment. "At least five different hands were all over that script during pre [pre production] and principal [photography]," the exec answered sharply. "God only knows who did what." Because last-gasp, ninth-inning script tampering can be a sign of an embattled project, a given studio is naturally inclined to muzzle such info. Postmortem: The movie opened two weeks later to mostly poor reviews and lukewarm grosses (audience attendance). The studio responded by pulling money from the expensive television ad budget, and three days after its release in theaters, the film had already been given a Viking burial.

During his days at Disney, industry chieftain Jeffrey Katzenberg was considered an ace "golden retriever" for his ability to track down such information about industry players, impending deals, and hot new scripts. So be prepared to indulge your exec a bit in this pastime. However, be wary of passing along such tidbits yourself, as it is an acquired art. Should you pass along a confidential second-hand tale of Jim Cameron clutching a Tickle Me Elmo doll and frothing at the mouth during your friend's pitch meeting, the exec will feign skeptical indifference, then phone 100 people with the story as soon as you leave. As stated above, be sure not to name any names that can come back to haunt you.

One thing to remember: If the meeting is truly for exploratory purposes only, you should also anticipate the obligatory naming of your favorite films. This topic comes up so that the gatekeeper can get a fix on your taste. Note that some execs pride themselves on thinking outside of the box, so you should also prepare for the curve-ball corollary to the above, which is "Tell me some movies you hate." What's important here is not to name a film made by the exec or production company where you're conducting your meeting. Remember that you are always skating well when you name movies that broke out (modest budgets but handsome earners) as favorites. Big budgets that went bust are always a no-brainer on a worst-of-the-year list. What you're doing is mirroring the exec's primary agenda (tight budgets) and concerns (green-lighting box-office bombs that claim careers when they detonate). That's why you should never blurt out, "Call me crazy, but I truly believe *Showgirls* was a misunderstood masterpiece, and I only hope that God grants me the integrity to create similar brilliance for *you!*"

USING MEETINGS TO LAND ASSIGNMENTS

Pitch meetings are more substantial than meet-and-greets, since there exists the potential to walk out with a job on a project that the production company or studio already owns. Usually they are looking for a new writer to take a pass through (further develop the material). And usually it is your agent or manager who has set up the meeting based on information they have regarding said open assignment. Note that dozens of writers will be auditioned until the gatekeeper hears a take (an idea of the new direction the story may now take) that inspires his confidence. The gatekeeper's agenda is surprisingly simple. Throughout your meeting, he—or, less often, she—will be asking mainly three questions regarding your spec: "Can I sell this to my superiors?" "Is it castable [actor bait]?" and "Is it cheap to produce?" Keep in mind that the exec will be also considering whether he or she might enjoy working with you for the period of time that a project may entail. If the answer is yes, then the gatekeeper may be thinking about in-house projects that require the "fresh take" or angle of a new writer for which you may be a good candidate. If a meeting is going well but you sense that the purchase of your project may not be the end result, you can shift gears and come right out and ask for a shot on anything the production company already owns: "You mentioned that final decision on my spec is up to the senior VP, and that's cool. In the meantime, if you have anything you want someone to crack, I'd love a shot." Note that I recently said this to a senior producer who promptly told me about three different projects he was struggling with. I chose one that I felt especially suited for, and over the next two weeks I pitched him various scenarios. We never quite found the right solution (remember, these producers may hear dozens or hundreds of takes on a piece of material); however, I benefited greatly from developing my relationship with the producer.

On the day of your meeting, you will feel "locked and loaded for bear" after spending days living, breathing, and researching every conceivable way you can rework the story. But before you release the geyser clamp on your brain like a Las Vegas fountain, stop and take time to listen. Generally, the tone of pitch meetings for assignments makes for an odd game of poker. For starters, the studio is playing with a natural royal flush of superior knowledge about the project, while you are trying to bluff with four of your five cards showing. Your hand can usually be summarized as, "Writer is desperate for work . . . needs money to mend holes in socks." Luckily, a good exec understands that you aren't yet up to speed on his agenda. Instead, he or she is looking to see if you can get up to speed, given your raw skills and experience. Thus there's no point in unleashing a monsoon of ideas upon the hapless exec until *after* he's tendered your contract. Listen for clues, and offer just enough to keep things moving.

In the Trenches

"I know why you called me in here. That script is a piece of crap, but I know how to fix it." Turns out that the P of C in question was written by the producer's brother-in-law. Whoops. Shutting your mouth until you're under contract, or at least until you know the parameters of the problem, would seem to be fundamental in such a situation. However, the director who actually uttered the above death phrase had previously helmed three features.

The moral is that in the rush to suit up for battle, remember that the most important aspect of film making is its collaborative nature. In other words, pick your spots carefully when you decide to voice the grocery list of your own ego and personal agenda.

Brevity is crucial in a pitch meeting. Its main function is to avoid boring the listener. Unfortunately, most pitches go on and on because they are filled with unnecessary minutiae of the story. So keep your pitch short and painless. That doesn't mean you are off the hook; you still need to have the story worked out in case some junior exec comes out of left field with a question. In fact, adding ideas to your pitch is a sign that the exec is enthusiastic and beginning to invest his own energies into the development of the project. So you should be enthusiastic, too. Go with the flow, no matter how skeptical you are. You can discuss creative differences *after* the contracts are signed.

Meeting the producer or development executive who is responsible for many of the movies you respect most and who has the power to bring you into such a coveted pantheon can be an unnerving experience. However, if you remember why you were brought in (interest in your work) and stay focused on your objective (communicating that you are a writer worth hiring), you will gradually relax and come to enjoy this part of the storytelling process. I've noticed that when writers are nervous or uncomfortable, they tend to show it by hyperactivity—feet that won't keep still, or hands rubbing the arms of their chairs. Other writers will be completely rigid. One trick I've developed is to plant my feet solidly on the floor as soon as I sit down, and just as I'm about to pitch or discuss my work, I lean forward a bit, as if I intend to impart some valuable confidential information. I believe such a posture implies earnestness, confidence, and a bit of familiarity, while cutting down the space between myself and the gatekeeper. Sometimes the exec will "mirror" this posture, and a good meeting will only get better. Keep in mind that many producers are simply looking for "partners" to join them on their moviemaking adventures. You can show them in word and deed that you are that suitable match.

-20-

SECTION 509:

SCREENWRTING COMPETITIONS

- What Are Screenwriting Competitions?
- What You Need to Know to Do Well in Screenwriting Competitions

EXTRA CREDIT READING:
   Writing Treatments That Sell by Kenneth Atchity and Chi-Li Wong

A man's reach should exceed his grasp, or else what's Heaven for?
                                                      —ROBERT BROWNING

WHAT ARE SCREENWRITING COMPETITIONS?

A plethora of short film, indy feature, and screenplay contests and competitions have sprung up in the last few years, generating notoriety, providing springboards to careers, and doling out upwards of a million bucks a year in cash and prizes. Many production companies, studios, and talent agencies are plugged into these events, so a strong showing can grant instant cachet. Meanwhile, competitions that are tied to festivals create incredible opportunities to meet colleagues and create synergy. I have been a judge on three screenplay competitions to date. My fellow judges have been producers, directors, agents, veteran actors, and studio executives. Industry experience is the common background for each. My own qualifications for a judge spot have been my credits and status as a working writer of fourteen screenplays and co-producer of one feature film, an instructor at UCLA and Santa Barbara City College, and a columnist who for several years has written about the business and craft of writing. I have also read at least 500 scripts, which is as important as any other experience. For the 2003 Screenwriting Expo Screenplay Competition (SESC), I ultimately read some 160 screenplays.

Some of those scripts were among the very best examples of our craft. On the other hand, I also survived a dozen or so postmodern "reworkings" of *Pulp Fiction*—the scripts that start "FADE IN: CHARACTER A steps from a bus and immediately has his lips blown off. Cut To: The Yukon."

WHAT YOU NEED TO KNOW TO DO WELL IN SCREENWRITING COMPETITIONS

It was during one long night of reading when I had a small epiphany about how a writer could go to *the top 10 percent of the script competition class* simply by adhering to the following rules:

1. USE SHORT, CATCHY TITLES

Short, catchy titles work best. Often a reader confronted with a stack of a dozen scripts will sift through the pile and extract the best titles. Scripts with great titles will elicit his or her freshest read. The others will be left until last. You, the writer, should imagine someone stepping up to the multiplex ticket counter on a Friday night. Certain titles like *Indiana Jones and the Temple of Doom* just sound more conducive to the Friday-night moviegoing experience. Contrast that with someone stepping forth to utter, "Two tickets for *The Worst Time of My Life*, please."

2. APPLY EARLY

Apply early, and don't wait for the last-gasp deadline. We received approximately 400 entries in the months leading up to the recent SESC deadline. Note that festival competitions have a much shorter lead time for judging entries than do stand-alone contests that can change their announcement dates to suit circumstances. In practical terms, this means that the festival readers or judges must consider the projects as quickly as they come in. In regard to the above-mentioned competition, many of the original 400 scripts were already through a second round of consideration when, in the final ten days of the competition, a biblical pestilence descended on the *Creative Screenwriting* offices in the form of nearly 700 more screenplays. It fell to the existing reading staff to throw itself into the new onslaught. A potential first casualty in such a situation is the subtle and slow-starting screenplay, the work chockablock with nuance that unfolds gradually or tells a small story simply. Personally, fifty reads into the process, I had little patience for storytelling missteps or over-used conventions. You may think it's the height of getting things started with a literal bang by opening a script with some anonymous person getting rubbed out in graphic fashion and excruciating detail during the first twenty seconds of your crime thriller, but after examining ten such setups, it just feels gratuitous and hollow to the reader. (I recently spoke with an agent who claimed he could tell whether a script had any potential based on the first page. Enough said.)

3. CONFORM TO INDUSTRY STANDARDS AND PRACTICES

The average, professionally written Hollywood script is 110–120 pages. That means a good judge can tell you, just by riffling the pages of your ninety-seven-page World War II epic, that it's a safe bet you don't have fleshed-out subplots or a true second act. Said reader will then begin reading with these shortcomings already in mind.

Cosmetically, your script should look "clean" on the page, with formatting that appears professional (e.g., no color graphics.) Books showcasing proper format for screenplays are abundant. *Writing the Picture* by Russin & Downs is my personal favorite. You should follow the industry standard of plain card stock cover, three-hole punched with one-inch, solid brass brads over solid brass washers. Artwork in the form of pictures of yourself, stick-figure drawings of a love scene or fight sequence will only out you as a rank amateur. Note that cheap brads feel like tin and are prone to curling and/or bending. When too long, such brads turn predatory in a stack of scripts—cannibalizing and mangling their own cover and then latching on to other screenplays. The result is a script that looks like a mess by the time someone gets around to reading it. Short brads often fall out (especially when multiple readers turn pages during successive rounds), and pages may get lost. Several promising entries I considered in the second round were missing pages; most of these scripts had short brads. In the end, I made the command decision that such scripts weren't strong enough overall to stop the process and seek out the missing pages. Washers are cheap and keep a script from coming unbound. It's a small detail that makes a big difference.

Three of the four competition finalists for the 2002 Expo Competition—and, I believe all of the twenty or so semifinalists—were completely professional in appearance. The lone exception garnered a special New Visions Award in 2002. This script looked as ragged and grizzled as the Unabomber, Ted Kaczynski, and indeed it broke many structural conventions. Printed with a smudgy nine-pin printer, the work was loaded with typos and punctuation errors from the fade-in to the fade-out. Indeed, it was a miracle that the script was discovered. The only thing that was clear was the writer's voice and talent. The moral is, if you break the rules, you'd better be brilliant on the page right from the get go.

4. FULL-READ YOUR MATERIAL BEFORE SUBMITTING

If you take the time and money to write a screenplay and submit it to a contest, please, please, PLEASE take a couple more hours to have it read back to you out loud in the form of a full read. That passive voice and alliteration that sounds so soothing inside your head will drag down your story to *Titanic* depths when uttered out loud, as will all the extra stage directions you have overwritten into your "fast paced" romantic comedy. More significantly, you'll quickly chafe under repeated lashes of expositional dialogue until your epiphanic realization that it isn't even necessary in the plot. That's why I full-read out loud every draft of my work. Most scripts change 25 to 30 percent during this process. Better still, get someone to read your script back to you. An entire read of a full-length screenplay can be completed in about three hours. Also remember that descriptions in your screenplay should create images and meaning in the reader's mind. Avoid "directing" the movie by calling for camera angles or instructions for how an actor should act in a scene.

-21-

In Hollywood, often you cannot escape the feeling that you are floating. Not floating in that transcendental, detached, Zen-state sense, but floating as if you have broken from moorings that give you a fixed place in society, floating like a wayward balloon in the stratosphere where the air is getting thinner and thinner. You'll receive well-meaning phone calls from family and friends and be told in the course of a conversation that Joe Blow, who couldn't carry your academic load in college, just made partner at his firm and has bought a house in the Hamptons. Such feelings are exacerbated when you are also faced with financial difficulties. Living in Hollywood is expensive. Meanwhile, putting pressure on your chosen craft to perform in a financial sense (sell this project today, or I lose my lease and am out on the street and living in a Santa Monica drainage ditch) creates a desperate mindset and doesn't foster creativity.

So let's further explore my aforementioned five-year plan for success, as well as various "job-jobs" to pay the bills while waiting to be discovered by Hollywood.

My First Job-Job

The financial pickings were mighty lean when I first arrived here. Sure, producers were interested in my work; however, the payments they offered barely covered my phone bill. Being ambitious and undeterred, I said to myself, "Oh, I'll take my $500 options and $5,000 assignment credits and do something that no one else with an advanced degree and a few hard-fought credits has thought of—I'll teach! Wahoo!" So I dutifully sent out my CV, writing samples and nothing happened. Nothing. Very soon I learned the sad, awful truth that every single writer with an advanced degree and a few credits has thought of that exact same course of action. Fast-forward to a year and a half later when I received a call from the coveted UCLA Extension Program. During the interview, I learned that the university had a variety of off-campus certificate programs beyond those listed in the glossy catalog. A week passed before I received a call from the California Institute for Men. "I'm not familiar with that university," I admitted. "Actually we're the Men's Prison in Chino. We have an opening in our education unit's writing program," said the EDU director. Despite some initial apprehension resulting from a misadventure en route to the interview when my car broke down in gang territory and had to be pushed uphill toward a strip club in searing 100-degree heat, the experience proved extremely rewarding on both a personal and creative level. I kept that teaching position for two and a half years, until I received my first studio assignment at Miramax.

Other Writers' First Jobs

A friend of mine lived above a mortuary where he paid a very low rent in exchange for assisting with the transport of bodies into the mortuary's embalming facility.

Another friend worked as a manager of the graveyard shift of a Kinko's. He says that flexibility of schedule and the ability to make mass copies of his scripts was the main draw. The downside was the often bizarre nature of the clientele in the wee hours of the night.

A TV writer/producer I know had been a university professor in Spain, when he became obsessed with the idea of coming to Hollywood. Unfortunately, his English skills were extremely limited and he struggled to find work. Desperation drove him to work at McDonald's, where he was assigned to the drive-through window. One week later he accepted a job offer writing a Spanish-language program for an Italian TV director who spoke no English (the American producer assumed that Spanish and Italian were "close enough" for the two men to communicate together). In a single day the writer literally went from earning the minimum wage of $6.50 an hour to $2,500 a week.

Not long ago, I heard about a writer who had his first breakthrough after eight years of trying. That's pretty much my definition of patience, but I'm not surprised that it took so long. Few writers are one-stop shopping, which means equally adept at writing in all genres and handling notes from directors, producers, executives, and actors, skillful at creating fascinating, fleshed-out characters, ironclad structure, and polished dialogue. Developing your voice to overcome deficiencies in other areas, as well as acquiring business savvy, takes a while. Simply put, the time element needed to find one's niche in no way reflects on a writer's ability. My own Big Break, a studio assignment, came four years, nine months, and two days after my arrival in L.A. Before the Big Break, I had four assignments and options ranging from $500 to $5,000 and a bevy of near-misses.

Your Five-Year Plan for Success As a Hollywood Screenwriter

Since your time is not open-ended, it's not enough to say to yourself, "Today's the day!" when setting your career course. Time limits should be set for attaining tangible goals. Producer Joel Silver (*Matrix, Die Hard*) personally delivering a Porsche Boxster filled with hundred-dollar bills in exchange for your writing services isn't a tangible five-year goal. Writers need to invest some brain cells into "what if *x* doesn't happen?" scenarios, because "instant careers" that don't happen instantly can take tolls on lives and relationships. Note that your long-term plan shouldn't put undue pressure on the actual writing. Early on, my girlfriend, who later became my fiancée, and I agreed on two things: To get married despite her knowing what I was attempting to do for a living (claiming to be a secret agent will only work for just so long); and to set a five-year time clock for a certain level of progress (a sustainable career with a year to two years' worth of projects in the pipeline), which would be discussed and evaluated quarterly or at least every six months.

What follows is a sample five-year Action Plan:

YEAR ONE

Action:

- Set aside $2,500 in order to relocate to Hollywood, or $750 (if you choose to stay where you are outside of Southern California) to set up meetings and visit Hollywood for two weeks.

Goal:

- Complete two polished screenplays that can serve as strong writing samples.

Caution:

Ninety percent of writing in Hollywood is rewriting. Many writers go from first draft to another first draft thinking that the next half-cooked but "brilliant" idea can be *the* ticket for success. Thus they fail to learn how to rewrite and strengthen existing material. One of my own projects, *Mea Culpa*, has been both optioned and sold by two different companies. I have written more than a dozen different drafts during a five-year period. Use your polished sample scripts as writing samples to introduce yourself to producers and directors.

YEAR TWO

Action:

- Place well—quarter-finalist or better—in major writing competitions like the Nicholl Fellowship, Chesterfield, Sundance, Disney, Christopher Columbus, Austin, and Worldfest. If you do, agents and producers will seek you out, or be willing to read your work.

Goal:

- Land an option or assignment of at least $1,000.

Caution:

Agents generally like to see two strong writing samples. If you skip Year One groundwork, you put yourself under pressure to rush completion of a second script, which will almost certainly turn out "green, or not ready for the marketplace." Often that will end the agent's interest in you. If, however, you have two strong samples, then the agent may sign you, or at least take you on as a pocket client. This agent may begin sending you out on meet-and-greet meetings where you may pitch your new projects, as well as pitch your take on available assignments.

YEAR THREE

Action:

- Option one of your scripts and land a production company assignment in the same year.
- Take a cable or straight-to-video assignment.

- Have a spec go out wide (this occurs when your agent gets behind the marketing of your spec and sends the script to all potential buyers throughout the industry while stipulating a deadline for all offers).
- Begin taking some high-profile meetings with gatekeepers and other key decision-makers. For example, for me, a story meeting with actor Jim Gandolfini was an important signpost.

Goal:

- Your work should garner interest from directors.
- Be able to answer the standard question "What are you working on?" with a list of projects you have in various stages of development.

Caution:

Since there is no standard-length option, the amount of time specified on your option contract can range from as little as three months to as long as two years, and will be up for negotiation. Weigh the length of the option period against the producer's credits and the amount of money offered. In general, the less money offered, the smaller the producer's actual commitment to the project. Beware of tying up and removing your promising project from the marketplace for too long.

YEAR FOUR

Action:

- Land an assignment or sell a script that is lucrative enough ($10,000 or above) to sustain you for three months.
- Have enough projects to keep you writing for the next twelve months.

Goal:

- See one of your projects made into a movie. If you haven't, consider writing and directing a short film (no longer than fifteen minutes) that can be shot on digital video.

Caution:

As well as a first sale or lucrative option or assignment, you may have an agent and/or manager representing you by this time, but beware of entitlement and complacency. Your agent takes only 10 percent of the money you earn, which essentially means that you are responsible for the other 90 percent. Don't count on someone else to ensure the success of your career.

YEAR FIVE

Action:

- Land a studio assignment or sell a script that is lucrative enough to sustain you for one year.
- Have at least six spec scripts that are in polished condition.
- Have at least two years of your own projects in various stages of development.

Goal:

- Sell a script off of a pitch.

Caution:

Continue to write your own personal projects on the side. Many working writers opt for the perceived easier money and easier task of assignment writing and neglect spec-writing stories that are truly their own.

Quit . . .

- only when both the writing and marketing of your material processes are no longer fun
- only when you can no longer financially sustain your dream

Every working writer will also tell you that even when success does come, you must still be patient. Production company deals sometimes collapse in business affairs offices. Even when they don't, contract negotiations, usually conducted by understaffed, backed-up legal affairs departments, take a very long time, especially in the summer, when everyone is on vacation. An accounting department can add another two to three weeks to the process. So before you quit your current Amway gig, commit the following to memory: Sell today, collect the first check of your step deal (usually 15 percent to 40 percent of the contract) *two to five months* from now. Further, according to the latest WGA figures, the average working Guild member writer makes about $80,000 a year. That's a far cry from the millions of dollars the studios sometimes pay out, of which we all dream. In other words, for most of us, screenwriting is a firmly middle-class endeavor—especially after factoring in federal, state, and city licensing board taxes; personal and business expenses; and agent, manager, and lawyer fees. While 40 percent of any given Guild contract is still a sizable chunk of loot, no one will mistake you for Bill Gates any time soon. George Jefferson, maybe.

POTENTIAL JOBS TO SUSTAIN YOU DURING YEARS 1-4

SCRIPT READER

If you want a crack at the Big Show and come to town, you must decide whether you want to be a heartbeat away from the people to whom you will inevitably sell your *North by Northwest Air* project. Many writers take jobs as assistants to producers and studio executives, while others work as readers. Coverage consists of two pages of synopsis and one page of comment, followed by a recommendation to "consider" or "pass." Readers cover from six to ten scripts per week, with production companies and studios paying $50–$60 per read. The workload often ebbs and flows depending on the season (August is dead, September is busy). A flexible schedule is the main benefit. On a personal note, I wrote coverage for a short time, but found the job psychically draining. The quality of 90 percent of the material submitted is troublesome. If you decide you might like this work, there are several books available on the subject. Also, you can gain experience by writing sample coverage of friends' screenplays or of scripts that you buy from Script City. Turnaround for a coverage is usually one day, so you will have to train yourself to read and write quickly.

TEMPING

Temp agencies can get you access to places where you might not otherwise be invited. But you'll need to know how to type beyond the hunt-and-peck method, and be able to handle a phone system. Usually, you'll be subbing for an assistant to an exec or a producer, someone who is away on vacation. Under no circumstances should you try to pitch your screenplays or drop a package of your work on someone's desk. Temping is a good opportunity for networking and making contacts, catching a worm's-eye view of the process, and building up your Rolodex. Check under personnel services and temp agencies in the Yellow Pages to find available positions.

WRITER'S ASSISTANT

Duties here run the gambit from errands to research, from typing notes to editing scripts, from setting meetings to returning calls. Successful writers often employ an entire staff. Most such opportunities are in the television industry and rare in the film industry, but do exist here as well.

The major benefit of this job is that if you continue to write on the side, the writer who pays your salary may take you under his or her wing, and offer to look at your work. Use your *Hollywood Creative Directory* to locate and query writers with production companies, as well as writer/producers and writer/directors, who are more likely to need assistance. You can enhance your chances by offering your services as an intern.

FILM EDITOR'S ASSISTANT

Editors don't really splice film anymore. Computers do that particularly arduous task. However, jobs abound for assistant editors whose primary task is to organize footage for the more senior staff. It's very good experience to learn more about how certain artistic and practical choices are made, how scenes are composed and stories told. Film school or tech programs like those offered by places like Columbia College and the Los Angeles Film School are where you'll learn basic proficiency with the two industry-standard editing applications, Final Cut Pro and Avid. For jobs, check out filmstaff.com for daily postings. Listings also appear in directories like *The Hollywood Reporter Blu-Book Production Directory,* (available by calling 323–525–2150, or at http://www.hollywoodreporter.com/thr/thrblu/letter.jsp), or *LA 411* (phone 323–4600–6304, or www.la411.com on the Web). You can also scan the trades, like *Variety* and *The Hollywood Reporter,* for lists and contact info for films in postproduction.

OUTSIDE THE INDUSTRY (DOESN'T HAVE TO MEAN STARBUCKS, BUT IT CAN)

Of course, you may opt to avoid the white noise of industry business and concentrate solely on your own work. You then will need to look outside the industry for the means to pay the bills. For example, several of my colleagues stay fresh by working in advertising on a freelance basis. Another managed the night shift at a copy shop until his big break came. Though such employment can't be mistaken for "living the dream," my friend's days were free to write, hang out with colleagues, and take the all-important industry meetings. Whether you are employed in the movie business or outside of it, the deliberate choice you make based on your personality and temperament will ensure balance and an environment to cultivate opportunity. The key is: To thine own self and the local electric company be true.

PART SIX

Extra Credit

-22-

Discourse has been the lifeblood of my "Belly of the Beast" and "Write Back" columns at *Creative Screenwriting* magazine since 1997. For that reason, I have prided myself on answering every reader e-mail sent to me. The bulk of the correspondence has consisted of specific queries looking for answers or advice regarding practical matters concerning the movie industry. What follows are actual reader e-mails and responses culled from the more than 2,000 letters I have received to date.

AGENTS

Q.—I recently pitched my latest screenplay to New Line Cinema. Four execs from New Line have read the script and they seem quite interested. Currently I don't have representation. At what point would I want an agent dealing with New Line?

A.—Revision notes from the studio on a script they don't own usually means that someone there finds certain aspects of the script "promising" and that they like dealing with you. However, right now, if push comes to shove, they will most likely pass on the project. So adding an agent to the mix is premature. The agent will sniff this out quickly, usually without even making a single phone call, then be reluctant to get involved. Execute the notes if you agree with them, figuring that you're building a relationship and getting world-class feedback for free, the result of which you can turn around and sell to someone else if New Line balks later on. The time to go agent callin' is when the script is done.

Q.—I have an extended short film I wrote, directed, produced, and edited, which was shown at a few of the smaller film festivals. Audiences seemed to like it, but now I can't get any agents to look at it. I sent out tapes more than a month ago and don't have a single response. What can I do?

A.—Be patient. Without the heat of winning a major film festival, a response can and most likely will take a couple of months. Agents have a pecking order for material, and it helps to think like Hollywood. First priority is given to the major motion picture from a big studio . . . then to the independent successful film . . . then big television . . . then the good art or festival film . . . then the bad one . . . then bad television . . . finally, schlock movies to bring up the rear. Sounds like your project rates between the good and bad festival film. When good agents finish chasing or pushing everything higher up on the food chain, that's when you'll hear from them. Until then, keep writing, while remaining confident that there is a twisted method to the madness.

Q.—What should I tell an agent in a query letter? Is getting an agent better than placing well in a screenwriting contest?

A.—Placing well in a screenwriting contest is a good way to generate interest from an agent. Barring that option, your query letter should include a one- or two-sentence pitch of the script you wish considered. Education, credits, and relevant experience can all help the cause. That stated, query letters face long odds because most agents receive hundreds and sometimes thousands of them each year. Many writers have better success cold-calling and pitching targeted agents via the *Hollywood Agents and Managers Directory* (www.hcdonline.com). K. Callan's book *The Script Is Finished, Now What Do I Do?* is also a big help. The secret to cold-calling is to make your call during lunch hours, when the agent and his or her assistant are away enjoying their nine-dollar mixed green salad. Simply leave your name and number. Don't offer much further information that could allow an agent the option of not returning the call, as in "Hi, this is Jerry Daumer. I'm a shut-in from Nebraska and I just finished my very first screenplay. It's a spec about the joys of befriending cattle and I hope you'll take a look. Call me!" Since agents are in the relationship business and never know when a deep-pocketed would-be producer may call, they eventually answer all messages. Generally, at the very least, the assistant will return your call and you can be ready with your pitch, hoping to receive an "Okay, send it" response.

Q.—I'm not happy with my agent. Should I be contacting other agents now, or should I wait until after I show my new project to my present agent? I hear it's easier to get an agent when you have one than when you don't.

A.—Assuming that your unhappiness stems from results to date and not personality issues, start calling the current agent once a week after he's had two weeks to read your script. Meanwhile, look for a new agent as soon as the two weeks are up. (Some writers like a clean break, so they would rather take charge and fire said agent beforehand.) Honestly, I think it's six of one, and half a dozen of the other, since any agent worth his ten percent will mainly care about your track record of working with people he's heard of or knows, the dollar amount of the deals you've done, or absent the first two, placing in well-known competitions. If all of these are not to be had, then a dynamite pitch can still deliver you to the Promised Land. Since query letters are a waste 99 percent of the time (agents rarely gain anything by reading them, while valuable time is lost for serving existing, earning clients), the key is to get out your *Agents and Managers* directory and phone the agents. In the past, I was able to get some A-list agents or their assistants to return my calls. Remember that most assistants are only six months from becoming agents themselves. Your message should be sparse but not cryptic: "This is Fran Savage calling regarding my project *Gerbils of the Mojave*. Reach me at 555–4355." Then write your eight-second premise and ninety-second pitch onto an index card. Tape the card to the wall over the phone (or to your forehead, if you are particularly forgetful like me), and be ready to rock when the phone rings, usually between 6:00 and 7:00 p.m. West Coast time (the time when many agents deal with any business they're not sure about).

Q.—What does it mean to be a pocket client?

A.—Most agents have as many as a couple of dozen "pocket clients" for whom they expend minimal energy. Such clients are beginning directors and writers who have no professional track record but who show promise, often in the form of a gritty, compelling student film or a screenplay that is tough to market. Becoming a pocket client is relatively easy: Place well (quarter-finalist or better) in a major competition, and an agent will be inclined to read your work. Plow through your trusty *Hollywood Agents and Managers Directory* (www.hcdonline.com), and then cast your net wide enough to make the connection.

Q.—I'm a published novelist, not a screenwriter, but I'm in the rather sad position now of being a pocket client for an agent at ICM—though I'm not sure yet whether it's pocket-client limbo or hell yet. I sent him the first 100 pages of a new project a couple weeks ago, but have yet to hear from him (in fairness, I'm sure he's got more pressing things). Any suggestions for getting out of pocket?

A.—If the new project is a novel, submit a complete manuscript. Crumbs of the bread only work for agents who show interest in being part of the developmental process. Apparently, your agent isn't sending such a signal. If you have a completed script, you can show initiative as well as your understanding of the business by tracking down suitable producers and pitching them. Pass along promising leads and budding relationships to your agent for follow-up. Don't pass along wild-goose chases. Agents are motivated by dollars and deals, and it is hard to move out of pocket status without them.

Q.—The agent I have been conversing with indicated that she has forwarded my scripts (TV shows) to the contacts I provided her with at NBC and Bochco Productions. Would it be okay to send her a thank-you note?

A.—That's exactly the right thing to do. Send it ASAP, and if possible, include some direct reference to your most recent conversation in order to personalize the note. All the small talk at the start of the conversation and all the small gestures are really about establishing that you get along with each other on a personal level that will fit nicely with a long-term professional relationship.

Q.—I submitted a project to an agent about three weeks ago. Is it okay to follow up with a submission by calling? If so (I know I shouldn't ask if she has checked it out, as it is not professional, or so I have read), what kind of question should I ask?

A.—Two and a half to three weeks is the proper waiting period. You should call and say that you are writer X who submitted script Y on [date] and are calling "to follow up." The assistant and agent will take it from there. If that call doesn't receive a returned call response (you may get voice mail or get put on a call sheet), wait ten days and make another call. As long as you remain professional, the agent will eventually get to you.

ATTACHING TALENT TO YOUR PROJECT

Q.—I have written a script whose protagonist was inspired by a B-list actor. When an agent agrees to represent it, is it all right to request the script be sent to this particular actor's production company?

A.—An agent probably won't be eager to forward the script to a B-list actor because in most cases, attaching such an actor to your project prior to financing won't help a movie get made. Sadly, few execs or directors get hot under the collar just because Tom Arnold or Emilio Estevez or Jim Belushi is on board. Further, most agents will feel that such a name encumbers them from going after A-list talent. The logic is, go for Tom Cruise, settle for Vince Vaughn, as opposed to, go for Vince Vaughn, settle for Kirk Cameron. Many fine B- and C-list actors get work simply because more-established box office draws are unavailable.

That stated, if what you have in mind is a $2-million straight-to-video flick, landing Michael Keaton or Robert Downey Jr. just might be the ticket. Just have your Visa or checkbook ready for such a cash-and-carry deal.

SHORT FILMS

Q.—I'm eighteen and an aspiring writer. I was wondering about your opinion on short scripts (for short films). Do you think that is a good practice for screenwriting?

A.—Short scripts are the early years of film school in a nutshell. The key is to write material that you can shoot yourself on hi-8, digital, VHS, etc. You'll be stunned how different things look and sound going from script to screen. For example, what works on the page doesn't always translate well visually, and some things that seem to be throwaways can suddenly leap out on the screen. Writing short films will help you see that.

Q.—I made a "quality" independent film for $24,000 that got some attention, but the only offer I received was for a straight-to-video horror movie. Is this a slap in the face?

A.—One of my award-winning but decidedly non-studio scripts landed me a studio assignment at Miramax for a horror movie called *The Hellseeker*, as well as a modest option on the "quality" piece. An unfortunate reality of Hollywood is that the industry will make dozens of *Chuckie* movies for every *Dead Poets' Society* they option. That's what audiences pay to see. So there's no shame in paying one's mortgage by virtue of one's craft and hard-fought experience. Spend enough time in Hollywood and you will learn this valuable lesson.

ANSWERING TOUGH QUESTIONS

Q.—I've been working at becoming a full-time writer for five years now. I've had some options on my work and near-misses. What do I tell people who ask, "What have you done that I've seen?"

A.—Studios produce one movie for every twelve they purchase. I know of one writer who has worked steadily for twenty-five years. None of his work has made it to the screen as a solo credit, so he writes and directs plays on the side. When writers get the so-what-movies-have-you-done, it's usually from people outside of the business, since fellow industry people inside usually ask, "So, what are you working on?" Unless you know the other person well, your answer is the same for both: "I'm in the hunt on several projects, so I have to be patient and let the process run its course." Follow the response with a Zen-like silence that puts the question back with the inquisitor. Those who don't mean well will beat a hasty retreat at this point—fearful that you have pegged their uncharitable motives, or afraid that they don't know anything about the "the process." Others will then ask, "What are you in the hunt for?" At this point, you can say, "I'm waiting for a response from Universal or director X or actor Y." Many times, the person will then say something like "Wow! Then I better get your autograph now!" Said person will walk away excited that you shared an interesting tidbit.

COLLABORATION

Q.—I'm forming a tight-knit screenwriting group. Including myself, the group will be made up of five highly imaginative individuals sharing the obsession to succeed as Hollywood screenwriters and the knowledge of how to work as a team. The concept is simple. Four other individuals will bring their screenplays to the table and then we'll decide, one by one, which projects to focus on and complete. We'll try to sell the completed screenplays as a team. Hopefully, we'll complete work faster and cover the market better due to our teamwork. What do you think?

A.—Collaboration *is* a very powerful tool. There are some major caveats, however, as exemplified by the following cautionary tale: A few years ago, a pair of writers worked out a first draft of a promising premise. The result garnered some meetings but went no further. Two years later, one of the writers had left the business, and the other revamped the script with an established producer. Several drafts later, the result bore little resemblance to the original, although the basic premise was still the same. Suddenly, every major studio and production company wanted the project, but the rights couldn't be worked out. The original co-writer surfaced, demanding a big pay day. Meanwhile, the producer saw himself as the logical co-partner. The end result was costly litigation while the project remains in limbo. Bottom line: Collaboration works well when the relationships are long established. Otherwise, let the collaborator beware.

Film School

Q.—I am an eighteen-year-old high school senior, and desperately wish to pursue a career in screenwriting and film directing. What should I study in college?

A.—I was an English and American History double major in college and didn't specialize in screenwriting until grad school, where I earned an MFA in Film, with Screenwriting as my specialty. In my opinion, it's important to balance film study with knowledge of outside fields, so that you avoid the trap of writing movies about other movies. That's fine for Tarantino, but not for most of us. I believe in casting wide your net of personal development to ensure a unique perspective about the world. Not a script goes by that I don't make use of my understanding of psychology, mythology, biology, world literature, biblical references, etc.

Other advice I can give is to see *everything,* from the worst movies to the classics. In film school, I saw an average of 250 films a year, which was and is the basis of my cinematic lexicon. Aim for half that number as an undergrad. Also, invest in a video or hi-8 camera and begin chronicling your experiences visually by making short movies. Directors such as Spielberg, M. Night Shyamalan (*The Sixth Sense*), and Bryan Singer (*X-Men*) started this practice very early on.

PRODUCERS

Q.—A producer liked one of my screenplays, but said the script needed work. I diligently did draft after draft without compensation or a contract, then last week the producer dropped out. He said he had other projects on his plate and couldn't devote any more time to do the script justice. What just happened?

A.—Interest you received in your project shows it has merit. I suspect that the premise was promising but the execution was problematic. Subsequent drafts may not have improved the situation enough to warrant the producer's continued efforts. On the other hand, some producers have dozens of projects going at one time. Inevitably, some good work gets lost in the shuffle. Remember that a time line and the ticking bomb are key elements for a good script. So take a page from your own work and establish reasonable time lines on the business side. If you feel you've delivered the goods and a producer doesn't get it together by such-and-such date, you're outta there. As a case in point, a rising producer put me on the free-draft merry-go-round when I first arrived in town. Twice around and I got off. I still see the producer around, and we're still friendly, but the producer knows I don't go for pie-in-the-sky schemes, so he doesn't waste my time. On the other hand, he knows I'm a good writer. If he ever gets some serious cash to develop a script, I'll be on the short list. It might take ten years, but that's fine.

Q.—Are most, if not all, screenplay sales handled by the Writers Guild of America in Hollywood? Is it possible to sell a screenplay without Guild intervention when dealing with lower budgets?

A.—The WGA doesn't "handle" screenplay sales. They simply have set guidelines for producers and writers who are Guild signatories. Most producers of low-budget films are not members of the Guild, so you can make any deal you like with these companies. Check out any of the books by Mark Litwak, as well as *Clause By Clause* by Stephen Breimer and *The Writer Got Screwed* (*But Didn't Have To*), for deal tips.

PROTECTING MATERIAL

Q.—I have a short film that I think would make a great feature movie. How do I protect the idea from being stolen if I send tapes of the film around?

A.—You can register the underlying screenplay of your short film with either the U.S. Copyright Office or the Writers Guild of America. However, be aware that material pilfering is a common occurrence in Hollywood. It generally doesn't happen in the blatant way most people think. In fact, most "borrowing" is inadvertent. For example, my wife and I were on a plane. The in-flight film was a silly one that I had pitched repeatedly (as an assignment) to a studio. Plot elements and characters from my pitch were right there on the screen. My stomach was in knots for the rest of the day. I know exactly how it happened. Exec listened to dozens of pitches over the course of a month or two. Exec then hired one that fit the bill a little more than the others. During the subsequent normal course of script development, Exec said, "Suppose this happened [in the story] . . ." Exec honestly believed that he was coming up with something off the top of his head when in fact he was thinking of an element (mine) from one of dozens of pitches three months before that he no longer consciously remembered. Most professional screenwriters learn to roll with it, realizing that they, too, are probably the unwitting recipients of such help. All this is to say that you should understand the nature of the beast before deciding on what is the appropriate remedy for your problem. A lawyer may protect the material (registration with WGA also gives recourse), but will not advance the cause.

QUESTIONS ABOUT THE CRAFT

Q.—What's a treatment? How do you write a good one?

A.—A good treatment should read like an exciting play-by-play (or blow-by-blow) description of the story with a bit of color commentary thrown in. Treatments will be different lengths depending on usage: eight to ten pages for a script you are pitching (don't leave the written treatment behind after a pitch); ten to thirty pages to flesh out a detailed storyline in preparation for going to script; three to four pages for a synopsis.

One of my first experiences in Hollywood involved the excruciating task of boiling a fifteen-page treatment down to a three-page synopsis for a high-level producer. I struggled for three days to get it down to four and a half, which wasn't good enough. Afterwards, the assistant told me that I wasn't ready for prime time because I couldn't follow instructions. So the moral of the story is the right treatment for the right usage.

Q.—I just attended a seminar where the term "high concept" was mentioned a couple times. Nowadays, what does it mean?

A.—Nowadays, not so much. Heyday for HC was the early eighties to the early nineties, although producer Jerry Bruckheimer is still sort of a keeper of the flame for "movie concepts that can be written on a match cover," (the HC definition for HC), e.g., "*Jaws* in space" (*Alien*) or "*Diehard* on a bus" (*Speed*). About five years ago, producers started realizing that such high-concept fare was getting a bit inbred and predictable. In contemporary Hollywood, writers are more apt to deliver concepts that are "short pitchable." A short pitch is a premise that can be delivered in three to four sentences.

Q.—I'm trying to think up a good story for a short World War II movie I intend to self-finance and produce myself. Suggestions?

A.—The key challenge to writing successful historical material is making it relevant to today. For example, *Saving Private Ryan* tapped into the sixtieth anniversary of the war by depicting a man as he is now and the life he has built, contrasted with the man he was and the sacrifices made by many others for him. Creating fleshed-out, complex characters is also critical. A few years ago, I was assigned to write a biopic of Muhammad Ali's boxing coach at the 1960 Olympics in Rome. The producer wanted to place the coach on a pedestal for hero worship, which unfortunately doomed the project. So show us warts and all. Another challenge is making the material exciting and unexpected—viewers don't like to feel they're in school and being lectured to, especially when they already know the outcome. A film like *Patton* is successful because it got beyond predictability and legend-made-of-stone. Same goes for *Amadeus*. You can easily imagine how both of these films could have been marble monument movies. So I think the keys to a successful project are contemporary relevance, solid characterization, and unpredictability.

Q.—Professional screenwriters who evaluated my work described it the same way: "quirky, edgy, quirky." Are there any producers, managers, or agents who even consider "quirky, edgy, quirky"?

A.—"Quirky" and "edgy" are generic catchalls used by producers, execs, and agents. Such vague terms have a slightly negative connotation more often than not—quirky sometimes meaning small, and edgy meaning outside of the Hollywood style. A big however, though, is that a reader who gets your writing and sensibility will see these two qualities as strengths: quirky meaning personal and edgy meaning unique, breaking the rules. As you can see, such valuations are highly subjective. It's kinda like Tex-Mex food—too out there for some, too spicy for others. However, if you have a fan (and there are many), they will be really passionate. Rogue agents and producers *dream* about finding quirky, edgy material. *Fade In* magazine just came out with its annual list of "100 Influential People in Hollywood to Know." Many are up-and-coming agents and producers who think outside the box of conventional material. Cross-reference this list with your *Agents and Managers* and *Hollywood Creative Directory* and track these people down.

Q.—In your opinion, what is the biggest mistake you can make in a script?

A.—Avoid the "giant talking heads" syndrome—long, theatrical speeches where there is no visual momentum. That is the true mark of an amateur. Audiences like to be shown, not told. Screenwriters should always keep in mind that film is a visual medium.

Q.—What are some of your duties and responsibilities in the movie development process?

A.—Screenwriters take interesting ideas or events and flesh them out into complete, visual stories with interesting characters. The stories are structured in such a way that actors and directors, etc., can transform them into film.

Q.—I finished my first original screenplay. It's a hundred pages. Should I make it longer, or is it fine?

A.—First off, congrats. Completing your first screenplay is really an accomplishment, so you should celebrate. Unless the script is low-budget (under $3 million) in which page length is a key financial consideration or is something you intend to direct yourself, 100 pages is a little thin (short). Most studio scripts come in at around 108–120 pages. In any case, you should first give your script to five trusted, non-producer or exec readers for their reactions (fellow writers, best friend, high school English teacher, film school professor, Aunt Ellie the librarian and movie buff, etc.). They can give you constructive criticism and notes, along with encouragement. Then you should submit the revised script to various competitions— Nicholl, Chesterfield, Sundance, Worldfest, Disney, etc. Making the quarter-finals isn't very hard, and many producers and agents will at least read the logline of your script (on the application you fill out). If they like what they read, they'll come looking for you. A friend who is a successful writer/producer with a movie and two TV series under her belt owes her career to placing top 250 in the Chesterfield.

Q.—What are the most important qualities that would be useful to a writer?

A.—You should be self-motivated, observant, detail-oriented, visually inclined, and like words and wordplay. In film school, I saw between 250 and 300 films a year, so it helps to like movies. A lot.

BUSINESS QUESTIONS

Q.—A production company has offered me an option on my script, but I've already heard that the first-time director they're working with wants to rewrite my draft. I don't know anything about the guy. What do you think I should do?

A.—There's the old joke about the screenwriter and the producer wandering the desert in search of water when they come upon an oasis. The writer drops to his hands and knees and is about to drink, when he hears a trickle beside him. He looks up to see the producer urinating in the water. "What are you doing????" he screams. "Making it better," the producer replies.

If the option is financially lucrative or the prodco is well established, there may not be anything you can do but grin and bear it and hope the changes will be minimal. Consult with your management to see if there's a way you can be kept on the project, perhaps as an associate or executive producer. Or offer a low-cost polish as part of your terms of contract. Barring these options, you pretty much have to just hope for the best. I feel your pain.

Some directors can write, but many, particularly first-timers, have never actually written a feature film script. That lots of things can go wrong when people start pulling apart the script doesn't seem to deter them. It takes years of practice to link words together to create characters and images that form stories with meaning. So even when the error is very small, most directors and producers don't have the necessary craft to fix it. Often what you get are ham-fisted attempts and clichéd elements tacked on. The creative, original stories that drew interest in the first place get flattened out and burdened with elements boosted from the current crop of successful movies.

I always look for project developers who don't presume to know how to write so they don't try, but they seem to be few and far between.

Q.—Is the screenwriting business really as bad as I keep reading? Not in terms of the odds of selling, but in the treatment of screenwriters?

A.—Mistreatment of screenwriters is a relative thing; you have to balance tremendous financial and creative rewards with tremendous disappointments and frustrations. TV writers do seem to be accorded more respect and are given many, many perks by the studios. For many of us, the trade-off is the medium (TV vs. the Big Screen). It's easy to get caught up in the my agent/my producer/the director/ the exec/the system blame game. Early on, I decided that my success or failure in the business needed to be squarely on my own shoulders. That realization has made a big difference.

Q.—What are some basic things a writer should avoid doing? For example, a producer told me, "Avoid writing stories about writers. Producers kind of roll their eyes with that."

A.—Never wear a suit to a meeting. Never bad-mouth someone else's work or projects. Avoid writing spoofs on the industry if you're not a Hollywood insider. Never send a producer (even when they beg) a script until you're sure it's rock-solid and the best it can be.

THE INTERNET

Q.—A friend has enjoyed some success with pitching and selling his script on the Internet. Depending on the site, can the Internet be a good way for a script to gain exposure?

A.—The Internet can be a great tool, if you adhere to the watchwords of "listen but verify." That is, protect your work and check credentials. Gocoverage.com is legit and gets notice, but you have to pay a small fee. Otherwise, I still think the various established competitions are best for gaining exposure to the industry while building bona fide credits.

FOREIGN MARKETS

Q.—Do other countries, such as England and Canada, pay similar fees for screenplays? Is it worth pursuing international production companies?

A.—Many films are financed via foreign money. Since Hollywood is the premier market for screenplays, studios here pay a premium price for scripts. So you can anticipate that a foreign company will pay less. Since these companies buy fewer projects, however, your chances of having your work produced are much greater.

LIFESTYLE ISSUES

Q.—What is a typical day like in the life of a screenwriter?

A.—Most writers have very personalized daily routines and sometimes bizarre rituals. I get up early, about 6:00 a.m. (Ernest Hemingway used to get up at four). I eat breakfast, read the newspaper and the trade papers, then read and respond to my e-mail until about 7:30. Answering reader and colleague e-mail kinda gets my juices flowing to write. Then, I put on earphones, fire up an ambient CD like Holst's *The Planets* or the soundtrack for *Thin Red Line* or *Field of Dreams,* then take a look at yesterday's work, make necessary changes (lots of them), and plunge into the next set of pages (90 percent of which is done directly on the computer). I write in two-hour stretches, with bathroom, drink, and lunch breaks in between. I'll take a late-morning break for phone calls, but if I'm on a deadline, then I don't answer the phone. Usually I can manage two to four writing stretches per day. Much more than that and I start to get cranky. On days when I don't have pitch or story meetings with producers or at the studio, I take the day's pages to the gym and ride an exercise bike while making stream-of-consciousness-type changes. I write six days a week, sometimes seven.

Q.—None of the professors who taught screenwriting in my university film program were actual professional screenwriters. As a working writer, what are some of the downsides of your job?

A.—Fighting the urge to drink Drano every time a script gets rejected or a deal doesn't go through—just kidding, you get used to it (rejection, not Drano). It takes about ten years for most writers to develop any sort of job security. Scripts take anywhere from two months to a year to complete. Meanwhile, the average Hollywood movie takes three to four years to go from script to screen. Only about one in twelve studio scripts make it through. So the enemy of screenwriters is time. But if you love movies and love to write, there's no better profession.

Q.—What is the average salary of people in your field?

A.—Some writers make millions (but generally not gazillions like actors, etc.). However, the average working Writers Guild member makes about $86,000 per year. The minimum price paid for a studio feature film screenplay is about $70,000. Most writers can do about two projects per year. But we really don't have salaries because we're paid per project.

Q.—What are some jobs related to movie writing?

A.—Sitcom writer, TV writer, Internet series or game designer/writer, novelist and teaching screenwriting at the college level. Copywriting for advertising is a distant cousin. Some screenwriters are also directors and producers.

AUXILIARY MATERIALS

Q.—If I carry business cards with my picture on them, then offer them to people I am talking with at seminars and workshops, would this be seen as inappropriate?

A.—Nix the pix, but carry a card with your e-mail address, etc. Nothing too elaborate, since, in general, the more successful the writer, the sparser the business card—the ultimate result being a writer who no longer carries a card. Gunslingers who come armed with a bandolier of easy-to-pitch loglines or a reel of clips from their completed projects do the best at meet-and-greets. For example, I currently have four active projects—all different genres—plus another that recently concluded with the studio hiring another writer (the drama!). I came up with a sixty-second "greatest hits medley" of concepts and hooks that I deliver like a verbal grenade (the tone being, "If I told you more, the resulting explosion might kill us all!").

244 **BREAKFAST WITH SHARKS**

The bottom line is that the work is the real jewel. Your sparkling personality, scorching appearance, whiplike wit, etc., are the black velvet box that showcase the gems of your craft. Execs, producers, and agents prefer to read the script, *then* want to meet the writer or director.

To conclude, if you're *already* standing there talking to the exec, producer, or agent, then the captivating pitch (really just a stand-in until they read the script) is all-important.

-23-

TOP TEN FILM FESTIVALS

At this writing, there are more than 600 film festivals worldwide. *The Ultimate Film Festival Guide* by Chris Gore is the bible for anyone interested in independent film. You can also check out www.filmfestivals.com for up-to-the-minute news and information on festival happenings.

What follows is contact information for the top ten festivals as listed in *The Ultimate Film Festival Guide*:

SUNDANCE

www.sundance.org
P.O. Box 3630
Salt Lake City, UT 84110-3630

California Office:
8857 West Olympic Blvd., Suite 200
Beverly Hills, CA 90211-3605

Phone: (310) 360-1981

Applications at: https://festival.sundance.org/2004CallForEntries/
   application.aspx

Festival date: January

Film submission deadlines:
August 1: Early submissions of features and shorts

(Early submission deadline is for American and international; dramatic and documentary features and all short films. Films submitted during this time will be granted a discount submission fee. For early-submission deadline the festival will be accepting *completed films only,* no rough cuts or works in progress.)

September 12: American short films, international short films, *and* all Sundance Online Film Festival applicants.

October 3: All Features.

TORONTO INTERNATIONAL FILM FESTIVAL

www.e.bell.ca/filmfest
2 Carlton Street, Suite 1600
Toronto, Ontario M5B IJ3

Phone: (416) 967-7371

Festival date: September
Entry date: June (international features)

CANNES

www.festival-cannes.fr
Association Française du Festival
International du Film
99 Boulevard Malesherbes
75008 Paris

Phone: 33-1-1-4561-6600

Festival date: May
Entry date: March

BERLIN FILM FESTIVAL

www.berlinale.de/
Internationale Film Fest Piele Berlin
Abteilung Programm
Potsdamer Strasse 5
Berlin D-10785

Phone: 49-30-259-20-444

Festival date: February
Entry deadline: Late November

SXSW: SOUTH BY SOUTHWEST FILM FESTIVAL

www.sxsw.com
1000 East 40th Street
Austin, TX 78751

Phone: (512) 467-7979

Festival date: March
Entry deadline: Early: mid-November; late: early December

TELLURIDE

www.telluridefilmfestival.com
379 State Street, # 3
Portsmouth, New Hampshire 03801

Phone: (603) 433-9206

Festival date: August–September
Entry deadline: July

CHICAGO INTERNATIONAL FILM FESTIVAL

www.chicagofilmfestival.com
32 West Randolph Street, Suite 600
Chicago, Il 60601-9803
Phone: (312) 425-9400

Festival date: October
Entry deadline: early August

FLORIDA FILM FESTIVAL

www.floridafilmfest.com
1300 South Orlando Avenue
Maitland, FL 32751

Phone: (407) 629-8587; (407) 629-1088

Festival date: June
Entry deadlines: Early submission deadline, February; late submission, deadline, March

SLAMDANCE

www.slamdance.com
5526 Hollywood Boulevard
Los Angeles, CA 90028
Phone: (323) 466-1786

Festival date: January
Entry deadline: Early submission deadline, October; late submission deadline, November

CINEQUEST: THE SAN JOSE FILM FESTIVAL

www.cinequest.org
San Jose Film Festival
476 Park Avenue, Room 204
San Jose, CA 95110

Phone: (408) 995-5033

Festival date: February–March
Entry deadline: October

TEN MAJOR SCREENWRITING COMPETITIONS

AUSTIN HEART OF FILM FESTIVAL

707 Rio Grande
Suite 101
Austin, TX 78701

Phone: (800) 310-FEST or (512) 478-4795

Deadline: June 15
Conference dates: mid-October

THE CHESTERFIELD FILM COMPANY

Writer's Film Project
100 Universal City Plaza
Building 447
Universal City, CA 91608

Phone: (818) 777-0998

CHRISTOPHER COLUMBUS SCREENPLAY DISCOVERY AWARDS

The C.C.S. Entertainment Group
Screenplay Discovery Awards
433 N. Camden Drive, Suite 600
Beverly Hills, CA 90210

Phone: (310) 288-1988
Fax: (310) 475-0193

CREATIVE SCREENWRITING MAGAZINE

Script Competition
6404 Hollywood Blvd.
Los Angeles, CA 90028

Phone: (323) 957-1405

WALT DISNEY FELLOWSHIP

Walt Disney Studios
500 S. Buena Vista Street
Burbank, CA 91521-0880

Phone: (818) 560-6894

NICHOLL FELLOWSHIPS IN SCREENWRITING

Academy Foundation
Nicholl Fellowships in Screenwriting

8949 Wilshire Blvd.
Beverly Hills, CA 90211

Deadline: May 1

SUNDANCE INSTITUTE

c/o S.P.E.
10202 W. Washington Blvd.
Culver City, CA 80232

Writers Lab deadlines: Postmarked no later than June 28 for the following January Lab. Postmarked no later than November 28 for the following June Lab (this one for filmmakers also).

THE WRITERS NETWORK

8306 Wilshire Blvd.
Suite 482
Beverly Hills, CA 90211

Phone: (310) 843-9838

WORLDFEST CHARLESTON

J. Hunter Todd, Director
P.O. Box 838
Charleston, SC 29401-0838

Phone: (803) 723-7600

WORLDFEST-HOUSTON

International Film & Video Festival
P.O. Box 56566
Houston, TX 77256-6566

Deadline: January 15

TEN ESSENTIAL BOOKS ON THE CRAFT OF SCREENWRITING

Ken Dancyger and Jeff Rush, *Alternative Scriptwriting: Successfully Breaking the Rules*, Third Edition
Alternative Scriptwriting goes beyond conventional three-act structure to explore more-innovative storytelling forms. Readers will come away challenged to take risks and attempt new ways to create characters, genres, and tones.

Lajos Egri, *The Art of Dramatic Writing*
The Art of Dramatic Writing is considered a trade secret by screenwriters. Egri emphasizes character analysis and psychological motivation to create natural story conflict.

Alex Epstein, *Crafty Screenwriting: Writing Movies That Get Made*
Epstein is a professional screenwriter willing to reveal plenty of tricks of the trade. Readers of *Crafty Screenwriting* learn how to create and polish hooks that will make their work stand out from the crowd.

Syd Field, *Screenplay: The Foundations of Screenwriting*
Field is considered to be the patriarch of the modern Hollywood three-act paradigm, and *Screenplay* is every writer's first bible for film writing.

William Goldman, *Adventures in the Screen Trade: A Personal View of Hollywood and Screenwriting*
Goldman is a screenwriting legend. His credits include *Butch Cassidy and the Sundance Kid, Marathon Man, All the President's Men, Misery,* and *The Princess Bride*. His book is the ultimate insider's glimpse into the world of movies and screenwriting.

Robert McKee, *Story*
Many readers will remember McKee and his writing principles from the movie *Adaptation*. McKee eschews structure in favor of substance and style. *Story* is an exhaustive tome that may be a tough nut for beginning writers to crack.

Robin U. Russin, William Missouri Downs, *Screenplay: Writing the Picture*
Writing the Picture is a very thorough but accessible guide to crafting screenplays, a true textbook/workbook. Beginning to advanced writers will benefit from Russin and Downs's own practical experience in writing for Hollywood. The book takes the reader from conception to completion, covering each part of the writing process in detail.

Linda Seger, *Making a Good Script Great*
Many writers consider Seger's book to be an essential companion piece to Syd Field's work. Scripts are broken down into their nuts-and-bolts components, like character development and subplots, to create an optimal three-act structure.

David Trottier, *The Screenwriter's Bible: A Complete Guide to Writing, Formatting, and Selling Your Script*
The Screenwriter's Bible is an A-to-Z guide for formatting your script properly, as well as a primer for crafting your screenplay and marketing the result.

Christopher Vogler, *The Writer's Journey: Mythic Structure for Writers*
Building upon Joseph Campbell's preceding work on mythic structure, *The Writer's Journey* establishes story archetypes for "the hero's journey." The paradigm is particularly useful for writers working in the genres of science fiction, fantasy, and action/adventure.

TEN KEY PERIODICALS FOR SCREENWRITERS

Creative Screenwriting Magazine
www.creativescreenwriting.com
(323) 957-1405

Daily Variety
www.variety.com
(818) 487-4554

Fade In Magazine
www.fadeinmag.com
(310) 275-0287

Film Comment Magazine
www.filmlinc.com/fcm/fcm.htm
(800) 783-4903

The Hollywood Reporter
www.hollywoodreporter.com
(323) 525-2150

Los Angeles Times
www.latimes.com
(310) 314-1218

Premiere Magazine
www.premiere.com
(800) 289-2489

Scenario Magazine
www.scenariomag.com
(800) 222-2654

Scr(i)pt Magazine
www.scriptmag.com
(888) 287-0932

Written By Magazine
www.wga.org/writtenby
(323) 782-4522

TEN VALUABLE ORGANIZATIONS, UNIONS, AND GROUPS

AFI—AMERICAN FILM INSTITUTE

www.afi.org

2021 North Western Avenue
Los Angeles, CA 90027

(323) 856-7600
(323) 467-4578 (fax)

Attend screenings and workshops or take courses.

ALAMEDA WRITERS' GROUP

www.alamedawritersgroup.org

P.O. Box 10727
Glendale, CA 91209-3727

E-mail: AWG@hotmail.com

Excellent networking, member script readings (weekly and bimonthly), guest speakers, +100 membership.

AMPAS—ACADEMY OF MOTION PICTURE ARTS AND SCIENCES

www.oscar.com

8949 Wilshire Blvd.
Beverly Hills, CA 90211-1972

(310) 247-3000
Fax: (310) 859-9351 or (310) 859-9619
E-mail: ampas@oscars.org

Screenings, seminars, exhibitions.

ATA—ASSOCIATION OF TALENT AGENTS

www.agentassociation.com

9255 Sunset Blvd.
Suite 930
Los Angeles, CA 90069

(310) 274-0628
Fax: (310) 274-5063
E-mail: agentassoc@aol.com

Executive Director: Karen Stuart
Administrative Director: Shellie Jetton

Seminars, round table discussions.

ATAS—ACADEMY OF TELEVISION ARTS AND SCIENCES

www.emmys.com

5220 Lankershim Blvd.
North Hollywood, CA 91601-3109

(818)754-2800
Fax: (818)761-2827

Foundation, seminars, events, screenings.

DGA—DIRECTORS GUILD OF AMERICA

www.dga.org

Los Angeles Headquarters
7920 Sunset Blvd.
Los Angeles, CA 90046

Los Angeles main number: (310) 289-2000
Los Angeles toll-free number: (800) 421-4173
Agency desk: (323) 851-3671
Communications and Public Affairs: (310) 289-5333
Contracts Dept.: (310) 289-2010
Directors Guild Foundation: (310) 289-2037
Membership Dept.: (310) 289-5350
Membership Screening Info: (310) 289-5300
Los Angeles main fax: (310) 289-2029

Guest speakers, screenings, workshops, networking functions.

New York Headquarters
110 West 57th Street
New York, NY 10019

New York main number: (212) 581-0370
New York Toll Free Number (800) 356-3754
New York main fax: (212) 581-1441

Chicago Headquarters
400 N. Michigan Avenue, Suite 307
Chicago, IL 60611

Chicago main number: (312) 644-5050
Chicago toll-free number: (888) 600-6975
Chicago main fax: (312) 644-5776

Functions, screenings, exhibitions, and workshop programs.

PGA—PRODUCERS GUILD OF AMERICA

www.producersguild.org

8530 Wilshire Blvd., Suite 450
Beverly Hills, CA 90211

(310) 358-9020
Fax: (310) 358-9520
E-mail: info@producersguild.org

PGA East Chapter:
E-mail: PGA-NY@producersguild.org
PGA East Chapter Chair: Nancy Goldman (ngoldman@producersguild.org)
PGA East Chapter Vice-Chair: Rachel Leib (rleib@producersguild.org)

Seminars, job postings, free consultations.

UCLA EXTENSION WRITING COURSES

www.uclaextension.org

10995 Le Conte Avenue
Los Angeles, CA 90024-2883

(310) 825-9971 or (818) 784-7006 (Registration and General Information)
(310) 206-6201 (Academic Advisement)
(310) 825-4246 (Financial Aid)
(800) 554-UCLA (Order a catalog)

Inexpensive, excellent courses covering the entire screenwriting field, easy to network.

WGA—WRITERS GUILD OF AMERICA

www.wga.org

7000 W. Third Street
Los Angeles, CA 90048

(323) 782-4528 (Credits)
(323) 782-4502 (Representation)
(323) 782-4532 (Membership)
(323) 782-4522 (Written By)
(323) 782-4603 (Interview requests: Gabriel Scott@Public Affairs)
(212) 767-7870 (Interview requests: WGAC)

Mentoring, guest speakers, screenings, wide range of writer services.

WOMEN IN FILM

www.wif.org

8857 W. Olympic Blvd., Suite #201
Beverly Hills, CA 90211

(323) 463-6040

Networking, seminars, classes, mentoring.

ELEVEN IMPORTANT INTERNET RESOURCES

AIN'T IT COOL NEWS

www.aint-it-cool-news.com

Harry Knowles is an industry legend, and this is his site. Get all the latest buzz on upcoming projects and soon-to-be-released films here.

DONE DEAL

www.scriptsales.com
http://pub130.ezboard.com/bdonedeal (for the Message Board)

Resources for script sales in Hollywood, along with interviews, advice, and contact information for agencies and production companies. The best part of the site is the industry chat room, where agents and professional writers mingle freely and post bulletin-board responses on hundreds of topics.

DREW'S SCRIPT-O-RAMA

www.script-o-rama.com

Frequently updated site for downloading movie and television screenplays. Contains over 600 scripts.

FILMBIZ RESOURCE GUIDE

www.filmbiz.com

Find entertainment industry goods and services ranging from camera equipment to wardrobe, as well as entertainment industry professionals.

HOLLYWOOD LITERARY SALES

www.hollywoodlitsales.com

Everything to help screenwriters sell to Hollywood. Free script listing service; interviews, articles, and classes from industry pros; books, software, critiquing service; postings from producers.

INTERNET MOVIE DATABASE

www.us.imdb.com

Extensive searchable database of above- and below-line film and television credits.

INZIDE

www.inzide.com

Submit scripts online for free. Read interviews with industry professionals. Message boards to communicate with other writers. Stories of development heaven and hell. Get your questions answered by the people who know Hollywood.

MOVIEBYTES

www.moviebytes.com

Features a database of screenwriting contests, script sales, literary agencies, film producers; publishes an e-mail newsletter.

SCREENWRITERS FORUM

www.screenwritersforum.com

Over 300 articles covering every aspect of screenwriting, including character development, selling your screenplay, and protecting your idea.

WHOREPRESENTS.COM

www.who**represents**.com

A quick but thorough guide for checking client representation and agent rosters.

WRITERS GUILD OF AMERICA

www.wga.org

Home of the Writers Guild of America, West. Register your script online, or check out the many resources that include research links, writing tips, industry articles, and interviews.

FIVE VALUABLE INDUSTRY DIRECTORIES

HOLLYWOOD CREATIVE DIRECTORY

(323) 308-3400 or (800) 815-0503 (outside of CA)
www.hcdonline.com

The *HCD* is basically the white-pages phone book of Hollywood. Here you'll find nearly 10,000 producers and studio and network executives representing over 1,750 production companies, studios, and networks. The *HCD* includes addresses, phone and fax numbers, staff and titles, credits, and studio deals. Updated three times a year, end of December, end of May, end of September.

HOLLYWOOD REPRESENTATION DIRECTORY
(AGENTS AND MANAGERS)

(323) 308-3400 or (800) 815-0503 (outside of CA)
www.hcdonline.com

The *HRD* is the way writers can locate agents and managers to read their work. Over 2,000 companies and more than 7,000 individuals are listed for talent agencies and management companies nationwide. Entertainment lawyers and publicity firms are also included. Includes addresses, phone and fax numbers, staff and titles. Published twice a year.

HOLLYWOOD DISTRIBUTORS DIRECTORY

(323) 308-3400 or (800) 815-0503 (outside of CA)
www.hcdonline.com

Everything you need to gain distribution for your film is here, including film festival listings and contact info. Over 800 companies and 5,000 names and titles are listed. Updated annually.

HOLLYWOOD REPORTER BLU-BOOK PRODUCTION DIRECTORY

(323) 525-2150
http://www.hollywoodreporter.com/thr/thrblu/letter.jsp

The *Blu-Book* contains more than 250 product and service categories with thousands of listings necessary to take a film, TV, commercial, or new media project from concept to completion.

LA 411

(323) 460-6304
www.la411.com

This is the directory that can take you from preproduction through post with everything from locating stuntmen to Porta Potties. You can procure production insurance or rent an elephant with the *LA 411*. The *Blu-Book* and the *LA 411* are often used in tandem by producers and production personnel.

AMERICAN FILM INSTITUTE LIST OF THE 100 GREATEST AMERICAN MOVIES OF ALL TIME

This list is both inspirational and crucial to understanding what kind of movies Hollywood sometimes aspires to make.

1. *Citizen Kane* (1941)
2. *Casablanca* (1942)
3. *The Godfather* (1972)
4. *Gone With the Wind* (1939)
5. *Lawrence of Arabia* (1962)
6. *The Wizard of Oz* (1939)
7. *The Graduate* (1967)
8. *On the Waterfront* (1954)
9. *Schindler's List* (1993)

10. *Singin' in the Rain* (1952)
11. *It's a Wonderful Life* (1946)
12. *Sunset Boulevard* (1950)
13. *The Bridge on the River Kwai* (1957)
14. *Some Like It Hot* (1959)
15. *Star Wars* (1977)
16. *All About Eve* (1950)
17. *The African Queen* (1951)
18. *Psycho* (1960)
19. *Chinatown* (1974)
20. *One Flew Over the Cuckoo's Nest* (1975)
21. *The Grapes of Wrath* (1940)
22. *2001: A Space Odyssey* (1968)
23. *The Maltese Falcon* (1941)
24. *Raging Bull* (1980)
25. *E.T. The Extra-Terrestrial* (1982)
26. *Dr. Strangelove* (1964)
27. *Bonnie and Clyde* (1967)
28. *Apocalypse Now* (1979)
29. *Mr. Smith Goes to Washington* (1939)
30. *The Treasure of the Sierra Madre* (1948)
31. *Annie Hall* (1977)
32. *The Godfather Part II* (1974)
33. *High Noon* (1952)
34. *To Kill a Mockingbird* (1962)
35. *It Happened One Night* (1934)
36. *Midnight Cowboy* (1969)
37. *The Best Years of Our Lives* (1946)
38. *Double Indemnity* (1944)
39. *Doctor Zhivago* (1965)
40. *North by Northwest* (1959)
41. *West Side Story* (1961)
42. *Rear Window* (1954)
43. *King Kong* (1933)
44. *The Birth of a Nation* (1915)
45. *A Streetcar Named Desire* (1951)

46. *A Clockwork Orange* (1971)
47. *Taxi Driver* (1976)
48. *Jaws* (1975)
49. *Snow White and the Seven Dwarfs* (1937)
50. *Butch Cassidy and the Sundance Kid* (1969)
51. *The Philadelphia Story* (1940)
52. *From Here to Eternity* (1953)
53. *Amadeus* (1984)
54. *All Quiet on the Western Front* (1930)
55. *The Sound of Music* (1965)
56. *M*A*S*H* (1970)
57. *The Third Man* (1949)
58. *Fantasia* (1940)
59. *Rebel Without a Cause* (1955)
60. *Raiders of the Lost Ark* (1981)
61. *Vertigo* (1958)
62. *Tootsie* (1982)
63. *Stagecoach* (1939)
64. *Close Encounters of the Third Kind* (1977)
65. *The Silence of the Lambs* (1991)
66. *Network* (1976)
67. *The Manchurian Candidate* (1962)
68. *An American in Paris* (1951)
69. *Shane* (1953)
70. *The French Connection* (1971)
71. *Forrest Gump* (1994)
72. *Ben-Hur* (1959)
73. *Wuthering Heights* (1939)
74. *The Gold Rush* (1925)
75. *Dances With Wolves* (1990)
76. *City Lights* (1931)
77. *American Graffiti* (1973)
78. *Rocky* (1976)
79. *The Deer Hunter* (1978)
80. *The Wild Bunch* (1969)
81. *Modern Times* (1936)

82. *Giant* (1956)
83. *Platoon* (1986)
84. *Fargo* (1996)
85. *Duck Soup* (1933)
86. *Mutiny on the Bounty* (1935)
87. *Frankenstein* (1931)
88. *Easy Rider* (1969)
89. *Patton* (1970)
90. *The Jazz Singer* (1927)
91. *My Fair Lady* (1964)
92. *A Place in the Sun* (1951)
93. *The Apartment* (1960)
94. *Goodfellas* (1990)
95. *Pulp Fiction* (1994)
96. *The Searchers* (1956)
97. *Bringing Up Baby* (1938)
98. *Unforgiven* (1992)
99. *Guess Who's Coming to Dinner* (1967)
100. *Yankee Doodle Dandy* (1942)

-24-

The following is a list of terms related to the entertainment industry:

ADAPTATION. Translation of a finished written work into film.

AGAINST. Refers to payment for a script or property. A specified amount of money is initially paid up front as a down payment toward a final and total sum of money. The difference between the two dollar amounts is paid at a later date, which is determined in the contract in advance. That date could be once the script is finished being written, after a rewrite or a polish is done, or even at the beginning or ending of the filming of the screenplay (production of the film).

ATTACHED. An actor, director, or producer who agrees to appear in a film or be involved with the production of the film. Whether oral or in writing, the agreement is considered contractually binding.

ATTACHED ELEMENTS. A director with credits (finished work) or a name actor (movie star) who has verbally or contractually committed to be part of a project.

BEAT SHEET. A breakdown of the key moments or scenes in a film. Lists the highlights and key scenes of the entire script or story.

BUMP. Refers to a meeting that is rescheduled at the last minute for a later date. Execs and producers give priority to projects already in principal photography, so bumping pitch meetings, etc., is a commonplace occurrence.

CAMERA READY. A screenplay that is considered ready to be made into a movie.

CHARACTER ARC. The emotional and spiritual transformation that the main characters undergo during the course of a story.

COLORS. Dialogue delivered in different ways and manners, alternating tone, speed of delivery, and varying facial expressions.

CONSIDER. A somewhat favorable response from a studio reader, which is usually noted on the coverage they do on a script or treatment. The "consider" can mean a certain ambivalence on the part of the reader. Not a *pass,* but not a strong recommendation that it be read, either.

COVERAGE. A reader's report on a script, which generally comprises three parts. The first page is generally the most basic of information on the material: Title, author, genre, date, draft, time period, to whom submitted, whom submitted by, etc. The report also consists of a synopsis of the script, which is usually a one-page to two-page description of the story (or events that take place in the script). The last part of the report involves comments by the reader on what elements, if any, they liked and/or disliked about the script's story, characters, writing, originality, etc.

CREATIVE EXEC. A studio executive evaluates literary material to determine whether a studio or company, etc., is interested in optioning or purchasing it. This person is above a reader in the chain of command. CEs also help to oversee the further development of a project once it is optioned or purchased, providing the writer with feedback, suggestions, and changes for rewrites.

CRUNCH TIME. Term used when time is short because a script is needed for production.

D-GIRL. An outdated and somewhat sexist term that refers to the women who at one time read scripts and evaluated them for producers, directors, etc. Today men and women serve in this role of looking at scripts for purchasing consideration as well as developing (hence "D") the material further by working with the writer and giving notes and suggestions on how to "improve" it.

DEAL MEMO. A contractual agreement that lays out specific terms for an assignment: Writer *a* will write *x* project or *x* scenes by *x* date for *x* amount of dollars (partial payment up front upon commencement and remaining amount upon completion and delivery is typical). Purchaser retains rights to *x* in exchange for *x* credit (if applicable).

DIALOGUE PASS. A writer focuses only on rewriting or "polishing" the dialogue in a draft of a script.

DEVELOPMENT. The process during which a story or idea is written and formed into a script, or a completed script is rewritten further to create a script ready to be produced.

DEVELOPMENT HELL. A situation in which the process of writing or rewriting a script continues over a long period of time. This usually involves numerous notes and rewrites along with frequently contradicting directions given by the various participants.

FEATURE. A full-length movie, usually ranging in length from 90 to 120 minutes.

FIRST-LOOK DEAL. An arrangement made by a writer with a production company or a studio, in which the writer must allow the company or studio the first right of refusal on purchasing and/or producing a project. If the studio passes, the project can then be "shopped" around to other interested parties.

FIVE TRUSTED READERS. Peers, former instructors, or industry people you have befriended, who are willing to read your new project and whose opinion you value and trust.

GATEKEEPER. A person with the power to *green-light* or say yes to a project.

GODFATHER. Someone established in the industry who is willing to make a phone call on your behalf to various *gatekeepers*. This process is called *godfathering*.

GUILD. Either the Writers Guild of America (WGA) or the Directors Guild of America (DGA). Both Guilds have set criteria regarding compensation, credit, and duties.

GREEN DRAFT. A raw and unpolished draft of a screenplay.

GREEN LIGHT. Studio or production company approval for a movie to go into production.

HACK. A pejorative term for a writer who delivers strictly formulaic work.

HEAT. When a project/script generates a great deal of interest—heat—from the filmmaking community, this generally leads to a high sale price for the material as companies and studios attempt to outbid one another for the rights. An individual can also be in high demand based on the selling success of their projects or a recently produced project.

HIGH CONCEPT. An idea that sounds very commercially marketable and in many cases unique and original. Usually associated with big blockbuster films, but can reference any idea or script that would appear to have great potential. See *low concept*.

HOLLYWOOD AGENTS AND MANAGERS DIRECTORY (HAMD). A directory that has contact information for thousands of actors, directors, literary agents, and managers in the film and television industry.

HOLLYWOOD CREATIVE DIRECTORY (HCD). A directory that has crucial contact information for thousands of producers and executives in the film and television industry.

INDIE. Short for "independent." Can refer to a film or production company that works outside of the Hollywood/studio system.

LOGLINE. A one- or two-sentence description of the story in a script or book, or of an idea.

LOW CONCEPT. A project that has limited audience appeal and is, therefore, a tough sell in Hollywood. See *high concept*.

MINIMUM BASIC AGREEMENT (MBA). A Writers Guild document that stipulates a foundation of creative protections and financial incentives for intellectual property.

MOW. Movie of the Week. Refers to a feature-length film that is made just for showing on a television network.

NOTES. Feedback and comments on a creative property. Can consist of changes, suggestions about tone, mood, etc.

OPTION. A situation in which a studio, production company, and/or producer pays a fee for the exclusive rights to a literary property for a set amount of time. At the end of the specified time period, the material can, in most cases, be optioned again, but if not the rights revert back to the original owner (or writer).

OUTLINE. A scene-by-scene breakdown of the story of a script, which shows each point and beat.

PACKAGE. A collection of talent and material that is put together by an agent or agency in which a script is tied together with certain actors, actresses, and/or directors and producers. This usually increases the chance of selling the property to a studio.

PAGE ONE (REWRITE). A complete rewrite of a script in which a major portion is altered, including the plot, scene order, character types, theme, etc. This can be done by the original writer or by another screenwriter brought in for the purpose.

PASS. A rejection from a studio, company, agent, etc. (When a writer rewrites certain elements of the script, including dialogue, character, action, etc., this is also referred to as a *pass*.)

PASSION PROJECTS. A story idea that may not be especially marketable but has great personal meaning for the creator.

PITCH. To verbally describe the story of a script or idea.

POLISH. The final touches made by a writer to a script to make a screenplay ready for production.

PRINCIPAL PHOTOGRAPHY. The first day of shooting a movie.

PROJECT SLATES. All of the scripts currently in development for which an executive is responsible.

PROPERTY. A script, book, or other literary material.

PURCHASE CONTRACT. The purchase by a studio or production company of all rights to a *spec* screenplay for a negotiated price, along with additional monies if the project is actually produced.

QUERY LETTER. A written request to ask whether a producer, agent, manager, studio, etc. would be interested in looking at a script, treatment, or story idea.

READER. A person hired by a production company, producer, director, studio, or agent to read a script, then write *coverage* on it. Readers generally work freelance.

RECOMMEND. A very favorable response from a reader, which is noted on the *coverage* of a script or treatment. Though not a guarantee that the material will be bought, in most cases it means the script will either be verbally discussed in a meeting or passed on to the next level for consideration by a development executive, or by an agent or producer.

RESPONSE AND REACTION. Feedback on a script from peers and others in the industry.

SALE. The outright purchase by a producer or studio of rights to a script written on spec.

SIGNATORY. A studio or company that is officially a member of the Screen Actors Guild or the Writers Guild of America.

SOLICITED. A script or project requested for review by a studio, company, or agent from a writer, agent, manager, and/or producer.

SPEC. A script written on the speculation that it might sell.

SYNOPSIS. A brief, usually one-half- to two-page description of a story or plot. Written in prose form, generally with little or no dialogue.

TAKE A MEETING. The term used for one individual meeting with another. In can also refer to an individual being the center of a discussion and thus leading the direction and pace of it.

TRACK. To follow the development of a project, either one's own or another's.

TRADES. Also called "trade papers," these are daily periodicals that report on the latest news and events in the film business, the two most popular being *The Hollywood Reporter* and *Variety.*

TREATMENT. Similar to a synopsis but much more detailed, this is a blow-by-blow telling of a story. A treatment generally includes every scene and plot involved. Treatments are written in a prose form, similar to a novel, and are used by writers to flesh out their ideas for a script. Note that treatments may be as short as a few pages or as extensive as thirty pages or more, depending on the purpose.

TURNAROUND. After a certain period of time, called the "turnaround," if a project/script is not produced, a studio or company will essentially offer the script to any buyers interested in acquiring the rights to it. This usually involves the other company or individual paying for all "expenses" incurred while the project was being developed. These are fees and expenses that were on top of the purchase price for the material. Due to the high cost of development, this can cause the project to then be very expensive and thus less attractive.

UNSOLICITED. A script or project, sent to a company, studio, and/or individual, that was not requested before it was sent—either in writing or by phone.

VOICE. A term connoting everything from a writer's uniquely personal style or perspective to a *Zeitgeist* grasp of specific themes or subject matter that is commercially viable. In practical terms, a voice means having something to say in an interesting way.

WEEKEND READ. The time period from Friday through Sunday that executives use to catch up on their reading of incoming scripts.

WORK FOR HIRE. An employment contract to write a script, which, under U.S. copyright law, vests the initial copyright with the employer.

Index

ABOUT THE AUTHOR

MICHAEL LENT is co-producer of the feature film *Hard Scrambled*. As an award-winning screenwriter, he has sold, optioned or been assigned to ten feature film projects including *The Hellseeker* for Miramax Studios. Since 1998, he has been a featured columnist for *Creative Screenwriting* magazine. His work also appears in the French film periodical *Tournages*, as well as *Screenstyle*. Michael has written for MTV, as well as *Billboard* magazine. He is a four-time writing competition judge, including the Screenwriters' Expo Script Competition which awards more than $30,000 in cash and prizes each year. He holds an M.F.A. from the University of Miami and has taught screenwriting in the UCLA Extension/Artsreach Program and at Santa Barbara City College.

Michael lives in Los Angeles with his wife, Sonia, and son, Willem. The family has two dogs, Pooka and Kiwi, both rescues from the Humane Society.

RELATIVE ORIGINS

Famous Foster and Adopted People

by
Maria and Aileen Dever

National Book Company
Portland, Oregon

Cover Illustration:
Ward Stroud, Avant-Graphics

Library of Congress Catalog Card Number
92-62062

ISBN 0-89420-286-3

402020